WAKA

IS LOVE ENOUGH

MICHAEL FOSTER

Dear Eva,
   Mitakuye Ogasin

Michael Foster

Nov. 2016

Book cover and design by Aaron Foster
Cover photograph 'Before the Storm' by
Edward Sheriff Curtis

ISBN-10: 1503031225
ISBN-13: 978-1503031227

Published by the author.

Dear Reader,

Historical fiction inhabits a special place in literature because it blurs the line between fiction and non-fiction. It also serves to anchor the writer and reader to a very real time and place. The author of non-fiction writing from his or her own perspective makes thoughtful choices of what to include in the work. Such editing inserts the author's viewpoint into the work and, even if the work isn't fiction, it certainly infuses the text with a personal slant. Even fiction, no matter how surreal, must be based on some reality both the writer and reader share. Fiction, non-fiction? Does it really matter?

Most would agree that <u>Wakanisha, Is Love Enough</u> is fiction. But, I have to admit to you that I'm not sure where this story fits. For me, it belongs in non-fiction. Let me explain.

One night, sometime during the winter of 1986, my wife and I had just gone to bed when our two young children came upstairs and, for some reason, wanted to sleep with us. It was a school night. Our kids had school the next day, as did my wife and I; we're both teachers. Our son and daughter were wiggly sleepers. It took me only a few minutes to realize that if I wanted to get any sleep at all, I'd need to find another spot to stretch out. I dug out my old sleeping bag and made myself a spot on the floor.

Just as I was drifting off, in a state of half-sleep, the entire content of this story downloaded itself into my brain. It was not a gradual process; it exploded in my head like a hammer blow! I didn't sleep at all that night. Who was telling me this story? This story of a tiny Sioux girl that made its way from somewhere out in the ethers into my consciousness consumed me that night and, to a great degree, obsessed me until I got it written.

That same winter, I tried to write down this story that I'd involuntarily received, but found it to be just too hard. I tried again in the early 90's and managed to get three of four pages written before giving up. The story was extensive – it was just too much work. The research was daunting. But the story would not let me be; the account of the Sioux girl's life was like a toothache in my head. It was always there, clamoring to get out. I finally surrendered my will to her and in the winter of 2013, her story flowed out of me in a torrent. Fiction? Non-fiction? Read her story. You be the judge.

Why did she choose me? That question nags at me. Dear Reader, perhaps the following facts are relevant.

Both of my grandfathers are of European descent and were born in the late 1880's. Also, both of them became landowners of large tracts of land in southwestern Kansas that had, just decades before, been 'owned' by Native Americans.

My grandfather Foster dealt strictly in farmland and the mineral rights that applied to land ownership in Kansas. My father inherited much of this land and I grew up the son of a farmer. My entire childhood from age five until I was drafted in the 60's was spent working this land. Many of the creeks, ridges and rivers frequented by the tribe in this tale are familiar to me from childhood.

My grandfather Breyfogle raised Angus cattle; he was in the business from the early 1900's. His breed: Dry Lake Angus. Almost all of the land in the Breyfogle Ranch was and still is native American prairie. Even though my grandfather took me out and showed me scars on the prairie from Indian cooking fires, and spent hours with me after hard rains scouring "Arrowhead Hill" for arrow points, I was never much interested in "Indians".

My older brother now owns the Breyfogle Ranch almost in its entirety. He has always showed much more interest in Indians than I did. He is also much more of a Kansas history scholar than I am. He collects books and artifacts related to whites and the natives alike.

So, fiction or non-fiction? Your call. Please know that this story takes place against a very real history in America's near past. And that history is sometimes laughable, sometimes ironic, often painful and amazingly interesting. If anything in our main character's story piques your interest, there are multiple website devoted to history by year.

In the end, whether this story is fiction or not is irrelevant. What is relevant is the loss humanity has suffered by the destruction of cultures that lived with the earth, not just on it.

Michael Foster – February 2014

Character Names – Alphabetical

Charles Allen – Pimp

Aponi – (Butterfly) Oldest sister to Itunkala and Chumani

Lieutenant Bart Ashby – Platoon commander, 19th U.S. Cavalry

Badger – Son of Yellow Knife and Horse Woman

Luther Bell – Driver

Julia Bulette – Prostitute

Dr. Cyrus Bartol – Reverend and unofficial leader of a wagon train

Black Cloud – Son of Yellow Knife and Horse Woman

Black Elk – son of a very important chief from another tribe of Sioux

Broken Knife – Chief Hunter and tracker, father to Itunkala

Chumani – (Dewdrop) Sister to Itunkala

Dull Knife – Chief Warrior and head of security

Ehawee – (Laughing Maiden) Wife of Broken Knife, mother to Itunkala

Horse Woman – wife of Yellow Bird

Itunkala – Mouse

Lotti Johl – Prostitute

Jondunn – Sioux nickname for John Dunn

John Dunn – Calvary Officer

Kangee – (Raven) Medicine Man, Shaman

Lark – Son of Yellow Knife and Horse Woman

Leftook – Nickname for John Dunn

Little Bear – Son to Aponi, Grandson to Broken Knife

Macawi – (Generous) Mid–wife, teacher, mother of Takchawee

Mary – Christian white woman

Rosa May – Prostitute

Spoon Woman – Nickname for Takchawee

Spotted Horse – Early name of Stone Foot

Stone Foot – Head Chief

Strong Wolf – Hunter, husband to Aponi

Takchawee – (Dove) Daughter of Macawi, Mother of Red
  Feather, wet nurse to Mouse, later called Spoon Woman

William "Bill" Moore – buffalo hunter

Yellow Bird – Chief of horses

Sioux Vocabulary

Awahtani – to sin, to break a taboo

Aphe – wait

Ate' – father (informal)

Berdache – a Two Spirit, homosexual

Chante – heart

Chesli – manure

Conala – little

Coonshi (*koo–she*) Grandmother, affectionate

Counting Coup – any act of bravery, often done by touching an enemy without harming them.

Ghost Road – heaven to the Sioux (The Milky Way)

Greasy Grass – Little Big Horn

Halhata – magpie

Háŋ – yes

Hau Kola – a greeting of great respect between warriors meaning roughly, "Hello, I would give my life for you."

Híŋhaŋni wašté – Good morning

Hiyá – no

HokšíyuzA – midwife, to act as a midwife

How Coula – traditional greeting

Igma – cat

Igma taka – mountain lion, cougar

Isnati Awicalowanpi – Four–day ceremony that celebrates a girl's coming of age after her first menstrual cycle.

Iyusking – happy

Kichi yungka, siksil hung – have sex, to lie with, perverted

Lala (Kaka) – Grandfather, informal (Grandpa)

Mashtíncala – rabbit

Maya Owichapaha – The Old Woman Who Judges

Maya owicha paka – fate/ he who pushes you off a cliff

Mila – knife

Nadowessioux – snake

Nagi – Soul

Oyúsiŋka – hate
Paha Sapa – Black Hills
Pilamaya – thank you
PhiláyA – please, to please me
Sunka – dog
Súnkawákan – horse
Suthung – seed, new growth
Tatonka – buffalo
Tawaiciyan – Freedom
Thawingya – to have sexual intercourse with a woman
Theȟíla – Love
Tȟokátakiya – future, in the future
Thunkashila – grandfather (formal) (God)
Uhcegila – Mastodon
Unj ya – we go
wablénič̌a – orphan
Wakan – sacred, holy
Wakan Tanka – God, part of the Sioux triolgy
Wakanisha – children, religious concept of the sacredness of
    family
Wasican (wasica) Original meaning – A person with special
    powers. Later became a negative slang term for white man.
    Another Sioux word that sounds similar means "greedy"
    and Wasican is now used as "White man who steals the best
    meat, fat, etc.
Watho haipajajablu – soap weed, yucca
Waúŋspe – To be learned, educated, have knowledge
Wič̌ála – Faith
Wichapi owanjila – North Star
Wiwilamni wahpe – watercress or "leaves from spring water"
Wóyawašte – grace, blessing
Wanzi – One
Nonpa – Two
Yamni – Three
Topa – Four
Zaptan – Five

Storms

1864 – 1865

A man's heart deviseth his way: but the LORD directeth his steps.
    Proverbs 16:9

Life is like a game of cards. The hand you are dealt is determinism; the way you play it is free will.
    Jawaharla Nehru

She awoke as a single black feather floated down through the opening of her tipi. It hovered in the updraft from her fire, sinister and prophetic. She looked up through the smoke flap and saw a crow sitting on her tallest lodge pole. The bird cocked its head to the side and looked down at her with its black, beadlike eye. Cawing loudly, it dove into her living space. In blatant disrespect of Sioux etiquette, the crow circled her tipi opposite the direction of the rising sun.

The early spring sun glinted through the opening at the top of her tipi and illuminated a swath of the western wall. This slender swath of light did not illuminate the pictographs she and her husband had painted on the outside of her tipi. Inside, the paintings seemed like negative space instead of the colorful history of two lives shared.

As the crow circled faster and faster, the sun reflected off the bird's plumage as it streaked through this tight beam of sunlight. It's feathers flashed, iridescent.

The hallucinatory quality of this interplay of color, the sound of the crow's breathing, its awful cry, the hiss of its wings completely erased Ehawee's reality. Gone for that moment was the ache from near starvation of the past brutal winter and the gnawing responsibility of her two young daughters asleep under the buffalo hide near her. For an instant, she was oblivious to the pain of her contractions. It was a moment and an eternity; she was acutely terrified and joyfully amazed simultaneously.

As if the crow realized Ehawee's spirit had separated from its physical tether, it flared its wings and perched on her cooking stone, the stone that had belonged to her mother and her mother's mother. Time seemed to stop as this apparition and the Sioux woman stared at each other. The crow broke eye contact, briefly looked at the two sleeping girls then looked at Ehawee's pregnant belly. As she raised her hands protectively to cover her unborn child, the crow again made eye contact. Then, with a hideous parody of a human laugh, it disappeared like the smoke from her sage fire.

Ehawee, whose name meant Laughing Maiden, was puzzled. She decided to ask the Shaman about this omen but when she stood, her contractions forced her to the floor. Her question went unanswered.

The young mother looked sadly at her two sleeping daughters. Normally a joyous event, now a birth meant another mouth to feed at the end of a cruelly harsh winter.

"Aponi, get up," Ehawee whispered. She waited a moment. Her firstborn rolled over under the thick buffalo robe but did not open her eyes. Another contraction gripped Ehawee, this one closer and more intense. "Aponi! Get up!" Her oldest daughter sat up, rubbed her eyes and frowned at her mother. "Run! Get our hokšíyuzA!"

Young Aponi shook her head. Even after a bitter, hungry winter that the small Sioux tribe had barely survived, this five year-old girl still was plump, a picture of the perfect woman to be. "No, Mama', Macawi scares me! Can't you get someone else to be mid-wife?"

"PhiláyA! Just go! The baby will not wait for you to show some manners."

"Ate can go. He's afraid of Macawi too but he's a grownup."

"Your father is out hunting with his friends. He would be here but we have no food. He does his duty even when I need him here."

"Laughing Maiden" wasn't laughing as another contraction doubled her over. She squatted on the earthen floor of their tipi and pulled her deerskin shift up to her knees. "Just go! The baby is coming!"

Chumani, the youngest girl peeked out from under the huge buffalo skin. "I'll go Mama." Chumani looked like her name, Dewdrop. She, too, was plump. Unlike her sister, however, she had learned to mind her parents. She had watched and learned to get attention differently than her older sister; instead of being contentious and argumentative, she knew she could earn her parents' favor by being sweet and compliant.

"One of you go!" grunted Ehawee as another contraction gripped her. Her name was an irony because she was, except for her pregnancy, cadaverously thin. The past harsh winter had made game scarce and her pregnancy had left her sick for almost the entirety. What little extra food that made it to their household Ehawee sacrificed to her two daughters. Her husband Broken Knife, the tribes lead hunter, always brought the better cuts of meat home but the game had been almost non-existent since summer.

Little Chumani quickly put on her moccasins and ran directly across the floor of their tipi. Ehawee grimaced; the pain in her stomach diverted her from chastising her youngest for her lack of manners. First it was the crow, now her own daughter ignored the Sioux tradition of circling the inside of the tipi in the direction of the sacred sun.

Moments later, Macawi arrived with several of the other women. Ehawee's door flap had been left open so Macawi entered and went directly to Ehawee in the customary clockwise direction. Macawi didn't speak; she lifted the pregnant woman's buckskin shift and looked. She nodded and stepped outside again.

The women of the tribe all deferred to Macawi. Even in the typical patriarchal order, many of the men in the tribe also acknowledged her authority. She dressed simply; her deerskin clothing was unadorned. She rarely wore jewelry; what set her apart was an inner strength, an earned knowledge that served the tribe. One look into her eyes was all it took for most to realize her will was overpowering.

As was their custom, the women chose a spot away from the main encampment, a sheltered spot out of the cold spring wind to prepare for the upcoming birth. They erected a small lean-to and lit a small fire. They brought extra hides for bedding, some water and as many fresh sage branches as they could find. The sage was used as a soft cushion for the baby to fall on because Sioux women usually stood or squatted during childbirth.

Takchawee, Macawi's daughter and the rest of the women gathered their herbs and powdered bark. They softly sang the traditional songs but in their hearts, they feared for this birth. The winters near famine and the exhausted condition of Laughing Maiden concerned them deeply.

Macawi helped Ehawee make the walk to her newly erected shelter just as the sun showed three fists above the horizon. Macawi, Takchawee and a few of the other women stayed but Laughing Maiden's contractions diminished then seemed to stop. The sun was not even overhead when Macawi said, "It seems that your baby wants to wait."

As Macawi helped her pregnant friend get comfortable, the few remaining camp dogs barked. The dogs were also thin and showed little aggression as a small group of Cheyenne appeared over a sand hill to the south. Dull Knife, the old alpha warrior of the tribe quickly readied his weapon and his warriors to challenge the approaching clan.

But the Cheyenne were long-time friends and trading partners of this little Sioux tribe. After they had been recognized, they were quickly led to the communal cooking fire for a pipe and a little food. Gathered around the communal fire, the Sioux sadly recognized that their Cheyenne guests were far hungrier than even they were. The ribs of the Cheyenne's' ponies stood out, almost as if the steeds were walking skeletons. These Cheyenne men from Black Kettle's clan were extremely thin and wraithlike.

Stone Foot, chief of the Sioux sat, tamped his pipe and got it going. As the pipe passed, Stone Foot stared at his guests with his intense, unwavering gaze.

The Cheyenne nervously began to speak. "Our Thunkashila Black Kettle led us to a bad place where the whites ordered us to live. He said we must do as the white man commanded if we are to live. We set our homes near their fort on Sand Creek three days ride from here. We flew the white man's flag and gave our word we wanted peace. But it was a bad place with no game; our people were hungry. Most of our men left to hunt when another white army surrounded our camp. Black Kettle put up the white flag but this army ignored his promise. The white men drank from their bottles and made big fires in the night. They laughed and acted like demons. When the sun came up, they fired their big guns into our camp from the four sacred directions. Then, the white soldiers ran into our camp with their rifles and shot our old men, the women and children. We are a few that got away by floating down the river."

Stone Foot listened to this testimony impassively, as if it did not pertain to his own destiny. Inwardly, this information made him furious and fearful; he knew the whites were close. He offered his guests a little food; all they could spare, and asked the Cheyenne what he could do to help them.

The Cheyenne sorrowfully told of yet another move their people had been ordered to make. Black Kettle had escaped the attack and had then talked to the white leader at the fort on Sand Creek. All Cheyenne were commanded to move to the Washita River in the Oklahoma Territory and share the land with many other tribes.

Stone Foot ordered that a small amount of their precious jerky be given to the Cheyenne for their journey. In return, the Cheyenne gave the Sioux a small container of dried corn, the only food they had.

As the Cheyenne rode away, Stone Foot called a tribal council.

Broken Knife, husband to "Laughing Maiden" was the last to arrive. He and his hunters had taken a scrawny mule deer and returned to share the meat. He had removed a part of one backstrap and went to his tipi for a needed meal and to check on his pregnant wife. He found his tipi empty and cold. Anxiously, he stepped outside. A neighbor women told him of the day's developments; the visit from the Cheyenne and of his wife's move to the birthing hut.

Broken Knife ran across the camp, past the communal fire and was stopped by Macawi. Her face smiled but her eyes did not as she said, "You know our customs Broken Knife. Men are not allowed at the birth house.'

"My wife. Is there a baby?"

"She will not birth tonight. Your daughters are being cared for." Macawi touched her palm to her heart and said, "Thank you for our food. You are a good man. Go to council; if there is news, I'll send word."

Five men made up the tribe's council; each member was informally elected not because of political skill but because of some specific knowledge that would help the tribe survive. Broken Knife was a voting council member because he was the most accomplished hunter and tracker in the tribe.

Although the council members' everyday buckskin breeches and shirts seemed similar, up close the men were very different. Stone Foot was a huge man, not tall but thick and powerfully built. Many simply referred to him as 'The Boulder' but not to his face. His eyes were flat, hard and appraising. He was intimidating. The chief of horses, Yellow Bird, was perhaps the exact opposite. Short and wiry, his wife decorated his shirts with feminine beadwork, and she kept his hair cut short on the top and long in the back. His face was long and narrow, resembling that of the horses he loved so much. Old Dull Knife, chief of the warriors, looked to be an older, smaller version of Stone Foot. His greying hair was long, tied in a tail and he had a long scar across his left cheek that extended down onto his chest, an old war wound. Kangee the Shaman was tall and thin. His face, now deeply creased, could have passed for a white man if not for his ruddy color. His eyes were deep set, inquisitive and lively and when he smiled, his somewhat somber face lit up and became childlike. Broken Knife seemed like an average man, unassuming and shy. He kept his hair short, just able to be tied in the back but he usually just ignored it. It was Broken Knife's eyes that set him apart from the other men. His eyes did not hold that aggressive, combative edge. He had no desire to lead and the others on the council often saw him as the lowest in their pecking order. But, during rare temper outbursts, his eyes could flash dangerously.

When Broken Knife arrived, the head chief's tipi flap was open. He stepped in as Chief Stone Foot was saying, "We must move from this spot." Yellow Bird, the horse master, nodded his head in agreement.

Their Shaman, Kangee, was the next to speak. "Game is returning. The nights are warmer. This is not a bad place."

The chief responded, "I feel the white man all around us. I do not trust them. We must move."

Dull Knife, the old warrior and chief of all the warriors, spoke. "I also feel the white man. We are weak from this winter. What happened at Sand Creek can happen to us. I say we move to the dry land near the mountains. There are no whites there.

The Shaman spoke next. "The Great Spirit gave us Tawaiciyan to live as Human Beings. We are not free men if we hide like rabbits from these whites. Our families, our Wakanisha deserve a life without hunger and fear. The winter has turned warm and game is returning." He held his hand over his heart then presented his open palm to Broken Knife in a gesture of thanks for the food he provided. "I vote to stay until our families are strong enough for the move."

Broken Knife was the youngest and lowest ranking man on the council and the irony of his ranking perturbed him. He and his hunters were the ones that provided the food that sustained his people yet the warrior commanded a greater respect. "There are two reasons not to move," Broken Knife said. "We have almost no dried meat and a little corn. Our people are weak. We must have food before we move. Also, my wife will have her baby soon. Would you have us leave as my wife brings a new baby to the world?"

Stone Foot shrugged his shoulders as if to dismiss the younger chief. "Our women are strong. They have babies always. We will trust the Great Spirit to bring us game on the trail."

Broken Knife raised his voice to the elder chief. "My wife is not strong! She feeds my two daughters and does not eat much. She is thin and is even now away at the birthing house. I vote to stay and feed our people!"

Kangee broke in, "I agree with Broken Knife. We must be strong to move. Our Creator will feed us here."

But Yellow Bird sided with the older men. "The horses are in fair shape. The spring has brought grasses for them to eat. If we travel easy, the horses will be fine."

Dull Knife looked from face to face. "There are three who would travel, two who will not. We must decide."

Broken Knife and the Shaman argued long into the night with the other three. After a long and sometimes bitter discussion, they reached an unusual decision. The families wishing to move west to the dry land near the mountains would go. The families wishing to hunt and replenish the tribe's food supply would stay behind. All agreed that there would be no more than ten suns until the tribe reunited. Broken Knife promised to bring much fresh meat to their planned reunion but in his heart, his argument was born out of fear for the safety of his family.

Broken Knife walked across his tribe's communal area. The central fire was smoking and almost out. Starlight and a new moon lighted his way to the tipi of Macawi and her daughter Takchawee.

Takchawee's husband had been a close friend and fellow hunter but after his death hunting, Broken Knife had stood for her and her young son Red Feather to be their provider and protector. Broken Knife would have offered this even if his wife hadn't insisted.

Macawi's tipi flap was closed and Broken Knife could hear no talking; the entire camp was silent. He considered walking to the birth hut to talk to his wife. He was tired, hungry and emotionally spent. His argument at council had split the tribe and his reason was only feet away. He deeply loved his wife and needed her support, her comfort. Instead, he trudged back to his own home.

He entered his cold and dark tipi. The meat, which should have been a warm and happy meal with his family, sat coldly on his wife's cooking stone. Broken Knife briefly considered rekindling the fire and cooking the meat but in his heart, he wanted his family's love as nourishment. Instead, he picked up his wife's robe and crawled under their buffalo hide. Broken Knife hugged his wife's garment and smelled her scent as he fell into an uneasy sleep. His disturbing dream began almost immediately.

He was last to join their council. There was no fire, no pipe to share and no ceremony. They sat or stood, as was their custom under a full prairie moon. There were no words, only understanding. The buffalo nodded to him in acknowledgment, the panther regarded him indifferently. Rabbit, badger and antelope sat near each other, as did the mule deer and elk. The bobcat and black tail deer stood and moved aside to make room for many snakes and lizards, a large rattlesnake at their center. There were many prairie dogs there as if all their clans were represented. Broken Knife looked around in wonder then realized that they had been waiting. He carefully sat cross-legged and as he did, all heads turned toward the animal that seemed to be their chief. A small mouse rose and stood on a stone and looked directly into Broken Knife's eyes. There were no words but Broken Knife felt in his heart and his head, "We are all equal and part of Wakan Tonka's plan. We are all related."

By sunrise the next day, Ehawee was pale and extremely week. Her contractions came but her water did not. The look in her eyes reminded Macawi of the eyes of a snared rabbit about to give its life for food.

That morning, some of the banter between the men was good-natured; some was not. Almost to a man, the hunters that Broken Knife led chose to stay behind. The wives of several of the hunters complained to their husbands; they preferred to stay with friends, sisters and parents. The disunion among these people was not uncommon but for this little tribe, it was the first time the presence of the whites split them. It would not be the last.

Strong Wolf, a young apprentice hunter of almost twelve refused to leave with his family and go west toward the mountains. He loudly told his father that his duty was to feed the tribe. The boy was in the painful stage between being a boy and a man, and when the argument between father and son became heated, Broken Knife finally had to intervene.

Broken Knife gently lectured Strong Wolf about Wakanisha. The boy had a fervent sense of duty to his tribe; he was almost the exact opposite of his father. Strong Wolf appeared a much younger version of Stone Foot, muscular and intimidating. Some in the tribe wondered if Strong Wolf's father was a berdache, a two-spirit; he was thin and effeminate and seemed to prefer the company of women. There was also talk that perhaps Strong Wolf was the son of Stone Foot; the boy was built like the chief and their personalities were also similar. Regardless, all in the tribe universally respected the boy.

Kangee and Broken Knife watched stoically as the tribe tried to sort out the tribe's good-byes. The families that stayed behind stood and uneasily watched as some of their friends and relatives prepared to depart. Faces on both sides of this divide showed anger, desperation, resignation.

The sense that two camps existed within the one was palpable. This uneasy stalemate was broken when Macawi, one of the women staying behind, stepped across that invisible anxious line and began helping another woman take down her tipi. Moments later, the women of the tribe fell to their traditional tasks regardless of which side of the line they stood. The tasks were simple. The buffalo hides were untied from the lodge poles and lifted down. The rawhide tethers were unwound from the point where the lodge poles intersected to make the tipi's unique cone shape. The poles formed into travois to transport the family's possessions. Macawi's simple act helped reunify these people.

Broken Knife and the several families that stayed behind watched as the rest of their tribe rode west. The separation made each one of them uneasy and frightened. In their hearts, they understood that the divide among them had come about because of the white man. The white man respected nothing, took what he wanted and left ruin behind. Broken Knife and his hunters simply wanted to hunt in peace and enjoy the prairie, the song of the meadowlark and the amazing thrill of taking a buffalo.

Before he left camp to hunt, Broken Knife attempted to see to his wife. Macawi met him outside the birthing house with her stern intense eyes and final say in women's affairs. "Your woman is near her time. The baby tries to come. I have seen it through the baby's caul. Hunt and bring us a feast to celebrate the birth of your new child. You know men are not allowed at the birth house!"

Broken Knife stood there, uncertain. His desire to see his wife was almost a strong as the force this intimidating woman radiated. The two stared at each other then Macawi's gaze softened. She smiled softly and placed her hand on the much taller man's heart. "When you return with our feast, I will have a new life to give you. Pilamaya. You are a good man."

Ehawee was now so weak, it took several of the women to keep her in a squatting position. By mid-morning, Ehawee's water had still had not broken so Macawi decided to help. She used a small but very sharp flint to puncture the protruding membrane that held the child. Water and blood gushed into the prairie soil.

A tiny, thin girl was born minutes later along with a great deal of her mother's blood. Ehawee, the "Laughing Maiden," held her third daughter briefly then quietly died. Whether it had been due to the mother's weakened state, a slip of the flint blade or simple fate, there was no blame.

* * *

Broken Knife and the other men who stayed behind made their preparations to hunt. Their ponies were painted, prayers were chanted and their weapons were made ready. But, in spite of the comforting, familiar rituals, the hunters were troubled. Broken Knife worried for his wife and family. Instead of the joy they normally felt just before a hunt, the hunters were uneasy for more than one reason. They knew that there was strength in number and they were now a divided people. Being such a small tribe, their difficult decision to divide into two groups made them much more vulnerable to attack.

They were also concerned because the brutal previous winter had left those behind with little to eat. Unspoken but troubling to each man in the hunting group was the knowledge that they were leaving their women and children guarded by two very old men and three older boys with few weapons. They also dared not speak of the reality that, without fresh game soon, there would be no strength left in any of them to face the world as men.

Their Great Spirit was kind that day. Spring had arrived early with rains and gentle winds. The buffalo grass was thick and green. The yucca was beginning to flower with its edible and delicious blooms: the tough yucca nuts wouldn't be edible until fall. The gaillardia and castilleja were blooming. The hearts of these hungry hunters were gladdened as if the flowers were a sign from the Great Spirit. These wildflowers, later named Indian Blanket and Indian Paint Brush by the white settlers, in years to come would be plowed under to plant wheat and corn.

This country was a vast open prairie. The land, which at first appeared to be flat, contained countless small hills with gentle slopes. The taller grasses ebbed and flowed with the constant wind that swept across the plain. There were no trees but miles and miles of sagebrush that smelled beautiful like the first day of creation.

Broken Knife and his hunters on this spring day were almost immediately rewarded with a rare bonanza, an antelope with a broken leg. The hunters would normally have tried for easier game; these skittish and fleet animals were difficult to take with bow and arrow. Also, the meat of these little animals was tough and stringy with a pungent taste. They quickly said a prayer of thanks to the Creator, killed and cleaned the animal. They shared what little they could of the liver and threw the carcass over the withers of the youngest hunter's horse.

The hunters briefly discussed returning to camp, but agreed that it was early and the day was beautiful. They thought that even if they managed to bring a few rabbits back in addition to the antelope, they would be returning with a feast in comparison to their meager winter diet.

Broken Knife and his band remounted and rode north again, into the spring wind to mask their smell and sound from any game.

Again, the Great Spirit offered them an unexpected prize. Not two miles from the antelope kill they came upon the carcass of a freshly killed mule deer. It was a doe marked by the claws and teeth of a big cat. The doe was still warm and only a few of her internal organs had been eaten. They realized that they were not the only hunters in the area; their numbers must have frightened the cat away. Their hunter's honor would not allow them to take the kill of better hunters than themselves. They left the warm deer carcass and rode on.

Less than a half–mile farther north, the hunters came upon two fawn only days old. The twin mule deer fawns were helpless and sure to die from lack of the protection of their dead mother, which would make them easy prey for a pack of coyotes or other predators. The Sioux quickly dismounted. After the briefest of chases, they had in their possession not tough, stringy meat, but the most tender meat imaginable, easily chewed even by the oldest of their tribe. The hunters gathered together to say their prayers of thanks and feasted on fresh liver, as was their custom. They started for home. For the first time in many, many months, they sat tall on their ponies and even began to sing.

Far to the northwest, the towering thunderhead of a prairie storm loomed. A menacing curtain extending from the cloud to the ground told the group that heavy winds, much rain and perhaps sky stones, hail, were falling. Broken Knife loudly offered another prayer of thanks to their Creator that, at least at this moment, they had soft, warm wind, sunshine on their faces and fresh food for their families. The others in the band yipped and yelled their own thanks as they rode home.

Broken Knife was in high spirits; he had returned with food for his family and his people. He had eaten his fill of fresh liver, ridden the prairie with his friends on a lovely late spring day and was returning to what he thought would be praise and thanksgiving. Instead, he was greeted by a group of weeping women outside his tipi. He found only sadness as he rode into camp leading his proud hunters. As he leapt from his horse, Macawi motioned for him to enter. Lying near the center of his tipi was the body of his wife wrapped in blankets.

After he had wept, prayed and sat in silence, Broken Knife stepped outside of his tipi, his home. Macawi and the rest of the women were there waiting. Macawi told Broken Knife of his wife's last moments. She then told him of his new daughter, alive and with her own daughter, Takchawee, who still was breast feeding her two-month-old son. Broken Knife asked that his baby daughter be brought to him then reentered the tipi to sit with his wife.

Broken Knife unfolded the small package Macawi had placed in his arms. Inside, the child was a tiny thin thing, not at all plump like his two other daughters had been. Her hair was not lustrous black, but a dark, dull brown. The girl did not cry; she barely seemed alive except for her eyes. Her infant's eyes looked directly into his with an intensity that made Broken Knife look away. When he looked back, her gaze had not wavered. He wrapped her up and held her to his heart. He wept again with tears of bitterness, joy, protectiveness, sadness and loneliness. The feelings washed over him again and again until he was utterly spent. Broken Knife held his newborn daughter close to his heart and lay down near his wife and wept.

Much later, he felt a presence enter this black and desolate place. He looked up and sitting on his wife's cooking stone sat a mouse. It was a very ordinary animal, seen everywhere the Sioux traveled. But this mouse did not seem timid; it sat there and stared at him with its curious, black eyes. When Broken Knife waved his hand to scare the little pest away, the mouse simply stood on its haunches and continued to stare. Broken Knife, never one to put much faith in portents, realized that the stone that his wife cooked on had belonged to her mother and her mother's mother before that. He looked at the tiny girl in his arms and began to think of the continuum of life, the unbroken cycle, the sacred hoop. He smiled grimly as he pictured this little girl grown and cooking for his grandchildren.

As the evening cooking fires were being lit and a much-needed feast being prepared, Broken Knife walked into the center of the village. Holding his daughter high in the air for all to see, he said, "This is Itunkala!" In Sioux, Itunkala means "Mouse."

The next days were a confused blur. Broken Knife endured the death ceremony of his wife Ehawee. Macawi and her daughter were caring for his new daughter, now a burden to him.

Aponi and Chumani, his two older daughters seemed lost in their own grief.

Aponi was almost six and Chumani was four. Little Chumani now cried most of the time; her tears made Broken Knife's heart ache. And since Broken Knife was the chief hunter and tracker, he was expected to lead hunts daily. Ironically, it was his argument that his group would stay behind and hunt.

Broken Knife was torn between duty to his family and duty to his tribe. His grief and responsibilities made him want to

just dig a hole in the prairie and hide; he was now solely
responsible for his own three daughters, Takchawee and her
son, Red Feather. Broken Knife longed to be a boy again
without these crushing responsibilities.

In truth, Macawi with her direct eyes and the way she
treated Broken Knife made him feel like a five year old.
Macawi just didn't act as a woman should.   Broken Knife
feared her!

On the second day after Ehawee's death, Macawi came to
Broken Knife's tipi just before sunrise and waited. His two
older daughters still asleep, he stepped out his tipi to greet the
day and say his morning prayers. He just wanted to walk off
into the prairie, relieve himself, and maybe not even come
back. He didn't get his wish.

Macawi stood in front of him holding little Mouse. She
paralyzed Broken Knife with her intense eyes. He shuffled
from one foot to the other, like a little boy caught being
naughty.

"You are the man of two families. All the families need
food. Today you must hunt. Tomorrow, we must join the
larger group."

Secretly, his heart leapt. He wanted nothing more that to
escape to the prairie with his little group of hunters. Broken
Knife did his very best at making his face look manly and in
control. "I was just coming to find you–"

"Your girls will stay with me. Takchawee and I will teach
them responsibility. You will hunt and bring us food."

They stared into each other's eyes for a long moment then
Broken Knife dropped his gaze. He said his thanks to this
powerful woman. "Pilamaya."

* * *

The creator was kind again as the hunters rode south. They
rode down a gentle slope, crossed a tiny stream and up the
other side. They spotted two young buffalo bulls, probably cut
away from a herd somewhere by the alpha male. Not far to the

east, the creek had cut a small cliff out of the underlying sandstone. There was not much of a drop, perhaps fifteen feet, but the small cliff was almost 200 yards wide.

Wordlessly, the hunters circled east around and behind the two young bulls to form a rough semicircle with their ponies. The bulls snorted as they caught the scent of the hunters and their ponies. As soon as the hunters saw the buffaloes react to their presence, they began yelling and galloped their ponies in formation behind the young buffalos. The two young bulls reacted perfectly. Within seconds, the two buffalo were lying at the base of the cliff with broken necks.

During the hunt, Broken Knife was able to live without his grief, his uncertainty and his worries. He lived in the hunt as a true man of Human Beings, the First People. He made the first cut and pulled out the steaming liver. He offered up a joyful prayer to the Great Spirit and took a delicious bite, the first spoils and a man's primal experience. It was after his prayer that the rest of his reality overcame him. He offered up to the Creator his grief, his uncertainty, and his terrible worries. The answer to his prayer came back to him with a certain amount of bitterness; he knew he could meet his responsibilities, his duty to his daughters, his tribe, his people, himself. He knew, too, at a deep level that he could never return to being a boy.

Macawi met Broken Knife as he rode back into camp. She looked him in the eye as always, but this time her eyes were smiling. "You are a good man. Pilamaya." She put little Mouse in his arms as Aponi and Chumani ran laughing to meet him. He sat on the ground and pulled his family close. He said another prayer, this one bittersweet. He thanked the Great Spirit for this moment. While earlier this day he had mourned the loss of his childhood, he now prayed his thanks for being a man, a Human Being. He closed his eyes and wished that this moment could be his eternity. His wish did not come true.

Wakanisha
1865

In the bitter, confusing days following the death of her mother Ehawee, the tiny infant Mouse was nearly forgotten. If it had not been for Macawi and her daughter, Takchawee, the little girl would surely have died.

Macawi, a woman of almost forty winters, dressed plainly. Her buckskin shifts were mostly unadorned, unlike some of the beadwork done by other women. Her hair was long, streaked with a small amount of grey that she kept tied in a long tail down her back. She was unremarkable looking but she stood out because of her erect stance, her intense eyes and the palpable force of her will.

Many members of the tribe secretly feared Macawi because of her forceful personality. They feared her because she seemed to stand outside the strict class system practiced by the Sioux. Despite her lesser status as a woman, she behaved as though she had no respect for traditional boundaries, insisting instead on treating all people as equals. Macawi refused to be intimidated. Occasionally, a young man would attempt to challenge Macawi with his bold patriarchal status. Macawi would respond by treating him like a child, recounting in front of his peers of some embarrassing incident from his childhood. Those who dared to taunt Macawi in this way always left red-faced, feeling humiliated and somewhat emasculated.

In spite of her rigid and seemingly unapproachable demeanor, many revered Macawi for the profound depth of her knowledge. The female version of a Shaman, her adeptness with herbal medicine helped her solve or cure many of their everyday maladies. While her wisdom made her invaluable, many of the men in the tribe deliberately refused to openly recognize her value. But the women of the tribe, as well as a few of the men, sought her counsel daily.

* * *

Although Mouse never knew her mother, Aponi and Chumani both missed her terribly. Looking back, Broken Knife realized his life had lost its harmony with the loss of his wife. Though his meals this past winter were meager, Ehawee had always been well prepared and had food ready when he was ready. She had kept his tipi tidy. But most of all, he grieved for the quiet love and support he and his wife of many years had shared between them. He found himself waking with her blanket or one of her buckskin dresses in his arms. Many nights, after his daughters were asleep, he cried himself to sleep. His tears, because he was a hunter and warrior, could never be shown in public.

As Broken Knife reflected on the past, he realized how much he depended on his wife for the organization in his life. Before her death, Ehawee kept their home running smoothly. His home was now sorrowfully disorganized, messy. Aponi and Chumani were no help. He began to realize how much he and his wife had doted on their daughters and had depended only on his wife for life's everyday needs. He also grasped how utterly indulged and irresponsible his two girls were. When Broken Knife asked his daughters to take over some of their mother's tasks, they either whined disobediently or did the tasks, but did them badly. His meals were abysmal. He wasn't able to find anything in the chaotic state of his home.

Broken Knife also felt painfully guilty regarding his children. Before her death, Ehawee had almost entirely dealt with his children and their needs.

Aponi was now almost six and an outgoing child. Though she was popular with most other children of the village, they knew to avoid her when she was moody. As a first child, Aponi learned that if being sweet didn't work, a good tantrum would. Since her father spent much time away from camp, Ehawee was teacher and disciplinarian. Mother and daughter developed a typical cycle. Sweetly, Aponi would learn the task, but when she performed in a sloppy or inadequate way, she would have a tantrum when her mother tried to correct her. Ehawee found it easier to do the task herself than suffer the outbursts and ill will of her manipulative young daughter.

Similarly, the girl had a way of getting complete control over her father when he was in camp. She knew that by being cute and giving him her complete attention, she could get his attention focused away from her mother.

Both parents knew in their hearts that they were shielding their daughter from the harsh realities of life but she was so precious to them they seemed powerless to change their ways with her.

When Chumani was born two years later, life abruptly changed for Broken Knife and his family. By then, the white man had firmly interrupted the natural cycles of Sioux life. The tribe avoided many of the routes and traditional hunting grounds in order to evade the white man. Broken Knife was forced to spend more and more time away from camp hunting.

Ehawee, now with a newborn, needed the help of her rather spoiled and petulant eldest daughter. But when Aponi was asked to help, she only escalated her difficult behavior. The cycles of their difficult family relationships made life increasingly unpleasant in the household of Broken Knife and Ehawee. Little Chumani learned very early how to exert her own personality into the mix. She quickly grasped that the best thing to do when her older sister became defiant and loud was to coo and smile and charm her mother. When Ehawee forced the disobedient Aponi to go away and play with the other children, Chumani was happy to have her mother to herself.

As she grew, Chumani easily learned the practical skills her mother taught her. She not only completed her own tasks, but willingly completed her sister's as well. Thus, it was Chumani, now, who spent most of her time with Ehawee, and it was she who often got most of her mother's attention. Aponi ran free and spent her energy waiting for and playing with her father.

Because she was sweet and dutiful, it was easy for Chumani to play up the contrast between herself and her rather incorrigible sibling. Aponi typically opted for the outrageous verbal tantrum while Chumani remained sweet and well behaved. Aponi began to resort to hitting and shoving Chumani, using her physical strength and the authority of her age over her little sister. Full-scale war was building between the two little girls.

The two sisters bickered and fought continually until one afternoon when Ehawee could take no more. She pulled them both by their ears into their tipi. With passion, Ehawee told them, "Girls, you must learn Wakanisha. As Sioux, in our beliefs, our lives, in everything we do, Wakanisha is the most important thing about us. We believe that children are holy. You are a gift from Wakan Tanka, and family is the most important facet of our lives. Without love and respect within the family, our way of life will leave us."

To Ehawee's immense frustration, the two girls looked at each other and, almost in unison replied, "I don't really care."

That night Broken Knife arrived home tired, hungry and dirty from a hard day of hunting only to find the three he loved most as mad as hornets. That same evening, Ehawee announced she was pregnant with their third child.

In his heart, Broken Knife questioned the truth of "Wakanisha".

A Cross for Mouse
1865

Chief Stone Foot led his half of the divided tribe west across the unbroken prairie toward the mountains as planned. Their first day of travel had been uneasy. The chief heard the women complaining about leaving friends behind; the children were cranky and uncooperative. Maintaining lookouts was a problem without Broken Knife's young hunters: they would typically act as scouts as well as bringing back game. Dull Knife maintained his usual aloof demeanor but his warriors felt skittish and unsure of themselves. Yellow Bird rode near the front of the column with the chief because his wife, who had not wanted to leave the others behind, was acidly verbal about her opinion.

Yellow Bird, like many of the men, had fantasies about being chief. He often chafed at being ordered around and at times, would question Stone Foot's decisions. He hated it when his three sons had to watch him take orders. Regardless, he usually saw the wisdom of the Chief's decisions.

But it wasn't wisdom that made Stone Foot a good chief; it was his presence. Stone Foot was not tall and did not loom over the other men. But he was a huge man, thick and muscular. Others had an undeniable sense that he would prevail in any physical confrontation, and the chief projected that self-knowledge in his eyes and in the way he carried himself. Stone Foot needed no badge or insignia; he was clearly the tribe's alpha male.

* * *

It was early afternoon when the tribe approached a small stream lined with cottonwoods and willow trees. Stone Foot called his two remaining minor chiefs to him and signaled for the tribe to stop. The women and children were pleasantly surprised when the message came to set up camp. The warriors were given orders for sentry duty as the women and children began to erect tipis. This journeying half of the tribe had expected to travel hard but they had only covered less than half of their normal day's travel.

Within minutes after the camp was set, several of the younger children began playing in the creek, laughing happily. The older children quickly began catching fish, much to the delight of the women who had little to cook for the evening meal. Singing and laughter could be heard throughout the camp. One of the scouts reported back that they had taken a mule deer and needed some women to help with the butchering. A day that started out unhappy and stressful had become pastoral.

* * *

Stone Foot sat down in front of his tipi, lit his pipe and called Dull Knife and Yellow Bird to him. The two minor chiefs sat near the head chief and waited for him to speak. "We must travel hard two suns. Today, the Great Spirit smiled on us. We will take the fish and venison with us for the trip. Also, if our young hunters take rabbit, we will have plenty for our journey. It is a hard day's trek tomorrow. We will leave early and make for another small river. The next day, if we travel well, we will make it to the place our Cheyenne allies have dug their well. It is a good place. The buffalo and deer follow their trail past there, so hunting should be good. But whites have built their strange houses close to their road. They are there for the men who dig the yellow metal. We must watch these whites carefully and never let them know we are close by."

Dull Knife spoke. "I will send two scouts out to look for any whites on our path. They will report back before dark so we will know if our way is safe tomorrow."

"Our camp at the Cheyenne well is an hour's ride from the whites' road and the river it follows. Again, you must have men watching the whites day and night." Stone Foot looked at his two friends as if to say, "You know what you need to do."

Only the Great Spirit could know that, as Broken Knife was mourning the loss of his wife and Stone Foot was enjoying fresh venison, a deadly, unexpected natural enemy was on its way to disrupt the lives of these Sioux.

* * *

The group that stayed behind waited anxiously for news from Broken Knife about the hunt. The morning after he and his hunters returned to camp with the news of their kill, Macawi organized the women and, with a few of the men, they butchered and packed the meat from the two buffalo dead at the base of the sandstone cliffs. It took three horses with travois to transport the meat back to camp. By mid-day, the camp was ready to travel. They were anxious to reunite. The remaining tipis had been disassembled and packed for the journey. The weighty meat was redistributed into more manageable loads. Broken Knife and those who had stayed behind to replenish the tribe's food supply began the trek to rejoin their kin and share their bounty.

Stone Foot's group had left traces of their journey across the prairie that were evident to even the least apt trackers. He had led his group west and north on a route the tribe had taken many times.

Just before nightfall, Broken Knife stopped his group at the same campsite his kin had used only days before. The stream lined with ancient cottonwoods, the one whites later would call White Woman Creek, was a welcome sight. The signs of their relatives' camp were obvious, joyous. Broken Knife's group found the remains of fire pits, the bones of rabbit and fish. The women used the same fire pits to cook fresh buffalo while their children played in the water.

* * *

Early in the fourth day of their traveling, Broken Knife and his band finally approached the Cheyenne well. However, from over a mile away, they could tell something was terribly wrong. The wind was coming from the south and at least two cooking fires were burning, blowing smoke toward the white man's settlement. Broken Knife could not believe Stone Foot would take the obvious risk that the white man might smell their fires.

He stopped his pony and stared. There was not one tipi standing. Urging their ponies forward, Broken Knife's group quickly approached the camp, or what was left of it. What they discovered was a path of destroyed earth, almost fifty yards wide. The destruction slashed a straight line going directly through the center of the camp from the southwest. The ground looked as if a giant had slashed the prairie with a knife. The sage and grasses were uprooted from the soil and scattered on either side of the wide swath. Many lodge poles lay splintered along the edges of the huge scar. Buffalo hides from the tipis lay entangled in the brush hundreds of yards away. The cherished possessions of these proud people were scattered wide in the prairie sage.

There were no joyous greetings. No dogs barked. No children ran around the group as they entered. They were greeted only by wailing survivors of a devastating, twisting, terrible wind.

Stone Foot, looking much older than his years, slowly approached the returning group. He had a long, fresh cut on his left cheek and a noticeable limp. His once regal buckskin leggings and shirt were in tatters. Oddly, some of the others seemed to have escaped any harm at all, but many were severely injured.

Stone Foot approached Broken Knife as he dismounted. The old chief held up his hand in traditional greeting. "How Coula?" His ordinary greeting was ironically at odds with the devastation that surrounded them.

Broken Knife stared, openmouthed. "What happened here?

Weak and exhausted, the old man answered, "Two days ago, a cloud approached. As always, we tied extra ropes to our tipis, secured the horses and moved our people to their shelters. You know, Broken Knife, the prairie often brings these storms; this one seemed no different. First, the cold wind blew one direction, and then came from the other. Then the rain came, very hard. Our tipis were warm and we said our prayers. Then, sky stones began to fall. The skins of Tatonka kept the sky stones out but there came a terrible noise, like the sound of the white man's smoking monster that runs on metal. Only a few moments later, the storm was gone but it took our camp with it. Many are dead, many more hurt. The sky stones hurt many of our horses and the herd scattered. What food we carried is mostly gone. We have few men left who are able to hunt. You are a welcome sight."

"We have food." Broken Knife replied. "What is your greatest need?"

Before the chief could answer, Macawi stepped up to the two leaders. "Send me all your women and girls that can work!"

Stone Foot barked, "Do not order me, woman!"

Macawi held her hand up in greeting, a very manly gesture. "We have little time for our old ways now. The women will erect the tipis that are not broken. We will begin to prepare food; we have brought much with us. I have tree bark for pain. There is much that needs to be done."

The old chief was clearly unsettled by this. He looked at the Macawi for a moment then his features sagged. "Is our Shaman Kangee with your group?" Broken Knife and Macawi answered "Yes," at the same time. Broken Knife called for the Shaman. Kangee had been tending a young man with a badly sprained wrist. He came and joined the small group.

Mustering back his self-control, Stone Foot asked the Shaman, "Does this woman rule *you*?"

The Shaman looked from face to face, perceiving the nature of the question. He spoke gently to the old chief. "This woman is wise about many things. If she were a man, she would be my equal but now is not the time for such talk. We must be strong. Macawi is a strong person. *All* strength is important now."

The chief thought for a moment, then nodded.

Kangee spoke respectfully, "Chief, if it is your will, Broken Knife and I will take all the uninjured men and see to our safety. Macawi will take all the women and see to our camp, our food, and our injured."

Stone Foot, Broken Knife and Kangee gathered all the men and older boys together; Macawi gathered the girls and women. The women assembled near one of the cooking fires, and the men walked to the south edge of the camp near the ugly slash that ran through the village.

Macawi chose two women. She said to the first, "You will see to our tipis. Take the women who can erect our tipis quickly and unload our horses. Use the Tatonka skins and lodge poles we brought in on our horses to set up all of the tipis. Erect them near the fires but not so close as to catch the smoke." She pointed to the east. "The doors must face the sunrise, as you know. We must not forget our Creator."

Then Macawi addressed the second woman. "Take seven or eight of our best cooks, gather all the food in camp and unload the food we brought. Begin cooking as soon as our horses are unloaded. Our people are hungry."

Macawi then spoke to the entire group, "Any woman with healing skills, come with me. There is much to be done. Draw water and begin heating it, bring whatever you can find that can be used for binding wounds or healing."

The women grunted their acceptance and nodded their agreement. They immediately began their work.

Kangee gathered and addressed the men. "Spread out and bring back to camp every Tatonka skin that blew away. Gather all the lodge poles, broken or not. Also bring back to camp any belongings or anything of value you find."

The men began to grumble until one finally spoke up. He said, "The skins and the poles are women's work. It is for others to find their own belongings."

Kangee quietly stared at the men until there was complete silence. "Tonight, there will be fresh meat, cooked and warm. There will be tipis to sleep in. The injured will be tended. If you prefer to sleep on the ground cold and hungry tonight, you may join the rabbits and snakes on the prairie. The Human Beings will sit around the fire tonight and thank Wakan Tanka." The men shuffled their feet, some looking at the ground, and began to move toward the site of the terrible destruction.

Stone Foot spoke. "Take all the unbroken lodge poles and the skins to the women. The broken lodge poles can be stacked near the fires for cooking. Bring all the belongings you find to the center of camp. We will claim what is ours or we will share."

As the men moved off to do the tasks assigned them, one by one they came to Broken Knife to speak. Those who had stayed behind with him to hunt and gather food thanked him for refusing to travel with the larger group. They said his vision had saved their lives and those of their families. Those men who had gone ahead confided to him that they wished they had stayed behind with him to hunt. They didn't speak the words aloud, but their eyes said that they questioned the judgment of old chief Stone Foot. Broken Knife smiled grimly at them but in his heart, he knew he had been given no grand vision when he argued to stay behind. He knew that he simply wanted to escape to the prairie to hunt, to leave behind his responsibilities. He knew he was just a man; he knew that he stayed behind to protect his own family.

The women all gathered briefly to admire little Mouse. She looked at each of them with her penetrating eyes and smiled her sweet baby smile. Each woman felt a slight chill as they looked into those deep infant eyes. It was the same feeling they got when Macawi looked at them and seemed to see through them, only stronger. One of the older women stared longer than the others into the baby's eyes and said, "This little girl has a large, old spirit. She seems to have wisdom of the ages in her face. I sense that she looks into my soul. The others nodded in agreement. The women broke up into groups and went about their tasks as ancient as their people.

In the same way that the men paid homage to Broken Knife for missing the storm, many of the women came to Macawi and offered thanks to Mouse for choosing to be born when she did. The group that stayed behind at first had been held in low esteem for not heeding the words of Chief Stone Foot. Now, that group was their savior. The women credited Mouse with their survival.

The work of restoring the camp to a functioning village was finally under way. All the men, women, boys and girls who were not seriously injured began the tasks at hand.

As the first tipis were being erected, a huge disturbance erupted at the north end of the camp. Broken Knife dropped the lodge pole he was carrying and ran toward the noise. He stopped in disbelief. Approaching the camp was a wagon drawn by a single horse. The wagon was moving at good rate of speed. Running behind the wagon were two of the tribe's young lookouts that had somehow let this intruder approach the camp unannounced. A white woman was driving the wagon. She was slender, wearing a long skirt, her gray hair tied in a bun. Around her neck glimmered a metal chain that held a small, silver cross.

After the woman reined in her horse and the wagon stopped, many of the tribes' younger men surrounded the wagon and made threatening sounds and gestures. The white woman simply climbed down into the crowd. She fearlessly looked each man in the eye. In fact, the men recognized the look. The force of her will reminded them of Macawi. Slightly intimidated, they stepped back and became silent.

As if this scene were momentarily frozen in time, a tense silence prevailed until Broken Knife and the Shaman stepped into the circle. Broken Knife stared at the stranger and said, "Leave, woman. You are not welcome!" The woman responded but no one understood her speech. Broken Knife stepped one step closer and loudly said, "Leave" and made motions with his hands to clarify his command.

Instead of getting back into the wagon and leaving as she was told, the woman went around to the back of her wagon and reached in for a bundle. Instantly, Sioux weapons came up and a deadly silence surrounded them all. She approached Broken Knife and made the universal sign meaning, "Come here!" Her demeanor, much like Macawi's, left little doubt about her personal sense of authority. She simply and calmly took over. Broken Knife followed her to the wagon. She reached into the bundle again and pulled out a package of cloth, torn into strips and a bottle. *"Whisky!"* she said. Broken Knife shook his head to show her he did not understand.

The woman pointed to a young warrior with an open gash on his arm. She made the "Come here!' sign again, and the young man moved forward almost against his will. The woman took his injured arm, opened the bottle and poured a small amount of whisky into the wound.

The young man jumped back immediately and began to howl. The woman did not react but many of the young men began to snicker. The warrior glared around at his friends and the snickering stopped. The woman took his arm again and very tenderly fashioned a bandage for his wound.

She pointed to another man with a cut on the back of his hand. The man immediately fell back much to the jeering of the group but Broken Knife grabbed the man's arm and dragged him to the white woman. She smiled at Broken Knife and again saying something indecipherable, repeated the treatment.

As a third "volunteer" was being treated, Macawi arrived. The two women eyed each other intensely. The men sensed some unspoken and profound exchange between the women but they had no idea what was happening. The white woman reached into the bundle on the back of her wagon retrieving another bottle and a bundle of cloth strips. She pointed to her eyes, then pointed to Macawi's eyes and selected another man with a serious gouge in his leg. She pointed to Macawi's eyes again and then at the man's leg. Using such gestures, the white woman instructed the man to sit on the edge of her wagon and showed Macawi the process.

Facing Macawi, the white woman gripped the cross around her own neck, placed her palm over her heart. She reached out and put her other palm on Macawi's heart. Slowly, Macawi repeated the gesture. Staring into each other's eyes, allowing some kind of mystical energy to pulsate between them. Both women understood without language that they were very much the same. Macawi knew that that this woman had come to help, and that they both spent their lives working for the Great Spirit.

Macawi made the "Come here" sign, and pointed to the tipi that was now being used for a hospital and treatment area for all the injuries from the storm. Without taking her gaze from Macawi's eyes, the white woman simply handed the reins of her horse to Broken Knife and followed Macawi to the suffering patients.

* * *

As sunset neared, after broken bones had been splinted and serious wounds treated, the white woman stepped out of the tipi and walked to her wagon. A flock of curious children had gathered around to watch her. The woman took a large crock with a wooden lid and sat it on the end of her wagon. She motioned with her finger for them to draw near. The children crowded around. The white woman took the lid off the crock, stuck her finger in. When she withdrew her finger, it was covered with a thick, golden liquid. The woman said something the children could not understand, then put the coated finger in her mouth and smiled. Holding a finger in the air she pretended to make it fly around as she made a buzzing noise. She then used both hands to make the "Come here!" sign to all of the children.

Finally, an older girl ventured forward. The woman pointed to the girl, pretended to put her finger in the crock then pretended to put her finger in her mouth. Then, pointing to the child, she held out the crock. Very tentatively, the girl touched the smallest tip of her finger in the crock then put her finger in her mouth. The wide-eyed children watched the girl with her finger in her mouth. She hesitated, smiled hugely and yelled their Sioux word for, "Honey!" sticking several fingers in the crock. The white woman smiled and attempted to say the word she had heard and handed the crock to the brave little girl. Utter pandemonium followed. All the children crowded around, each trying to reach the crock. In moments, the band of happy, screaming children disappeared into the prairie carrying the crock with them. Several adults followed but were unable to get anywhere close to the children's treasure.

Macawi stepped out of the tent to see what the children were doing. She walked over to the white woman's wagon and a group of women gathered around. The white woman touched herself on the chest and said, "*Mary.*" Macawi smiled, repeated what she had heard then pointed to herself and responded, "Macawi." The two women smiled and as they shook hands they again repeated the name of the other.

Mary turned to her wagon and unloaded a small cask of salt, an old ax and a slightly rusty but very large knife. With gestures indicating that these gifts were for everybody, Mary handed the items to Macawi. She also gave several unused bolts of cloth to Macawi. Softly touching her heart, Macawi said warmly, "Pilamaya."

A young woman broke through the circle, carrying a young child who was wrapped in a muddy blanket. Mary looked at the child. Even before she touched its cold skin, it was obvious to her that the child had been killed during the storm. The Sioux woman said something to the white woman that she could not understand but the fervent pleading in her eyes was clear. The white woman shook her head and the Sioux woman began to cry softly. Soon both women were crying, bending over the little child's body. As the Sioux woman fell to her knees, Mary knelt down beside her. The white woman held the cross at her neck and the Sioux woman looked to the skies. Holding one another, the two women cried until no tears were left.

One at a time, women and a few men came to the tent where Macawi and the white woman were working. They asked for help with preparing their dead for a proper Sioux Keeping of the Soul ceremony. The white woman, Macawi and the other women quietly washed the bodies. Softly, the white woman began to sing. Her song, even though completely foreign to the Sioux, conveyed to them the feeling of Wakan Tanka.

One young man who was fatally injured by the storm had already been dressed by his loved ones in fine buckskin with beautiful beadwork. But many other affected families were not so fortunate. Their belongings had been blown and scattered; they had no finery with which to send their loved ones to the Spirit World. When Mary realized the need, she went to her wagon and returned with several bolts of brightly printed cloth.

The white woman tore off a small amount of cloth from the first bolt and went to the young mother. She put the cloth on the ground and held out her hands for the child. The young mother quickly understood and wrapped her child in the beautiful new cloth. One by one, the families of the dead accepted shrouds of cloth from the white woman until all of their beloved departed relatives were clad for their journey.

As day broke, the tribe used broken lodge poles to erect burial platforms. They chose a site far south and west of their camp, near the beginning of the great scar left on the earth by the deadly storm.

Families gathered with friends near their loved ones. The mourners spoke to their dead, forgiving them, praising them, but mostly releasing them from all things undone. In Sioux culture, the journey to the spirit world could not be made without the healing of release. The white woman walked among them praying in her own language. The Sioux women as well as many of the men expressed their respect to the white woman by placing their palm over Mary's heart, over her cross.

As Mary began to climb back into her wagon, Macawi and her daughter Takchawee walked toward her carrying the infant

Mouse. The baby had developed a cough in the night and both women were worried. The two Sioux women placed the infant in the white woman's arms. Mary opened a little wooden box that held a very small bottle and spoon. In the bottle was a clear, green liquid. The white woman gestured to her own eyes and then, pointing to the eyes of the other women pulled out the bottle stopper and poured a very small amount of the green liquid into the spoon. She gently poured the liquid into the baby's mouth. She then handed the bottle and spoon to Macawi and gestured to make Macawi and Takchawee understand that they were to keep both.

Mouse cried briefly, coughed, then lay quiet. She stared up into the white woman's eyes. Mary held the baby's gaze and in that moment, it was if her entire world existed only in the eyes of this amazing child. They were not the eyes of an infant but those of an ancient soul – one who had already experienced joy, pain, grief and the challenges of humanity many times over. There are no words that could define the love and wisdom that passed between the two during those few moments. Recognizing she was in the presence of a magnificent spirit, Mary removed the cross from around her neck and placed it around the child's.

Silently, the white woman handed the baby to Macawi, and put her palms on the hearts of the two Sioux women. She rode away, north, back to the settlement of the white man.

Pilamaya
1 8 6 5

Some normalcy of life returned to camp. The memory of the storm was still as raw as the gash it had left in the earth. The women had many serviceable tipis standing. Thanks to Broken Knife and his hunters, there was enough to eat, though they were now using broken lodge poles as fuel for cooking.

Lodge poles were extremely valuable, perhaps the second most valuable thing a Sioux could own. Their ponies were the most valuable and defined the life style of these people. One decent pony was worth four or five lodge poles but the pole, if cared for, lasted sometimes longer than the owner. Poles were often passed from one generation to the next. Families also passed the story of their poles and how they came to be family possessions. The same was true of the buffalo hides that were the other part of their homes. A hunter could point to any hide covering his home and tell his children of the danger, humor, or both that had taken place during the killings that fed them and clothed them. Family histories were drawn in picture form on the outsides of their tipis.

Stone Foot called a council and discussed the need to make the four to five day journey west to the mountains to get new poles to replace the ones that were lost. Evenings were spent planning and debating the best place to go for the poles.

The tribe was happy with their plan to be going to the mountains, where there was easier living and an escape from the prairie heat in midsummer. They did not look forward to the difficult work of harvesting the lodge pole pines using stone tools. The gift of the metal ax from Mary the white woman would make the pole harvest much easier.

The tribe looked forward to erecting their tipis in a mountain meadow, surrounded by aspen, mountain streams and cool, crisp air. They happily anticipated eating venison, elk and rainbow trout and with the nutritious mountain grasses for their ponies. They longed for long summer days -- the women sitting together and gossiping, making their beautiful buckskin clothing, children playing in the streams, the men with easy hunting, being a little lazy and putting on a bit of fat for the winter.

Broken Knife got much thanks from tribal elders and the women; even the children approached and thanked him for providing them food. His honor and prestige had never been higher. However, the esteem he enjoyed was like a hollow shell. On the outside, he was a true Human Being, a man, the provider for his people. Inside, his life was a shambles. He often returned to his own tipi to find his cooking fire out and cold. On such evenings, he would have traded everything he owned to have his lovely Ehawee meet him at his tent flap.

Little Mouse, now weeks old, spent her days with "Spoon Woman", Macawi's daughter. The white woman's spoon had become Takchawee's most prized possession. It was one of just a few metal items in camp and now everyone in camp called her "Spoon Woman".

One evening after a difficult and unproductive day of hunting, Broken Knife returned to his tipi. The fire was out, the inside a mess. Both daughters, with strict instructions for keeping the fire lit and having at least a semblance of dinner waiting, were nowhere to be seen. He walked through the camp. Most tent flaps were closed but Macawi and Spoon Woman's flap was open. He heard childish laughter inside. He walked in and there were his two daughters enjoying a dinner prepared by a Spoon Woman from meat that he himself had risked his life to kill.

He politely greeted the women as custom dictated then said, "Girls, it's time to go home." There was an uncomfortable silence. Chumani responded by looking to her older sister. Aponi simply glanced at her father and said, "We'll be home later."

Broken Knife experienced a sudden flare of nearly uncontrollable anger. His ruddy face turned a deep, bloody red; his fists clenched at his side. Only his last shred of self-control kept him from physically dragging his older daughter out of the tipi. As it was, he had displayed a loss of Wakanisha in front of the most important, powerful women in his tribe and her daughter, the one caring for his newborn.

Macawi looked from face to face. Calmly she stood. "Girls, go with your father. Chumani, little one, take this corn cake and venison with you for your father's dinner. Aponi, carry these coals from my fire to your tipi and tend to your fire." She picked up a small, bowl shaped stone and deftly removed several coals from her fire and handed the stone to Aponi. "Go now. Make the fire. You're father will be there soon."

Aponi quickly accepted the coals and, with her eyes on the floor, scampered out the tent flap and fled for home.

Macawi busied herself wrapping food and tending the fire. Then, she looked at Broken Knife. "Tomorrow, talk to Kangee about your daughters. They grieve for their mother as much as you. Spoon Woman and I will keep Itunkala at night until she is able to eat solid foods."

Suddenly, Broken Knife's anger was replaced by sadness. It took all his self-control to keep from weeping in front of this woman. He stepped out of the tent and quickly rubbed the tears from his eyes as little Chumani emerged carrying his dinner. Together, they walked back to his lonely and cold home.

Little Mouse, wrapped tightly, watched and listened.

* * *

Early the following morning, Broken Knife gathered his hunters together and gave them instructions. He told them of tracks he had noticed and that today, the winds were favorable. What he did not tell them was that his family needed him. Today, he would not join them. The young hunters, happy to be free his of supervision, rode their ponies north. Strong Wolf was jubilant. It was his first time out as a hunter without supervision, an equal with the other hunters.

* * *

A tent flap conveys a simple but important part of Sioux culture; if the flap is open, any person is free to come in. If the flap is closed, you may not enter unless invited by the person in charge of that household, usually the woman. This morning, the Shaman's flap was open so Broken Knife entered. The men shook hands and Kangee indicated where the hunter should sit. Broken Knife sat at the Shaman's left, a sign of respect from the host. Kangee sat at the back of the tipi, directly facing the door. Broken Knife had followed polite custom and had walked to his spot circling the tent clockwise.

Now that protocol and politeness had been observed and Broken Knife was seated in the spot of honor, they spoke. And as it is with men when the subject at hand is sensitive, they spoke of other things. They discussed hunting and related several stories. They spoke of the weather, past, present and future and its effect on the hunt. They talked about the upcoming trek to the mountains for lodge poles and the possibilities of weather and hunts that might affect their move. Finally, Broken Knife managed to blurt out, "My daughters have lost their mother. They seem to have lost their way." The old man thought for a moment. "They are young. They will learn."

Broken Knife responded, "They have no mother to teach them. They ignore what they know and they play like children." The Shaman thought for another moment and replied, "I will speak to them. They are women; they will do what a man tells them." Broken Knife shrugged. "I am a man. I am their father. I tell them and they still act like children." The older man abruptly stood up and said, "I will talk to them now!"

Moments later, the two men stood outside Broken Knife's tent, somewhat unsure of how to proceed. The tent flap was closed and, with no woman to bid them enter, there was a sad moment of waiting. With a sigh, Broken Knife opened the flap and both men entered. Kangee cleared his throat loudly and the two sleepy girls sat up with very wide eyes. Both girls had just awakened.

The shaman spoke in his deep voice he used when making pronouncements. "You are the women of this household. You will have food ready for your man. You will keep this area clean as a woman should. You will be obedient and do as your man says." With that said, he stepped out of the tent without another word.

Both girls looked at each other, at their father, then burst into sobs. Broken Knife tried to remain stoic until little Chumani crawled out of her bed and snuggled into bed with Aponi. The girls hugged each other and cried even harder. Broken Knife, even without realizing what he was doing, found himself with his girls on the floor, sobbing with them.

Very little goes unnoticed in a small village. And what gets noticed gets talked about. When Broken Knife finally emerged from his tent, Macawi was sitting near his tent flap holding Mouse. She stood as he appeared and handed the infant to her father. Macawi looked him very directly with a sad smile. "I will teach your girls if you approve."

Itunkala looked from face to face as her father said, "Pilamaya."

Corn Cakes
1 8 6 5

Macawi smiled to herself as Broken Knife rode off in the early morning.

During the hunt the day before, the young hunters had used more enthusiasm than common sense. Strong Wolf had spooked the small herd of mule deer that they had been sent out to harvest. In his haste, he had drawn his bow and fired at a deer before being told. The other young hunters had been none too kind in their comments; he was reminded of his age and status. That night, there had been leftover venison, some jerky and corn cakes for dinner, but no fresh meat. No one laid blame on the young hunters but many smiled at the numerous excuses the young hunters made for their empty hands. Strong Wolf was told by the other hunters to stay home until he grew up.

Macawi walked to Broken Knife's tent and stood outside the closed tent flap. She listened for a moment. "It is Macawi. May I enter?"

After a few moments, there was a small voice from inside that said, "You are welcome."

Macawi smiled and entered the tent. She asked, "Do you know why I asked to enter?"

Both girls shook their heads "No" and little Chumani asked, "You are an adult; why would you ask our permission?"

Macawi smiled at the girls. "Please dress and go make your toilet. Clean yourselves and come to my tent. The flap will be open. Come in and there will be some breakfast for you. Today, we begin."

The two girls arrived a short time later as instructed but, as they were about to step into Macawi's tent, she stepped outside. "Show me your left hand."

Aponi shifted from right to left twice then finally held up her left hand. Chumani copied her sister.

Macawi exclaimed, "You are two very smart girls! Please step inside." The older woman stopped the two young girls as soon as they were inside. "Please show me your left hand again."

Both girls immediately held up the correct hand.

"When you enter any tipi, it is our custom to circle the tent in the direction of your left hand. It is the direction the sun circles the sky." Macawi told them. "All life depends on the sun. We honor it by remembering it in our homes." She turned and circled her tent in a clockwise direction and sat down directly across the tent from the doorway. She invited Aponi to sit on her left and Chumani on her right. "Aponi is on my left side because she is my guest with the most honor."

Aponi smiled smugly at her sister and little Chumani began to frown. Macawi watched this exchange. "Aponi showed the greatest knowledge this morning; I'm showing her respect by having her sit on my left. Sometime very soon little sister, you will sit on my left for some knowledge you have gained." Then Macawi asked, "Which sister invited me to enter this morning when I found your tent closed?"

Aponi answered, "I did Coonshi. May I call you that?"

For the first time, the girls saw a genuine smile light up the older woman's face. Macawi answered, "I am not your grandmother but you show me much esteem with that name. I am honored by your respect. Thank you!"

Both girls lit up with smiles of their own and in almost perfect time with each other they said, "Thank you Coonshi!"

Macawi began, "We are Human Beings. We are not animals. Human Beings show respect. We show respect to our Creator. We show respect to each other. We show respect to this world, made by our Creator. When you called me Grandmother, I felt great joy. I admired that you chose the word Grandmother for me. Your faces showed joy. We shared joy together, did we not?"

Both girls nodded eagerly and smiled.

"We Human Beings have many customs and traditions to show respect." Macawi said. "You learned two very important customs already this morning. Chumani, tell me one custom you have learned?"

The little girl smiled and held up her left hand. "Always go this way inside."

"Excellent! You are a quick learner little one!" "Aponi, tell me what you have already learned."

"We are Human Beings and the most honored person sits on the left side." Aponi exclaimed. She smiled smugly again.

Macawi said slowly, "Those are two things you have learned. Little ones, we must also know honor. It is important to know honor because by honoring a person, you are showing them respect." Then she added, "To honor a person, to respect them, you must know about them, what they have done, how they have helped others, what they know and what they can add to the strength and protection of all other Human Beings. Your father is much honored and respected. Watch how others treat him. They admire him because he is the best hunter in our tribe. He feeds us. He deserves great respect. When he comes home tonight, how can you show him your respect?"

Both girls were caught off guard by this question; they weren't expecting to have to apply their learning quite so soon. Aponi quietly said, "He asked me to keep our fire going today. Yesterday I let the fire go out even though he asked me to tend it. We could make sure the fire stays lit."

Macawi looked at each girl. "Earlier, I asked you which girl gave me permission to enter your tent. I recognized your voice Aponi and it was right for you to answer. Another tradition we Human Beings have is that someone needs to be boss. Inside the tent, the woman of the house is the boss. When the tent flap is closed, no one, not even the man of the house should enter without the woman's permission. That is our custom." Macawi sadly shook her head and said, "Your mother Ehawee has gone to be with our Creator. You Aponi are the oldest and now the house is yours. You are the boss. You have much to learn about being in charge and showing respect."

Both girls' eyes began to fill with tears. Macawi said, "It's time to check on your fire. Do you know how to find dried sage branches and other things that can be used to burn in your fire?" Both girls immediately brightened up. "Your father will be so surprised and happy to find his fire going when he returns. Each of you, go now, and find at least one armload and take to your tipi. Notice where I store my fuel on the other side of the tent near the door. That is also our tradition. When you have taken the firewood to your tent, play with your friends for a little while. When you are hungry, come back here. We will make corn cakes and talk.

Aponi and her little sister began running as soon as they stepped out of Macawi's tipi. They headed directly across camp through the common area where the central fire burned. Several men and some older boys were sitting around the fire talking quietly. The girls knew enough that it was impolite to run in the common area so they slowed to a walk and took the traditional clockwise direction around the circle.

As the girls passed the men by the fire, they clumsily postured as women are to do in respect to the men. Stone Foot and several of the other men nodded to the girls and continued talking quietly. Yellow Bird, who had been talking to Stone Foot, did not acknowledge the girls but his two oldest sons, Badger and Black Cloud sneered at the girls. Then Badger said, "Good morning little wablénica." The girls continued on hanging their heads but several of the men and Strong Wolf, a large boy of about 12, glared at the two disrespectful boys. Stone Foot looked sideways at Yellow Bird, as if expecting a reproach, but the minor chief either ignored or was oblivious to the rudeness of his sons.

A few minutes later, Aponi and Chumani returned, each carrying arm loads of dry sage branches. Their path through the center of camp this time took them past the boy's side of the fire. As the girls respectfully postured again, Aponi dropped several branches and her little sister tripped over them and fell, spilling her entire load. The men stopped talking as Badger and Black Cloud laughed.

As the girls were attempting to pick up the little girl's armload, Badger said, "It's about time you orphans did some work around here." The two boys laughed again. The men around the fire looked from face to face, to see how this little drama would play out. Yellow Bird sat quietly.

Strong Wolf who had been sitting near the fire stood and quickly helped Chumani retrieve her sage. Then, as the girls went on their way, he faced Badger and Black Cloud. "One day, these girls will be strong women and they will remember this day, this day you forgot the teaching of the White Buffalo Woman. Remember, there are two paths to choose."

Stone Foot stood and walked over to Strong Wolf. He put his arm around the boy and sat with him on the boy's side of the fire.

The sun was not quite overhead when the two sisters returned to Macawi's tipi. The tent flap was open and both almost tumbled over each other during their entrance. "The fire?" Macawi asked.

Both girls nodded. Aponi said, "We gathered sage like you said. We found lots of dry sage not far from the well. We both took two arm loads."

Chumani chimed in, "We just checked, it was still burning so we added a little. Our home is very warm and it smells good."

"Good!" said Macawi "because we will use some sage leaves when we cook. It will make your lunch taste like your tent smells."

The girls smiled and rubbed their stomachs. "Good, we're hungry!"

Macawi took out two stones; one was shaped like a bowl and the other like a ball. She asked, "Did your mother have stones like this?"

Both girls smiled. "Yes Coonshi!"

Macawi smiled then pointed to a large, flat stone sitting partially in her fire. "Do you have a stone like this?"

Both girls nodded yes and Chumani spoke, "I watched my Momma cook on our stone."

Macawi said, "Go to your tipi and bring your mother's grinding stones but leave the cooking stone there. We will use mine to cook your lunch."

Aponi pushed past her little sister and ran for home, her little sister trailing behind. Moments later Macawi heard Chumani wailing as they came back. Aponi entered with both stones and little Chumani entered seconds later crying. She sniffed, "Aponi wouldn't let me carry a stone; I wanted to help!"

Macawi gave Aponi a look and said, "Remember, respect." She turned, pulled out a buckskin bag and took out a handful of corn. She had both girls sit down near the fire and said, "We're going to make corn cakes for your lunch. And since Aponi carried both stones, I have a very important job for you, Chumani." Immediately, the little girl smiled. Macawi asked her, "Do you know what sage looks like?

Beaming, the little girl said, "Yes".

"Good" said Macawi, "because I want you to gather a few fresh sage leaves. Can you do that for me?"

Again, Chumani nodded yes and bolted for the door. Moments later she was back with a handful of fresh sage.

Macawi took out another handful of corn and put it in both grinding stones. "Watch, and do what I do. Take turns so you both learn."

Aponi grabbed the round stone and little Chumani began to frown again.

Macawi took her stone and by holding the top of the stone, struck the corn in the stone bowl with a crack. Many of the kernels cracked. She struck again several times until the corn had been transformed into meal. She added another handful of corn to the bowl and repeated the process. "Your turn, do what I did then rub the corn with the stone. You want the corn to become almost like dust."

Aponi had little trouble with the first handful.

Then, Chumani said, "My turn!"

Macawi put another handful of corn into the girl's stone bowl but Aponi continued to make meal leaving her sister to watch. Chumani only lasted about five seconds before she tried to grab the round stone out of her sister's hand. Aponi shoved her sister away and began to grind corn again.

Chumani grabbed again but this time her bigger sister shoved her completely over onto the floor. Chumani was up instantly and did a full-body hit on her sister's chest, grabbing for the grinding stone. Girls, the stones and the corn meal tumbled to the floor.

Macawi ordered, "Stop!" in a surprisingly loud voice. She took the girls by their shoulders and sat them in front of her. To Aponi she said, "What did you do?"

Aponi whined, "She tried to take ---"

"Stop!" said Macawi. "What did you do?"

"She tried to ---"

"Stop! What did you do?"

"She -"

"Stop! What did you do?" said Macawi in a low monotone. In a little voice Aponi said, "I wouldn't share."

Macawi turned to Chumani and said, "What did you do?"

Chumani began in an indignant voice said, "She ---"

"Stop! What did YOU do?" Macawi said in the same low voice.

"I tried to grab it out of her hand." the little girl said.

Macawi turned to Aponi again and asked, "What you did, who did that help?"

The older sister said in a quiet voice, "Nobody."

The woman then turned to the little girl and asked the same question.

Chumani quietly said, "Nobody."

Macawi then turned to Aponi again and asked, "What you did, who did it hurt?"

Aponi thought a moment and said, "It hurt my sister."

"Who else?"

Aponi looked at the woman. "Did I hurt you?"

Macawi responded, "You hurt my feelings very much. Who else did you hurt?"

Aponi said, "There's no one else here."

Ignoring the remark Macawi said, "What about your father?"

Aponi thought for a moment. "I didn't I hurt my father, did I?"

Macawi said, "Think girl. Tonight when your father comes home, will you and your sister have a hot meal ready for him? How will you show him honor and respect for the work he does for you?

"I won't fight with my sister. We'll cook together."

Macawi then turned to Chumani and asked, "Who did you hurt?"

Little Chumani burst into tears and sobbed, "I hurt everybody! I'm sorry!"

Macawi said, "Stop crying. I have one more question for each of you but it is the same question. After I ask, both of you talk about how to answer me." Macawi hesitated for a moment then asked, "What do you plan to do about how you treat each other?"

The two girls looked at each other for a moment then Aponi answered, "We will work with each other. We won't fight." Little Chumani nodded her head.

Macawi looked at each girl directly in her eyes for a long moment then said, "You will start *now!*"

Mouse sat wrapped in her blanket, watching and listening.

* * *

Broken Knife arrived back at camp late afternoon. He and the other hunters had taken two large mule deer. He was happy about the hunt and graciously accepted thanks from the other villagers. He quickly took his knife and removed one backstrap from one of the deer and headed for home. He secretly dreaded another difficult evening with his daughters but when he entered his tent, he was completely surprised.

As soon as he stepped into his tent, he smelled the sage smoke of his fire. His girls ran to him, hugged him and laughed. "Coonshi taught us to cook for you!"

The girls began to cook corn cakes on their rock and while the smells drifted about the tent, Broken Knife cut thin strips of venison and showed the girls how to cook it next to the corn cakes.

The three gathered around the fire and said prayers to their Creator.

Broken Knife had never tasted worse corn cakes in his life but silently in his heart, he thanked the Creator for the best meal he had ever eaten.

Mouse, who was propped up near the fire, smiled.

Council
1865

More than half a moon had now passed since the storm. Those less badly injured were now mostly healed. Game was plentiful. Repairs were made to the existing tipis. New garments were being fashioned out of the many deer and antelope hides the hunters brought back to camp. As the people explored their surroundings near the Cheyenne well, more and more articles of value were found, brought back to camp and claimed.

Sadly, some of the found articles belonged to those who perished in the storm. Stone Foot ruled on the distribution in these matters. He knew the needs of every family in camp and often, knew more about them than he wanted to know. Stone Foot understood that every human village, regardless of race, religion, time or place contained the same types of people. Any human tendency among members of his tribe, whether greed, generosity, hatred or love, petty gossiping or secrecy, was known well to Stone Foot and he judged his people accordingly.

The cooking stones and corn grinding stones did not blow away in the storm. Stone Foot made sure every family or young woman nearing marriage age had these necessary household tools. The remaining stones and any other unclaimed or unwanted artifacts found after the storm were lovingly placed under the funeral platforms of their previous owners.

The prairie was in bloom from the abundant winter snowfall. A soft breeze was blowing in from the northwest. Snatches of song and laughter could be heard as Stone Knife's people went about their tasks. Their horses had lost their gaunt, starved look after a spell of grazing on the lush prairie grasses. Thanks to the hunters and an abundance of game, food was being prepared and stored. It was time to move.

That evening as Aponi and Chumani were preparing dinner, they told their father of the rudeness of Yellow Bird's sons. Broken Knife smiled bitterly as he heard about the kindness and courage that Strong Wolf had shown. In his heart, Broken Knife secretly felt that this young, inexperienced hunter was like the son he would never have. He recognized the same selflessness in Strong Wolf that he felt in himself. This young hunter often made mistakes but his intentions were always focused on the good of the tribe, not recognition.

After they had eaten, Broken Knife said, "Girls, go to the tipi of Strong Wolf and give him my thanks. Give his family this backstrap for their dinner."

That night, the two sisters didn't return until much later. When Broken Knife asked his daughters about the evening, they said, "We heard many stories of our mother." From that day on, Aponi and Chumani spent many hours with other families that accepted them as sisters, daughters.

As the sun set, Stone Foot could feel the psychic pull of the mountains to the west. In two days' ride, they would be able to see the mountains and in two or three days after that, they could be there.

Stone Foot got up from sitting cross-legged near his outdoor cooking fire. He approached Kangee and said, "We need to council." Stone Foot motioned with his head in the direction of his tent. The old man entered his tent and, moments later, Dull Knife, Yellow Bird the horse master, and Broken Knife joined him. Dull Knife took his usual position of honor directly to the left of the host. The other three men did their usual shuffling to find their spots, much like any other species of male mammals determining their assigned spot in the pecking order. Broken Knife, the hunter, usually had the spot furthest from the host at these meetings. But today, he claimed a spot closer to the host with no objections from the others.

Stone Foot took out his pipe, packed it and got it burning. As he passed it to his left, he began. "Yellow Bird, how is your lame horse?"

"She's much better but my white one still has a bad spot above his eye from the sky stones."

The talk of horses continued for a while, and the discussion eventually turned to their upcoming move. Like a general asking his transportation officers about readiness, Stone Foot needed input from his most trusted men. As usual, there were minor problems, but nothing to stop them from what was to come.

Stone Foot told the men, "We are 141 Human Beings. There are 37 strong men. Many of the older children are able to carry and work. The Creator has been kind; only three injured people will need to be carried. We have more than a 100 horses."

Dull Knife spoke. "What of the whites? Our traditional path along the Big Sandy River takes us close to Sand Creek. We are not strong enough for battle. We have few rifles and little powder. My warriors have been helping rebuild, rather than making arrows and preparing for conflict. We should avoid the whites and go south to the mountains. There are many small streams along the way that will have water because of the snow. We may have to carry water for our last travel day before the mountains, but I do not want to meet any whites."

There was much conversation about the route they might take, as well as bitter talk of the killings of their allies the Cheyenne at Sand Creek.

The group turned to their Shaman for words of wisdom. Kangee looked at each of them then said, "The Great Spirit has taught us to be free men. We have spoken with wisdom tonight. We will go to the mountains as free men, but we will use caution and sound judgment. Our Creator tests us to see if we still are wise and brave. There is no reason to delay."

Even though Broken Knife was not sitting in last place as he did in the past, the other men, out of habit, waited until the end to ask him about provisions. Briefly considering the irony of their priorities, Broken Knife thought, "Food gives life. All life must eat and we thank our Creator for each meal, each animal that dies for our food. Without food, we would die, but always war is more important than the one that brings food."

He silently took a deep breath and sighed before he spoke to the men in his usual even tone. "We now have fresh meat for several days. The women have dried much more meat. If our travels take more than three days, we may have to camp and hunt for one day. The prairie grasses will feed our horses but we need corn. The women complain that they only have a few days of corn left and the harvest is months away. We may need more game to trade for corn if we meet any on our journey that will trade. If the Creator will smile on us and send one or two large Tatonka, we could have much to eat and trade."

The five council members discussed some finer points of travel, such as who would ride, who would walk, who were now the best scouts. Kangee assured them he had recorded the momentous events of the last few weeks on the hides of his tipi.

There was a short, uncomfortable silence. Stone Foot fixed his eyes on Broken Knife. "We grieve with you. Your wife was a good and honorable woman. Kangee and I have both lost our women. We have felt that weakness."

Broken Knife looked directly at the old man. "Speak your heart. Am I less of a man now I have no woman?"

Stone Foot continued, "We respect and honor you for the work you do. You now have three daughters and all three are very young. Macawi and 'Spoon Woman' are being mothers to them. We worry that you will break your heart feeding our big family while your daughters are cared for by another."

Broken Knife hesitated, sighed then said, "My heart is mending. Aponi and Chumani have learned much and are doing well. They are cooking for me and keeping my tipi. We are a stronger little family. I will continue to work for the good of our big family if this council wishes it." He looked each man directly in the eye as he said this.

Kangee broke in. "Your two older daughters have learned much. Each of us sees them growing in wisdom. But, Broken Knife, the women talk. Your little one, Mouse, makes them nervous. They say it was her and not you that saved us from the storm. All of them think your group stayed behind because of her, because she chose to be born at that time, during the storm. The women feel strange when she looks at them."

Broken Knife jumped up and spoke. "She is just a baby! She was born when the Creator planned it. Yes, I know her spirit seems larger than she is."

Yellow Bird spoke, "There's more. When Spoon Woman takes her out in the pack, the children stop playing and follow them. When Spoon Woman walks with her past the horses, the horses become quiet and follow her with their eyes. When Macawi props Mouse on the ground while cooking, the camp dogs gather and circle her, growling if one of us comes near. This child makes us nervous."

Broken Knife began to clench his fists and rose up on his toes when Kangee gently stood and put a calming hand on Broken Knife's arm. "Yes, Broken Knife and our group stayed behind and missed the storm. We stayed partly because this man's wife was about to birth her baby. We also stayed behind to hunt. Now the baby is here and much good has come into our lives. The Creator sends us abundant game. The weather is perfect. The white woman came and helped us. We have many things to be thankful for. We should not fear a mouse."

The Shaman continued, "A mouse is a wise animal. Mice can live everywhere. Yes, they can be annoying and sometimes chew our things. But, a mouse can live in the desert or in the forest. If we would but watch, there is much we could learn from these little animals. I think we may learn much wisdom from our little Mouse. We must let her be who the Creator wants her to be."

Broken Knife turned, shook hands with the Shaman and said, "Pilamaya."

Cheyenne Wells
1867

As in many cultures, the Sioux's stories and their history were linked to significant events. The great storm was one of those events. Almost two and a half years had passed. Families that had lost one or more of their beloved relatives told their stories of pain, hardship and sorrow. The families with the luck to have been safe with Broken Knife and those who survived the storm intact described those years differently. The hunting had been very good. The tribe had avoided confrontations with whites and had maintained their Tawaiciyan. They had traded well with the other tribes that grew corn. For the first time in many years, the coming winter did not concern them. Life was good.

Even so, Broken Knife and Spoon Woman worried, but not about the coming winter. Like most parents, they worried about their children.

Broken Knife's two older daughters seemed to be doing well given that they were motherless. Macawi and Spoon Woman were wonderful, natural surrogates. Spoon Woman had been wet nurse to Mouse and was now a strong mother figure. But the two older sisters now spent more and more time in the tipi of Strong Wolf and his family. And during moves, Strong Wolf and Aponi often rode double on the young hunter's pony. Broken Knife's two older daughters seemed to have integrated themselves into tribal life and Aponi's friendship with this young man seemed natural.

What really worried Broken Knife was the mental life of his strange and unusual daughter Mouse. She was nearly two before she began to walk. In a culture that relied on physical ability, he initially feared some handicap. But when it came to her mental abilities, Broken Knife was feeling fear more than worry. Now, at two and a half, Mouse seemed almost as mentally capable as an adult. Her ability to learn and use language was staggering. She could easily count over fifty, could name most of the animals the tribe saw and was already conversing with almost everybody as an equal.

The male population of the tribe was clearly annoyed by Mouse. The entire tribe believed in Wakanisha but the male population also believed that women, and especially children, should defer to them. Mouse simply would not be intimidated; she treated others as equals. The men were irritated with her attitude and abilities because, in their hearts, they feared the person they knew she might become.

Spoon Woman had other reasons to worry. Her son Red Feather was fatherless. He was a happy boy. He had walked early. He could run, throw, jump; do all the things a boy should do. But little Red Feather had only been speaking for about six months. She didn't really worry that he was somehow handicapped; she just wished he didn't rely on Mouse. Mouse did all the talking. When the two children were together, as they were almost daily, Mouse was the dominant child. Red Feather seemed to be content with Mouse as his boss.

Many fine fall days passed. The buffalo herd grazed nearby and hunting was easy. The herd showed no signs of its annual migration, so the tribe waited and enjoyed the ease of life. Broken Knife had trained his many young hunters well. The tribe needed only to harvest one or two of the huge animals each day. The meat was boiled or fried and eaten fresh and abundance was being dried and stored for winter.

Broken Knife stayed in camp more often now that his young hunters were having success. He enjoyed these relaxing days and took pleasure in them. Aponi and Chumani now showed him a greater respect and enjoyed his company. Their cooking had improved significantly thanks to days spent with Macawi and Spoon Woman. Broken Knife sometimes carried little Mouse around with him but she often toddled along behind.

For the children, days in camp were joyous. Mornings were usually a time for learning and stories, although there was no set time or mandatory attendance. Often, Aponi and

Chumani would take little Mouse to the tent of Macawi and Takchawee where they would gather with a growing pack of children. From there, one of the women would take the group to visit different tents in the camp.

Each tipi had family histories and stories drawn on and around the openings. When the group came to visit, a family member from the tipi would come out and tell their stories and point to the pictures or the children's guide would read the stories to them. Some of the older children were learning to read the pictographs and would often relay the story themselves.

A favorite place to visit was the home of Broken Knife. Most of his stories were of hunting adventures. The young boys especially enjoyed it when Broken Knife relived encounters with mountain lions or bears, or incidents when the huge bulls fought back.

Kangee's stories for the children were different. The children sat raptly listening when he told the ancient Sioux legends of The White Buffalo Calf or the many stories of Coyote, the Trickster. The old Shaman told these stories in his deep resonant voice, often telling of the seven sacred rites, of birth and death and the afterlife. He was, after all, their spiritual leader.

One day, the old shaman was telling a story about two warriors who had been killed in battle and had to face Maya Owichapaha, the old woman who judges souls. When Kangee finished the story, he asked the children what they thought. One older boy wanted to know why the warriors were in battle. Aponi wanted to know why one warrior got to go to the Ghost Road and the other didn't. Kangee answered their questions with authority and grace.

Then Itunkala stood and looked at him with her disconcerting eyes. "Are these stories true?"

The old Shaman hesitated a moment then answered, "Yes!"

"Can you show us the story on your tipi? Show us the pictures." she asked.

"There are no pictures of Maya Owichapaha. No one alive has seen her."

"Then how do you know she is there?" asked Mouse.

The rest of the children had begun to squirm a little. A few adults had drifted over and had joined the fringes of the group. The little girl stared calmly into his eyes with her intense gaze. Kangee had been questioned for years by adults about the religious beliefs of the Sioux and had always answered convincingly. For a reason he could not understand, the questions coming from this tiny girl went straight to the core of his being, to the place where his own private questions were hidden.

"I do not know that she is there. I believe that she is there. The story of Maya Owichapaha is very old. It was an old story when my father's father's father was a little boy."

The little girl thought a moment. "Macawi taught me to believe what I see. But she also teaches me to believe what my heart tells me. Is Maya Owichapaha in your heart?"

The old man raised his hand to his heart and said, "Yes, Maya Owichapaha is in my heart."

Itunkala walked over to the old man and asked, "Will you teach me more?"

* * *

That night, Itunkala began to develop a cough. By the next morning, she had trouble breathing. Broken Knife first went to Macawi's tent with the little girl.

Macawi said, "She coughed the last time we were here. Remember. The white woman Mary gave us the bottle and spoon with the medicine. We have none left. This place must be bad medicine for little Mouse."

Broken Knife and Macawi took Mouse to the Shaman. Kangee said a Shaman's prayer and had the little girl breathe some smoke from burning sweet grass. The smoke only made her congestion worse.

By afternoon, Itunkala's cough was much more severe and the entire village was concerned. Dull Knife, Broken Knife, Kangee and Macawi had a brief discussion about what should be done. Kangee put into words what the other adults were thinking; Mouse should be taken to white woman's place. But, Dull Knife protested loudly. He reminded them about the tribe's policy of avoiding whites at all costs. Macawi reminded him of the kind white woman's help with the victims of the storm two years ago. Finally, Broken Knife said, "I'll take her myself. Send scouts to watch and if there are problems, leave and go east with the tribe."

Macawi said, "I'll go too. The white woman Mary may remember me. Broken Knife, go to your tipi and get the metal necklace with the cross. We will put this on Itunkala so the white woman will remember."

Late in the afternoon, the three approached the white settlement. Both Macawi and Broken Knife were extremely nervous. They rode their ponies up the last hill before the settlement and dismounted. They tied the horses to some sage and peeked over the ridge of the hill down to the riverbank where the houses were built.

The houses were constructed mostly of sod. Each had small openings for windows, some even had glass. Thankfully, the houses were quite far apart. Many of the houses had several horses in corrals and some had wagons parked near corrals. One house, smaller than the rest, had no horses outside but had a large garden. As they watched, Mary came out and harvested some plants from the garden. Macawi and Broken Knife smiled at each other.

After some quiet discussion, Broken Knife and Macawi decided to circle the settlement, cross the shallow stream and use the trees as cover to approach the white woman's house from the back. They hoped no other whites would see them.

They quietly approached the back of the white woman's house. Macawi then said quietly, "Mary, Wóciciyaka wácin." which in Lakota Sioux means, "Mary, I wish to speak with you."

There was no response from the house. So Macawi repeated "Wóciciyaka wácin!" much louder.

Suddenly, the white woman stepped around the side of the house holding a rifle. The rifle was pointed at the ground but in their direction.

Macawi said, *"Mary"* as she looked directly into the woman's eyes.

The white woman hesitated. *"Macawi?"*

Macawi held one hand over her heart and held her other hand up, palm facing the white woman.

At that moment, Itunkala coughed and the white woman then saw that Broken Knife was holding a toddler. The little girl coughed again. Broken Knife held the baby out to Mary and he said, "Aké iyúskinyan wancínyankelo." (I'm glad to see you again.)

Immediately, Mary leaned the rifle against the house and walked up to Broken Knife and Itunkala. The man placed his daughter in the arms of this white woman. Macawi stepped up and exposed the cross around the baby's neck.

Mary gasped then smiled at them both. *"Bless you!"*

The three adults stood there for a moment until Itunkala made eye contact with Mary. Mary remembered that feeling of falling, being sucked into another dimension. Then the little girl said, "Táku eníciyapi hwo?" (What is your name?) "My name is Itunkala."

The woman said something the Sioux couldn't understand. She then made the universal hand gesture meaning, "Come in."

The afternoon sun was setting behind the surrounding trees when they all stepped into Mary's sod home. The home was neat and clean but not at all airy and light like a tipi. It was dark; little light came in through the two small windows. A single bed sat against one wall under a window. On the other side of the room was a small, pot bellied wood stove, some cabinets and a table with two chairs. On the wall above the stove was a small shelf that held a kerosene lamp and another cross. On an adjacent wall was a sturdy, handmade bookshelf with many books.

Mary took a match out of a box, struck it and lit the lamp, much to the amazement of the three Sioux. Mary took the lamp, set it on the table and motioned for them to put Mouse on the table.

When Mouse was on the table, Mary first held her hand on the little girl's forehead. When she didn't feel any fever, Mary smiled and said, "*OK! Good!*" and nodded her head. Both Macawi and Broken Knife showed their understanding by smiling and nodding.

Macawi attempted, "*OK!*"

Mary laughed, pointed to Macawi and said, "*OK! Good!*" Everybody smiled. Next, Mary undressed the little girl and looked her over for bites, bumps and rashes. Mouse had beautiful skin and no sign at all of any problem. Mary smiled again and said, "*Good! OK!*"

Macawi repeated, "*Good! OK!*"

Mouse sat up, smiled and said, "*OK! Good!*" Everybody laughed.

Just then, there was a scratching at the door. Mary opened the door and an old dog walked in, sniffed the strangers and lay down on the floor.

Mouse excitedly said, "Sunka!"

Mary looked from Mouse to the dog then pointed and said, "*Dog.*"

Mouse pointed to the dog again and said "Sunka!"

Mary smiled and said, "*Sunka, dog!*"

Mouse repeated, "*Dog, sunka.*"

Slowly, Mary pointed at the dog and said, "*This is a dog. This is a dog.*"

Slowly, Mouse said, "*Dis – is – dog.*"

Mary smiled hugely and said, "*This is a dog. OK! Good!*" Everybody laughed again. She then held one finger to her lips.

The three Sioux looked at her quizzically. Mary then held her hand over her mouth then held one finger to her lips again. All three shook their heads in understanding. Mary then put her ear to Mouse's chest and listened to her breathe. She motioned for the other two adults to listen as well. Mary then pointed to Mouse, pointed to her own chest and mimed being short of breath.

Mary went to a cabinet, took out a bottle and a spoon and poured a small amount of green liquid into the spoon. She motioned for Mouse to open her mouth but Mouse just held out her hand. When Mary hesitated, Mouse pointed to herself and shook her head. Mary looked at Macawi then to Broken Knife. They both shook their heads "Yes." Mouse, said in English, "*OK! Good!*" The child then took the spoon and swallowed the liquid, making a terrible face.

In a far corner of the dark house, a cat woke up, stretched and rubbed against Mary's leg. Mouse immediately said, "*Igma! Dis is igma.*"

Mary pointed to the cat and said, "*This is a cat.*"

Mouse pointed and said, "*Dis is a cat.*" There were smiles all around. Then she pointed at the dog. "*Dis is a dog.*" She pointed again and said, "Dis is a cat."

Mary smiled and pointed at the cat and said, "*Dog?*"

Mouse frowned and said, "*Heyah! (No), cat.*" All the adults laughed again.

Mary looked intently at Mouse and said, "*This is NOT a dog. This is a cat.*" Then the woman pointed at dog and said, "*This is not a cat. This is a dog.*" She then pointed at the dog and asked, "*Is this a cat?*"

Mouse quickly said, "*Dis is not cat. Dis is a dog.*" Mary clapped, smiled and hugged the little girl.

Mary pointed to herself. "*My name is Mary. Mary.*" She pointed to Macawi and said "*Macawi.*" She then pointed to Mouse. "*What is your name?*"

The little girl pointed to herself. "*Itunkala.*"

Mary attempted the name a few times and finally got the inflection close. The two then shook hands and smiled at each other. Mary then turned to Broken Knife, held out her hand. "*I'm Mary, what is your name?*"

Broken Knife told the white woman in his language his name but after many attempts, she could not say it. He then slowly drew his knife and held it in his the palm of his hand

and said, "Mila." He pretended to break it and said again, "Mila."

The two shook hands and said each other's names. From that day on, Broken Knife was called Mila in this little group, Knife in Sioux.

Mary then pointed to Macawi and Mouse and again pantomimed sleeping, and then pointed to the bed and back to the woman and the little girl. She then pointed to the bottle of medicine and held up three fingers.

Mouse immediately said, "Wanji, Numpa, Yamni" and held up three fingers.

Mary held up three fingers. *"One, Two, Three."* She then held up three fingers again and pantomimed taking the medicine three times. She pointed to Mouse then Macawi again and pantomimed sleeping again.

Macawi and Broken Knife had a brief discussion; he was torn between his tribal duties and his love for all three of his daughters. "I must return and direct the hunt. I also must watch over Aponi and Chumani. I will return tomorrow." That night, Mouse began to learn the language of the whites.

* * *

Instead of staying one night, Mouse and Macawi stayed three. Mouse soaked up words like the prairie soil drank in rain.

By the end of the second day, Mouse was using humor in her new language. She would say things like, *"Dis is not sunka, dis is tatonka."* while pointing to Mary's dog. She would giggle and all the adults would laugh. She got her biggest laugh when she pointed to her father. *"Dis is no Mila, dis is knife."*

It was late afternoon of their second day that Mouse discovered Mary's books. Mary did not have the Lakota language skills to explain the books but when she finally pulled out a book of animal drawings, all three of her Sioux guests became utterly amazed. They were like awestruck children. They chattered and named familiar animals. Mouse sometimes said the name in both languages, sometimes in one or the other. When a page was turned and an unfamiliar animal appeared, they all gasped and pointed. When a picture of a zebra appeared, the three were speechless with amazement. Little Mouse finally asked, *"Is dis a Súnkawákan, a horse?"*

Mary said, *"This is not a horse. This is a zebra."* All three of the Sioux said 'Zebra' at the same time.

When Mary turned the page and showed them the picture of an elephant, she could not understand their reaction. Mouse was no help. Both Macawi and Broken Knife pointed to the elephant picture over and over saying, "Our stories tell of this animal. Our ancestors hunted and ate this animal." Mary would understand many years later when she gained a sense of the enormity of Sioux history.

Mouse's cough only lasted through the first night, but powerful friendships were formed among them. Macawi and Mary became as close as sisters but without a common language. But Mouse was making short work of that. By the third day, Mouse was starting to translate. Much of what was said was via hand signals and acting out. The process had started. Relationships became bonds.

On the third afternoon, the three Sioux left sadly. Broken Knife had come every day, usually with some prime cut of fresh meat or with fresh corn cakes with local berries baked in. On the last day, Broken Knife arrived with two enormous backstraps. It was easily enough to feed fifteen to twenty people. When Mary tried to have him take it back, he used sign language and Mouse to say, *"Feed friends."*

The next day, Mary took the meat to all her neighbors. She told all the white settlers living near her about her Sioux friends, the storm, everything. For as long as Mouse lived, the area around the Cheyenne wells remained a haven with the whites as friends.

* * *

The whites who settled there on the Smokey Hill River were mostly Methodists, the remnants of a wagon train that passed through. They had regular visits from passing miners and the occasional Methodist circuit rider, but Mouse's little band of Sioux was their only regular visitors. The Sioux passed through at least twice a year.

For the first several years of Mouse's life, the friendly folks near the Cheyenne well were the only whites she knew. She loved stopping there, loved her time with Mary and she loved learning, rarely forgetting anything she was taught. Years later, Mouse would learn that not all whites were so friendly.

Macawi and Broken Knife told their stories back at camp. Broken Knife gained more prestige in the tribe, Macawi had greater respect among the women, and the stories of Mouse grew and grew. But only the women recounted the stories of Mouse -- not the men. The men continued to see women as inferior. They told their stories of the hunt and battle glories, and seemed to remain unaware of the amazing little girl growing in their midst. Soon, they would think differently.

Nadowessioux - The Snake
1 8 6 8

Articles of a treaty made and concluded by and between Lieutenant-General William T. Sherman, General William S. Harney, General Alfred H. Terry, General C. C. Augur, J. B. Henderson, Nathaniel G. Taylor, John B. Sanborn, and Samuel F. Tappan, duly appointed commissioners on the part of the United States, and the different bands of the Sioux Nation of Indians, by their chiefs and head-men, whose names are hereto subscribed, they being duly authorized to act in the premises.

ARTICLE 1. From this day forward all war between the parties to this agreement shall forever cease. The Government of the United States desires peace, and its honor is hereby pledged to keep it. The Indians desire peace, and they now pledge their honor to maintain it.

From The Ft. Laramie Treaty, 1868

Stone Foot took a calculated risk and set up camp near what the whites called White Woman Creek. There were white settlements on and around the area but his scouts had reported that the route they were taking was safe. The region was dry prairie land, much like most of the land the Sioux called home. They were on their way west and north, away from the Arkansas River headed to their traditional hunting grounds. The creek and its scattered cottonwood trees offered some shade and a welcome diversion. There were some fish to be caught, water for their horses, bathing and cleaning. They were also very near the border of the Colorado territory. The chief knew that by leaving Kansas and entering the Colorado territory, there was less chance of being pursued by the Kansas authorities.

It was fine late afternoon on a very hot early-summer day. The adults had done most of their chores; many were in or near the creek. Small cooking fires were lit and the camp was relaxed and content. There was fresh fish to cook and several of the young hunters had snared rabbits.

On that first afternoon the tribe had arrived at the sandy bank of White Woman Creek, Macawi helped Chumani and Aponi set up their tipi with the help of Spoon Woman. The older girls badly wanted to explore, wade in the creek and play with the other, older children. But, as Broken Knife rode off with his hunters, he said, "Mind Macawi; watch your sister." They knew it meant babysitting.

Aponi angrily clenched her fists at her side but her slightly wiser, more diplomatic younger sister Chumani responded, "Háŋ Ate." As Broken Knife rode away, Aponi glared at both her sisters and grabbed Mouse by the hand. She led them out onto the open prairie. Almost immediately, the girls scared a jackrabbit from under a patch of sagebrush. In the spot where the rabbit fled were several young kits, so young that Aponi was able to catch one without much of a chase.

Aponi smiled to herself and led her two sisters farther onto the prairie carrying the kit in one hand. Aponi knew full well that her actions had doomed the baby rabbit. The human scent on the kit's fur would keep the mother away. Aponi handed the kit to Mouse and said, "Stay here until the mother rabbit comes back then put them back together." The two older girls left Mouse there as they returned to the creek and their friends.

Mouse took her instructions seriously. She was afraid that maybe the mother rabbit wouldn't return with her near so she took the rawhide from around her waist and tied the kit to a sage twig and waited yards away, hidden in a thicket. Almost immediately a huge bird, a golden eagle, swooped down and flew away with the kit. Mouse was astonished and about to cry out when the rawhide snapped the eagle back to the ground with a shriek. The bird thrashed on the ground for a moment, pulled the kit out of its noose and flew away with its meal. But lying on the ground were several of the bird's feathers, one of which was an enormous tail feather.

On some level, Mouse recognized the significance of the feather; she picked it up and walked back into the camp. Several of the men including Kangee and Stone Foot had just settled in near the communal fire with their pipes when Mouse entered camp.

Stone Foot was facing away from Mouse as she approached. She solemnly pulled on his leggings and waited for his response. At first, the chief scowled at Mouse then he saw the feather. His face did not convey the wonder he felt but he was unprepared for what happened.

Mouse very slowly raised the feather in her open palm, balancing it as she presented it to this mysterious and important man. Slowly, Stone Foot stood and turned to face this tiny girl. The two locked eyes for several seconds, long enough for the old chief to feel pulled into a place he always imagined where the Great Spirit lived. His consciousness narrowed to only one place, the depth within the eyes of this little girl.

With a huge effort, Stone Foot broke eye contact and leaned over. He accepted the feather with dignity. Then very slowly with his other hand, he touched his heart and extended it towards the child. She smiled and walked away.

The following morning, Aponi and Chumani were unhappy about the lectures they had had both from their father and Macawi. The girls still wanted to play in the creek. But instead, Macawi ordered them to look after not one but two three- year olds, Mouse and Takchawee's son Red Feather.

Red Feather, two months older than Mouse was an easygoing boy. He did what he was told and rarely fussed or caused trouble.

Mouse was another story. Her gift to the chief was the talk of camp and seemed to give her some immunity to her older sister's anger. An unruly child might have proved easier for her older sisters, but instead, Mouse often simply outmaneuvered them as she had done unconsciously with her gift to Stone Foot.

Red Feather and Mouse played together quietly for some time and it seemed as if they might just crawl into the shade and nap. Aponi and Chumani could stand it no longer and sneaked off to the creek to play, leaving the three year olds behind.

The evening meal was about to be served when Macawi found little Red Feather asleep near the children's area. Mouse was not with him. It wasn't a new development; Mouse often left camp to explore. Macawi woke her little grandson and asked where the three girls were, but the sleepy little boy didn't know. She trudged down to the creek and found Mouse's two older sisters playing in the water. Aponi and Chumani sheepishly confessed that they, too, had no idea where their younger sister had gone.

Macawi pulled the two girls from the water by their ears and made it painfully clear that they had failed in their duties. They were now to accompany Macawi until little Mouse was found.

Strong Wolf, who had been swimming nearby, stood nearby. "I asked Broken Knife's daughters to join me." he said. They are the daughters of my teacher. I asked them to be here. I will help find the little one."

The four started at the center of the camp and worked outward in a circle. Mouse was not in camp and no one had seen her for a while. No one down at the creek had seen her either so the search party started up the gentle slope from the creek to the level prairie. Not far from the rim of the creek basin was a large area of fresh mounds of earth, a prairie dog town. In the midst of this field of bumps and holes stood little Mouse. Macawi called out to her but Mouse stood fast, staring at something on the ground.

Macawi, Strong Wolf and the two sisters walked toward Mouse to find out what was so fascinating to the little girl. What they saw was terrifying. A large snake was halfway down one of the prairie dog holes as it looked for prey. As they got closer, they recognized the rattles at the end of the large prairie snake's tail. Before Macawi could react, Mouse reached down and pulled on the snake's tail until the snake came completely out of the hole. The snake displayed its displeasure at being interrupted. It buzzed its rattles and coiled, as if to strike. Frozen in fear, Macawi and Mouse's sisters felt that time stopped in that moment. The snake's head was now at the same height as Mouse's. The two stared into each other's eyes. Mouse seemed completely fearless, as if she didn't comprehend the danger she was in.

Then, in a high, pure soprano, Mouse began to sing a song Macawi had taught her earlier in the year, the Song of Happiness, a traditional Sioux children's song.

As Mouse started through the song for the second time, the snake stopped shaking its rattles, dropped to the ground and briefly wrapped itself around Mouse's right leg. Mouse looked down and smiled as the snake crawled away.

* * *

Itunkala's encounter with the snake was the subject of talk around the fires that night, and for weeks to come. Broken Knife took pride in his unusual daughter but was also perplexed and troubled by her antics. Gossip about Mouse brought him esteem with the tribe yet her spirit seemed much too big for her tiny slender body. He worried that Mouse would never attract a husband. She was too small and her attitude was far too large. Aponi and Chumani were bigger girls and would grow into desirable women. As with most Sioux fathers, Broken Knife looked forward to his daughters' coming of age ceremonies. The ceremonies would come with offers of horses in exchange for the hands of his daughters in marriage. In fact, Horse Woman, the wife of the Yellow Bird was the most prestigious woman in the tribe because her husband and his family had paid three ponies for her hand in marriage. Her father had become wealthy and she became the highest-ranking woman in the village although, perhaps, the most obnoxious.

After dinner Macawi and Broken Knife sat down with Mouse to teach the little girl a lesson that perhaps would save her life in the future. Broken Knife had argued before dinner for strong discipline, but Macawi simply skewered the large man with her eyes and said, "This child has an immense spirit. We must let it grow."

Macawi squatted near the child and said, "Girl, do you realize that the snake kills before it eats?"

"Yes." said the girl, "so do we."

Broken Knife, needing to speak, said, "The snake could have killed you. Do you know that?"

The girl looked at them both then replied, "You taught me that Human Beings only kill for food. Nadowessioux would not eat me. He has honor like us."

Macawi looked at the girl's father and smiled. "Girl, just like the Human Being, the snake will also kill to protect itself and its family."

Mouse looked at them both and said, "Snake knew I was his friend."

Broken Knife lost patience and snapped, "Nadowessioux has no friends. He kills. He could have killed you!"

The little girl looked up at her father and said, "Father, you taught me that Nadowessioux helps keep a balance. He helps take the small animals. You said he looks for mice. I am Mouse. I wanted him to know me."

Broken Knife began to lose his patience so Macawi put her hand on his arm. "Girl, you have a wise spirit. Learn from the animals but also learn from Human Beings. You can learn by asking instead of doing. Ask your father or me for the lesson you want to learn. Your spirit is precious and we need you with us."

The little girl thought a bit and asked, "Do I own my spirit?"

Macawi looked at Broken Knife again. The man seemed completely lost, bewildered. Gently, the old woman said, "Girl, you and the Creator own your spirit."

"When do I see him?" Mouse asked.

The two adults looked at each other and a subtle shudder passed between them. Her father whispered, "When He decides."

The little girl, sensing the conversation was over hopped up and began to walk away then turned and said, "I'm ready!"

Lessons

1868

In some ways, Macawi and her daughter Spoon Woman were very different. Macawi could be abrupt, rude, even scathing. The men of the village grudgingly treated her like an equal. She didn't carry a weapon except for her tongue and her wit. If it weren't for her knowledge of herbal medicine and her ability to teach the young, the men would have been much less tolerant. In her own way, Macawi had earned her rank in the village the same way the men gathered prestige. She simply refused to be cowed by anybody, and earned that right by her contributions to the welfare of all. If she had been a man, she would surely be part of the tribal council. Only her gender and Sioux tradition kept her from that role.

Spoon Woman was soft and endearing where her mother was contentious. She was just as knowledgeable as Macawi, having learned all the same skills. After all, her mother was a gifted teacher. What the men of the village failed to realize was that the gentle Spoon Woman was just as successful at exerting her will as her ferocious mother. The men felt more comfortable around Spoon Woman because she fit the image most Sioux men had of a woman. Their male egos felt more intact when they found themselves doing some task for her. Where Macawi would have used the force of her will and sharp tongue, Spoon Woman softly gave compliments. But, the end result was the same.

There was one belief, one force that both women embraced completely. Wakanisha! They believed in the holiness of the family as the foundation of their way of life. Even though these two women were not a traditional family, their devotion to Wakanisha encompassed and permeated the entire village.

Macawi was the teacher of every person in the village in their early twenties and younger. Spoon Woman, with her vastly different style, was now following in her mother's footsteps as a natural teacher and her gentleness attracted the children. Now, the children of the village had not one but two

amazing women to learn from.   Had Macawi and Spoon
Woman not been widows, life for the village would have been
very different.   In their way, Macawi and Spoon Woman had
more influence in the tribe than the council members.   The
council made decisions on day-to-day issues but these two
women influenced the tribe's very thoughts and values.

Red Feather, son of Spoon Woman, was born into this
remarkable household of women after his father died. He did
not miss his father because the Sioux tribe was his family; he
had many father figures. But, because of his father's absence,
his mother and grandmother both tended to focus extra
attention on him.

The camp gossip this day was centered on Mouse and her
encounter with the rattlesnake the day before. A few in camp,
mostly older men, were of the opinion that Mouse was
somehow defective and would not survive her childhood. But
most of the women and many of the men as well saw Mouse in
an entirely different light.   Her encounter with the snake was
one of the growing numbers of tales being told about this
unusual little girl.   Many thought her birth had saved them
from the disastrous storm.   The fortunate appearance of the
white woman and her intense connection with Mouse was
another. Others laughed about how even Kangee lost his stoic
composure when Mouse questioned him. Even the horses and
camp dogs responded to her undeniable presence. At three
years old, Mouse seemed completely unaware of her
uniqueness.

Broken Knife came to the tent of Macawi and Spoon
Woman early. He was still quite concerned. His daughter
seemed not to know fear and he knew that fear is a useful
emotion; it tends to keep a person alive.

Macawi, Spoon Woman and Broken Knife sat in the early
morning sunshine in front of the women's tent. He said, "Our
two little ones are like brother and sister. They learn quickly."

Macawi said, "Broken Knife, you are troubled. Speak your
heart."

He thought for a moment then spoke. "I fear for Mouse. Her spirit is big. Her body is not. She learns much from us, but not about danger. There is much that can hurt her. That is what she should learn."

Spoon Woman spoke. "I love her like a daughter. She fed from me; Red Feather is like her brother. Because of her, I fear for him. They should learn together."

That day and the next, the two helped Mouse and Red Feather learn about fire, and all about the ever-present prickly pear cactus that could make life miserable. They began to learn the ways of the horses. And they began to learn about water.

When the sun was warm, Broken Knife took Red Feather and Mouse to White Woman Creek. Earlier, he had found a spot where the water was so deep that it came to his shoulders. He let them play naked in the water for a while until the inevitable happened, Red Feather slipped into deep water. Broken Knife pulled him out and the three had a talk. He explained that water was important, that it had a spirit like all things. He told them that water means life to all living things but it could be dangerous and kill. "Water, like fire, must be respected!"

Broken Knife asked several of the older children of the camp, the ones who could swim, to be his assistants. He showed the two little ones that it is easy to float by holding their breath. He had the older children paddle around and dive for stones.

Then he asked, "Which of you is ready to try floating?" Mouse immediately volunteered but he chose Red Feather to go first. After some coaxing and promises to not let go, Red Feather managed to float on his own for several minutes.

Then it was Mouse's turn. Before her father could pick her up she said, "I'm going to do this myself." and plunged into the water. She proudly floated for a moment or two and then sank like a stone. Broken Knife quickly dove under and pulled her to him. She didn't cry. After she stopped coughing, she said, "Ate', it's beautiful under there!"

Broken Knife held her and laughed into her wet hair. "What did you see my little Mouse?" She pulled back and looked into his eyes.

"It was so quiet and peaceful. Some fish smiled at me and there were many shiny things like the stars in the Ghost Road. If that is like where we go when we die, why are we afraid?"

Lessons
1870

AMENDMENT XV
Passed by Congress February 26, 1869. Ratified February 3,
1870.
Section 1.
The right of citizens of the United States to vote shall not be
denied or abridged by the United States or by any State on
account of race, color, or previous condition of servitude.

A light snow covered the prairie during the night. The morning dawned clear and cold without a hint of wind. One by one, tipis began to emit the pungent smoke of burning sage and dry buffalo chips. Breakfasts were cooked, plans were made, children begged to be allowed out to play. A communal central fire was lit. Some of the men gathered around the fire in the center of their movable village wrapped in thick buffalo blankets. One of the men produced a pipe and the men settled in for a long warm visit. They smiled at each other and said a brief prayer of thanks. Wind or more snow would cover hunting tracks so today was a gift.

Without having to speak of it, the tribe knew that any tracks left in the snow could potentially bring attention. And since food was plentiful and water nearby, the snow offered a day off from many of the men's responsibilities. For the women, it was a workday like any other.

Aponi was about to get her robe and gather fuel when she heard a voice. "May I come in?" She looked at her sisters. "Macawi, is that you?"

"Yes. It is a perfect day for Itunkala to learn the snare. Do you need her for chores?"

Aponi and her sister looked at Mouse and smiled. "You can have her if you promise to bring us some rabbit for dinner. Come in. Have you eaten?"

The older woman stepped in. She was not wearing a buffalo robe but had tied an elk hide over her shoulders. "I'm not hungry. We had some of that young deer your father brought in yesterday." She smiled at Mouse. "Today is the perfect day to learn how to take a rabbit. Have you seen the snow?"

Mouse did not respond to the older woman's question. The girl looked at Macawi with her large, solemn eyes. "Will we take the spirit of a rabbit?"

Macawi took off her robe and sat on the floor cross-legged and met the little girl's gaze. She reached behind her and pulled out an object wrapped in a small piece of deer hide and unwrapped it. Inside, was a large slightly rusted metal knife sheathed in beautiful elk hide.

"Soon after you were born, your friend Mary, the white woman gave me this mila. I have saved it for you for this day. We will use this mila to take the spirit of the rabbit. Do you accept this gift?"

Mouse looked at the knife, looked gravely up again at Macawi and looked at the knife again. The girl held out her hand and Macawi placed the knife in her hands. Had Mouse not been so serious, the scene might have been comical. The blade was nearly as long as the little girl's thigh. Macawi adjusted the leather thongs attached to the sheath and tied the knife on the little girl's waist and again around her left leg.

Mouse reached across her body with her right hand, drew the knife. She held it in front of her face and looked up and down the blade. "I accept this gift. Pilamaya."

Macawi and her older sisters fussed over how Mouse was dressed. Mouse had a robe similar to Macawi's but hers was made of deer hide. After the hide was tied over her shoulders, Macawi asked her, "Can you draw your mila easily? Is anything in the way?" Mouse drew her knife easily, resheathed it and tried again.

Macawi knelt down again. "This mila will be at your side all your life. Care for it. It will help feed you; it will help make your tipi when you are a woman. And in a time of danger, it will protect you. It is a powerful gift." Mouse reached out and nearly toppled the older woman as she hugged her. "Pilamaya Coonshi!"

The two walked into the slight breeze across the prairie. Macawi stopped and knelt down. "Look behind you. What do you see behind us that you don't see in front of us?"

"Our feet made marks in the snow."

"Can you tell how many people made these marks?"

The girl smiled. "There are two of us."

"Not us. Look at the marks, the tracks we made. Can you tell from the tracks how many people walked here?"

The little girl nodded. "Two. I see two tracks."

"Good." Macawi slipped off one of her moccasins and made a footprint. "Now look closely at this track. What animal made that track?"

Mouse smiled. "You made that track Coonshi."

"You must watch carefully. Each animal makes its own track. A deer track is different from a raccoon. A rabbit is different than a prairie chicken. If you watch and learn, you will find food for your family. Your father is the best tracker in our tribe. Learn from him, learn from everybody. Now, watch the ground and tell me when you see a track that is different from ours."

They walked on and soon, they flushed a rabbit and it loped away. Macawi stopped the girl and whistled quietly. The rabbit stopped and turned it's large ears in their direction. "When you learn to use the bow, remember this trick. Rabbit is curious and will stop and listen to a sound he does not know."

They walked over to where they had spotted the rabbit. Macawi let Mouse find the rabbit tracks. She began to follow the tracks but Macawi stopped her. "Now follow the track back, and you will find where our friend rabbit was hiding."

Macawi showed the girl some gnawed sage bark and cropped prairie grasses the rabbit had eaten. Nearby, they found rabbit pellets. "Now we look for more tracks. The rabbits follow a trail. We will set our snares on their trail."

"Watch how I set my snare. Then, you will set one further down their trail." The two had found a concentration of rabbit tracks in a thick stand of sage. Macawi set her snare in a spot where the trail was narrow. She tied a slip knot into a noose from the strong, thin cord made of deer gut. The noose was circular, large enough for two fists to easily fit through. She suspended it a hand's width from the ground directly in the rabbit trail. She tied the other end to a thick sage branch nearby and used twigs to hold the noose open and steady. "Can you do the same, little one?"

Mouse nodded. "I think so Coonshi." Macawi showed the girl another good spot several yards down the trail. Mouse set her snare very well for a first try. Macawi helped Mouse make a few adjustments and they set off for home.

As they walked back across the snow, Macawi continued her lesson. "Our friend rabbit guards his spirit as we do. His ears are big. That is why we must be quiet. He can smell us. That is why we walk into the breeze. He also hides or runs very fast. These are the ways rabbit guards his spirit. He does not want to be our dinner."

"Coonshi, why do we hide like rabbits from the white man? The white woman seems to be a Human Being like us. She says her God is a God of love. We are not afraid of her."

The older woman put her hand on the girl's shoulder as they walked. "Many whites are evil. They seem not to have a Great Spirit to guide them."

Mouse thought for a moment. "How can they be alive if they have no spirit? You told me that all living things have a part of the Creator in them?"

"I can't answer your questions little one. Talk to your father or Kangee."

"My father says they are like children, Wasican, greedy. Other men call them terrible names my father tells me not to say. If they are Human Beings like us, why can't we share?"

The older woman wrapped her arm around the little girl as they walked. "Our chief Stone Foot believes the whites see us as animals, animals to be removed from this land. That is why we hide like rabbits."

The sun was two fists above the western horizon when Mouse and Macawi returned to their snares. The Creator was smiling on them; each trap held a rabbit.

Macawi solemnly looked at the little girl. The rabbit was trembling, pulling at the cord around its neck, frantically trying to get away. Macawi pulled her knife, grabbed the rabbit by its ears and said, "Thank you Thunkashila for this life. Thank you mashtíncala. Your flesh will feed my family; your fur will keep me warm many winters. Pilamaya." She quickly drew the knife across the rabbit's throat. Its life gushed out onto the snow. "Pilamaya"

Mouse looked at the rabbit, dead in the snow, surrounded by a spray of red against the white. "Where is its spirit, Coonshi?"

"Every living thing only borrows its spirit from Wakan Tanka. One day, every spirit must return to be with the Great Spirit. Rabbit's body is here but its spirit is now home." Macawi walked over to the snare that Mouse had set. She pulled her blade and began to repeat the process.

Mouse stepped in front of the woman, drew her knife and said, "I'm going to do this myself."

Out of the Fog
1873

While protecting a railroad survey party in Montana, the United States 7th Cavalry, under Lieutenant Colonel George Armstrong Custer, clashes for the first time with the Sioux.

August 4, 1873, Tongue River, Wyoming

Stone Foot sat in his tipi and brooded. He wondered about the nature of tawaiciyan. Were his people really free if they lived in hiding? Almost all of his life, he and his people had gone where and when they pleased as long as agreements with other groups of Human Beings were honored. Now it was more difficult to elude the whites. He was tempted to stay at the Cheyenne well and set up a permanent camp. The whites there had proved to be trustworthy and honorable. In the several years they had camped there since the white woman had appeared the interactions between his people and the whites had been beneficial to both.

Mouse and the white woman Mary continued to learn from each other. The little girl learned the white talk rapidly. Broken Knife and Macawi continued to trade with the other settlers. All in all, it was a good place. If only the buffalo would stay there instead of following their ancient migrations, Stone Foot's little group could be happy here.

* * *

It was late summer and the buffalo herd had moved southeast three weeks before. Meat was not running low but they had not yet dried enough for the winter. Also, the hunters had to keep ranging farther out to find game. Stone Foot reluctantly called for a council.

When Kangee arrived, the two older men sat near the entrance to Stone Foot's tipi enjoying the soft summer breeze. Kangee was the first to speak. "So we move south." It was not a question. It was just a statement of fact, of understanding between the two men. Old Stone Foot didn't speak. He just nodded the affirmative. No other words were spoken until Yellow Bird arrived with his oldest son, Badger.

As a boy, Badger was headstrong, selfish and was a veritable bully. But, Badger was almost as skilled as his father with horses, and the other young men of the tribe seemed to respect his knowledge of horses. But, the rest of the tribe still had misgivings about the young warrior; it was true he was good with horses but still tended to treat people badly.

Without having to speak of it, the older men treated Badger with a degree of respect and listened to him when he spoke but gently refused him admission to their council. The honor of leadership required many years of proving oneself before a spot could be earned on the council.

Mouse arrived at Stone Foot's tipi minutes later. She greeted the assembled men with the respect due from women. "My father has not returned from the hunt. I have told my sisters to tell him of this meeting when he returns," she announced.

The men nodded to her and, one by one, followed old Stone Foot into his tent. The men had just started their customary camp discussion when Mouse entered through the open tent flap. She nodded to each man and she appeared to be preparing to sit at Kangee's left. Old Stone Foot and Dull Knife were completely taken by surprise, baffled. Although Kangee showed no outward reaction, he smiled inwardly.

Mouse was about to sit when Stone Foot recovered from his shock enough to bark, "Leave, child! This is a man's gathering!"

Mouse slowly turned and looked the old man in the eye. She said, "My father is not here. I can speak for him."

"You are a girl child. You do not speak for anybody." rumbled the old man.

Mouse looked at them calmly and said, "My father talks to me like an equal. He asks me advice."

Stone Foot was now red in the face and clearly losing his temper. He said, "Leave! This talk is for men! We do not need women or children to tell us what to do!"

Mouse walked toward the door but stopped and faced the old man. She held his gaze for a moment then said, "I talk to the whites when we're here and I'm learning their language. They trust me and I trust them. I talk with them; I ask them questions. Sometimes I ask them things my father wants to know. I tell him about my time with the whites. What he learns from me he brings to you. My father is not here to tell you what I have learned this week, so I can speak for him."

Kangee nodded but Stone Foot pointed at the door and yelled, "I will not be ordered about by a woman child! Leave!"

Mouse held the old man's eyes for a moment longer. It wasn't until he dropped his gaze that Mouse deferred to the men in the usual way women show respect to men. She stepped quietly out of the tent.

* * *

Four days later, the tribe had passed out of the Colorado Territory and crossed into the state of Kansas. They were following the tracks of the tatonka herd almost directly east. The scouts reported back daily. The herd was perhaps only a day away and appeared headed to a familiar area. Stone Foot knew if they followed the path they were on, in one day, maybe two, the buffalo and their tribe would be back in the area the whites call Dry Lake.

It wasn't just Stone Foot's tribe that attempted to stay away from the whites. The buffalo also sensed the whites' frequently malevolent ways and had begun to change their ancient migration patterns.

The Sioux had nearly arrived at the place where the tribe had camped for centuries, White Woman Creek. The scouts returning in the late afternoon of the fourth day reported that there were even more white settlements there now and that the herd of tatonka had veered to the north.

Stone Foot ordered camp to be set up in a shallow depression between several small hills. They had carefully crossed White Woman Creek, passing between white settlements without being seen. They had filled bladders and other containers with water and camped away from any water.

Just before sunset, Stone Foot's people heard gunshots from the north. He called the scouts to him for a report. The scouts reported that several young bulls that had been driven away from the herd were in the vicinity of the gunshots. The old man cursed the whites again for their stupidity.

The following morning, the tribe broke camp and headed north, again picking up the herd's trail. The herd was now traveling almost directly east and would miss the tribe's traditional wintering spot near Dry Lake. Following its usual direction, the herd had chosen a new path that was almost twenty miles north of their usual route.

About midday, a scout reported back that the herd had been spotted. An hour later, the rest of the scouts returned, tired but happy. The herd appeared to have stopped and was pasturing a few miles to the east.

Stone Foot ordered the tribe to stop and set up camp. Swiftly, the work was done. Tipis were erected; women and children fanned out looking for fuel for cooking and a spring for water. As was their custom when setting up camp in unfamiliar territory, the tents were erected in a circle with the tent flaps facing the center. Normally, all tent doors faced the east to honor the creator. But in times of uncertainty, the women only allowed the children to play in the center of their circle. This way the women's work could be done while watching the children.

Just before sunset, strangely unfamiliar and alarming noises came from the north including a whistle that sounded like a very large bird as well as clanging and hissing. The women quickly called all the children inside while a few men rode north to investigate.

The men rode back a few minutes later with amazing but troubling news. A little over two miles to the north of their camp was a small white town. In the town was a smoking, rumbling monster that rode on a metal road. A few of the men had seen the whites' trains before and explained the concept to the rest of the group.

This town, called Grigston, Kansas by the whites, was just a collection of a few houses, a blacksmith shop and a large corral. The train was stopped there to pick up cattle to sell in the Colorado territory.

After an uneasy night, the scouts returned early with more bad news. The noise of the train had not only scared the Sioux but had upset the buffalo herd as well. The herd had now moved several more miles east and south, much too far for the women to walk to the site to do their butchering. So, once again the camp had to be struck and the organizing process repeated later that afternoon. New springs needed to be found, more fuel gathered. The tribe prayed that their good hunting could return and they could provision themselves for the approaching winter.

A brief, fierce wind had come up in the night. It rained but no sky stones fell. Many shuddered remembering the storm from years ago. The rain and wind eventually stopped and the stars reappeared. For the rest of the night, there was no wind at all.

The first person up and out early the next morning was Aponi. She stepped out to find an unusual sight: fog. A dense misty fog filled the small depression where they were camped. She enjoyed the novelty for only an instant. Standing silently in the fog were two long lines of horses that stretched away to the north and disappearing into the mist. On each horse was a white soldier. Every soldier had a rifle but the man at the front of this column also had a long knife at his side. He had seen her before she saw him but he just stared at her silently with his strange blue eyes.

Aponi panicked and ducked back into the tipi. She shook her father Broken Knife and whispered to him what was waiting outside. He sat up quickly, dressed and headed out to Dull Knife's tent. Mouse and Chumani were instantly awake.

Within minutes, the girls could hear the men gathering weapons, whispering instructions to their families. A tense Broken Knife reentered the tent. He instructed the girls to take food and water and run to the brush in the opposite direction. He ordered each of them to take a knife.

Mouse looked at her father and said, "I will talk to these men."

Broken Knife almost yelled but then whispered, "You must run. You have heard the stories of Sand Creek. You must get away."

Mouse replied, "They have horses and guns. We could not run. I will speak to them. If I run or walk up to them, the result will be the same."

"Please daughter, these whites have no honor. You must try to escape."

"Father, I have talked to the white woman Mary and her people. They are no different than us. Maybe this man is a good man. I'm going to do this myself." Without saying another word, Mouse stepped out of the tent and walked toward the soldiers.

There was no movement within the ranks of soldiers. They sat on their horses in the fog like statues. Mouse walked to within ten feet of the lead officer and stopped. She said, *"Good Morning!"*

The officer blinked; there was the trace of a smile on his face. He asked, *"Do you speak English?"*

Mouse smiled back and said, *"Yes, a little. I have friends that speak it with me."*

The officer stopped smiling and said, *"Your people must report to Fort Laramie. Tell your leader what I said."*

Mouse replied, *"Please come down from your horse so we can talk."*

"Tell your people what I said."

Mouse asked, *"Are we your slaves? A slave must do what she is told to do."*

The officer was a bit taken aback. He answered, *"No, you are not a slave. But you must follow my orders."*

Mouse replied, "*My white friends told my about your leader in the east. He made a law that says that all people are free. Do you know this law?*"

The officer smiled again and said, "*Yes I know this law.*"

Mouse smiled back and said, "*Please come off your horse and we can talk like free people. May I give you some food?*"

The officer smiled again and climbed down. Mouse sat on the prairie and indicated that the man should sit with her. He sat down and said, "*I thank you for your offer but my men would not understand. I'm here to tell your people to report to Fort Laramie in the Wyoming Territory.*"

Mouse said, "*If we are not slaves and we are free, we wish to stay here.*"

The officer said, "*You must go, it is the law.*"

Mouse sighed then said, "*Is that a white man law or the law of your God?*"

The officer began to get flustered and said, "*It is the law of our people.*"

Mouse said, "*My name is Itunkala; Mouse in your language. What is your name?*" She held out her hand.

The officer shook her hand. "*My name is Lieutenant Jordan Bent. I am pleased to meet you Mouse.*"

Mouse and Jordan made eye contact as they shook hands. "*This law that makes us go to the north is a law of men. Do you obey man's law or God's law?*"

Jordan stuttered, and then replied, "*I try to obey both, but it is hard.*"

"*My friend reads from your Bible to me. She tells me that men should not kill each other. She tells me that men should live together in peace. Do you believe those words from your Bible?*"

Jordan Bent, in that moment not Lieutenant Bent, stood up and mounted his horse without a word. The Lieutenant gave the order to turn around and leave. The soldiers with their weapons and horses disappeared into the fog.

Two Scalps
1874

Kangee awoke with a sense of unease. It wasn't a noise, but the absence of the usual morning sounds that awakened the old Shaman. The quiet talk among women while cooking the morning meal, the noises of children scuffling, dogs barking and even the warble of meadowlarks songs were missing. All was silent.

Without taking time to even put on his breeches, the Shaman opened the flap of his tipi. In all his years, this seasoned man had never experienced a morning like the one he saw outside his tent. An enormous horse painted in strange figures was tied to his tipi poles. The horse was clearly not one of theirs. Kangee observed a woman kneeling and weeping next to the large horse. The entire village was sitting in a rough semicircle in front of his tent. He rubbed his eyes and then saw the real reason for the silence, the gathering and the weeping. Tied to another of his tent poles was a stranger's scalp, with hair trimmed in the feared Pawnee style. A second scalp, lovingly placed on a beaded ceremonial piece of deerskin, was one of theirs, familiar.

Kangee quickly dressed and stepped out to face this strange new day. He walked to the sobbing woman and put his hand on her shoulder. Horse Woman, the wife of Yellow Bird and mother of three boys, looked up at him and shrieked, "My man is dead!" She reached out and touched the smaller scalp and collapsed wailing.

The Shaman looked around. Everyone seemed to be in a state of shock. He approached Dull Knife and asked, "What can you tell me?"

"The women tell me that Mouse came here about sunrise leading this horse, and put the two scalps here at your door," Dull Knife answered.

The shaman asked, "The honored scalp, is it her husband's – is it Yellow Bird's?"

Dull Knife held up his hands. "I don't know. It looks like his hair. The women tell me he was with the horses last night and he hasn't been seen today."

"Bring Mouse to me!"

Dull Knife and most of the tribe pointed toward the corrals. The corral was about 200 yards from the main part of the camp. It was nothing more than a rough circle of trees with two rawhide ropes encircling the herd. Mouse was sitting on the ground about halfway between the camp and corral holding her head. Dull Knife walked to her and gently pulled her to her feet. As he escorted her to the Shaman's tent, all could see that Mouse had been crying for some time. She seemed unsure of herself, behavior that was, for her, disturbingly unusual.

The shaman took Mouse's hand and indicated she should enter his tipi. She walked in without a word and circled inside the tent counterclockwise, a very impolite thing to do. He came in behind her and watched as she sat near the right side next to the firewood and other supplies. She had been in his tent hundreds, perhaps thousands of times. Throughout every lesson, every conversation or exchange of information they'd ever had, Mouse sat on his left, an honored guest in the Shaman's tent. But not today.

The shaman gently ordered, "Tell me!"

She spoke in a quiet voice, "He died as easy as a rabbit."

The shaman walked over, put his hand on her head. "Start at the beginning and explain, help me understand, please."

Mouse shuddered, took a deep breath and began to talk. Once the words began to flow, they became a torrent. "The horses were restless, I could hear them. I walked down to the corral with my rawhide and knife. It was dark. Yellow Bird was with the horses; they were stamping and snorting. We talked for a few minutes. He thought maybe there was a big cat or coyotes near. I sat down and was working on my rawhide like you taught me. I had braided maybe 30 feet of rawhide rope when an arrow hit Yellow Bird in the throat." She paused, tearful. "He died without a sound. Behind me a big man, a warrior with the hair we fear, came up and cut off

Yellow Bird's scalp then he started for me. I jumped back and hit him in the face with a rock. He ignored me and began to untie the horses when I remembered a lesson you taught me. You showed me how a prairie hen will act hurt and just barely stay out of the fox's teeth and lead the predator away from her nest. So, I hit the man with another rock and then another. He kept ignoring me, trying to take the horses. I cursed him with the words you told me never to use. I said, "You live like you have no relatives!" I began to run." In one breath she said, "He chased me to the bluff over the river and he was about to turn back when I hit him with another rock and called him a white man thief. I ran down the bank and out onto the little ledge overlooking the rocks below. I tied my rope onto some brush and walked out onto the ledge. I had tied the other end of my rope to my waist; when the big man saw me he must have thought I was trapped because I couldn't go any further." Gathering her strength, Mouse continued, "My rope was tight. He started out onto the ledge. He told me he was going to eat my liver. I yelled back that I would slit his throat and take his scalp. He laughed and came out on the ledge after me. Just as he was about to grab me, I jumped out. The rope pulled his legs out from under him. He fell to the rocks. He was alive but not moving so I climbed down. I took my knife and cut his throat." Now even more distraught, Mouse said quietly, "He died so easily, Kangee, just like a rabbit. But I didn't thank the Great Spirit for his life. I cut his scalp instead. Will the Great Spirit forgive this death? I've taken deer, I've taken rabbit and many fish and I've always given thanks for their life. I've never killed a man. I feel happy for his death but I cry from a pain inside. I hurt in my heart. My spirit feels pulled away from our Creator. I feel I owe a death. Kangee, tell me what to do!"

The Shaman sat down cross-legged near Mouse and gently touched her forehead. "We believe that all life is sacred. We also believe that our people are the only true Human Beings. I can't speak for Wakan Tanka; he may see us all equally and the man you killed may also be a Human Being. But, Mouse, he killed without honor from a place of hiding and he was a thief. What you did kept us safe and that is an honorable thing." Tenderly, Kangee said, "We believe that the Great Spirit gives life and takes back that life. You acted with purpose, with honor to keep your people safe. No Human Being will judge you badly. You have acted like a great soul. We thank you Mouse! The man you killed may have taken all our horses and then led more murderous people back here. You are welcome here in my lodge always. Wait here if you wish while I tell the others what happened. You acted rightly."

The Shaman stepped out of the tent into the crowd and relayed Mouse's story. He gave instructions to have Yellow Bird's body brought to camp. He asked others take a horse to drag the dead thief far downwind from the camp and burn the body. Kangee declared to the men that any possessions of the dead man now belong to Mouse. If any had taken a bow or knife or any other thing from the corpse, it should be presented to Mouse with dignity and thanks.

* * *

That day and the next, the tribe observed their rituals of death. Yellow Bird's body was dressed in his best buckskin and placed on a raised platform. His wife Horse Woman and their three sons prepared Yellow Bird's soul bundle and placed it inside the tatonka skin in which they had wrapped his body. One by one, the family and other mourners said their prayers. Many of the prayers asked for the release of the man from his duties and from things left undone. The Sioux believe that the soul rises up to the Ghost Road and finds its way to Maya Owichapaha, "The old woman who judges each soul."

The following day, the Shaman called the three sons of Yellow Bird to his tent and ordered them inside. The boys were 16, 14 and 11. The two younger boys, Black Cloud and Lark, were very nervous. Badger, the oldest, lived up to his name. He had always been belligerent and defiant, often a bully. Many times these three young men had been ordered into the Shaman's tipi to be disciplined. The process was usually unpleasant and painful.

However, this time when they entered the tipi, the Shaman did not let the young men choose their direction but instead walked them in the correct, polite clockwise direction. Kangee then sat them near the firewood and supplies, a clear sign of his disdain for their behavior.

With little preamble, the Shaman said, "Your father was a good man. He knew horses better than any man in our village. Hopefully, one of you will take his place. Today, his horses become your horses; his wealth becomes your wealth. Our traditions and laws are very clear. Badger, because you are the oldest, you will choose first and take half of your father's horses. Black Cloud, you will take half of Badger's number. Lark, as the youngest, you will choose last and take half of the number of Black Cloud's number. Your mother will decide which of the household goods you young men will each receive as is the women's tradition and law." Kangee's voice became stern. "Hear this! The choices you make at this time and the manner in which you make your choices will remain with you always. Do you understand?"

Black Cloud and Lark had tears in their eyes as they nodded their understanding. But Badger held his head a little too high. "I will lead my brothers through this difficult time."

The Shaman stood and indicated the boys should stand. Rather than thank the Shaman and offer words of respect, Badger walked across the center of the tipi floor and opened the flap himself. The two younger boys looked from the Shaman to Badger and back again, hoping for a sign of how they should act but Badger plunged out the door and almost ran to the corral without waiting or even acknowledging the Shaman. His disrespect was palpable. The two younger boys followed without a word. The Shaman shook his head and thought, "There is a bitter lesson coming for these children."

By the time Black Cloud and Lark arrived at the corral, Badger had already separated out his father's horses. Yellow

Bird had owned seven fine horses, a fortune in terms of tribal wealth.

Rather than wait for his brothers, Badger selected two of the best horses and was looking at a third when his brothers arrived. The two younger boys waited a moment then began to bicker and argue about the selections Badger had made. Badger sneered and reminded his two brothers of the Shaman's words. It soon became evident that it was impossible to take half of seven horses without cutting one in half and a dead horse was worthless for anything but food. Black Cloud argued back and even Lark began to show some of his young boy's temper.

The brothers' arguing escalated to yelling, then screaming, and finally to threats followed by shoving. The brawling at the corral had attracted a small crowd; each person there had an opinion about what was fair.

Badger, shoved Black Cloud against a tree and selected another horse. Black Cloud stood up and hit Badger in the chest with a closed fist. Badger responded and leapt on his younger brother's back and held him around the neck. As the two older boys staggered around screaming and cursing at each other, Lark jumped on Badger's back and the three fell into a shrieking, clawing, crying, punching pile on the ground among the horses' hooves.

At that moment, the enormous, painted foreign horse appeared with Mouse on its back. She gracefully dismounted. The three boys stopped fighting as if by magic and stood with their mouths open at this strange sight.

Mouse softly said to the three boys, "This is not you. It is only grief for your father. You loved him and now the pain of his death has made you angry. Do not be angry at each other. You are family. Our Creator is testing you and you must complete this painful task of settling your family's affairs. But if you allow me, I will help.

I give you this horse. It belonged to the man who killed your father. In this way I can help you honor your father's memory and you can remain a family. Years from now you will not have to look back on this moment with pain and regret, but you can celebrate with your own children and their children and the children of your brothers."

There was a frozen moment when not even the wind moved. Everybody stood rooted to the ground as the future of many Human Beings hung in the balance. Lark, the youngest, solemnly took the reins to the big horse and handed them to Badger. In that moment, Lark was the first of Yellow Bird's sons to become a man. Badger and Black Cloud recognized the moment and also felt changed. They began to realize their future as a family.

It was Black Cloud who first recognized the solution. "Badger, we now have eight horses; you can choose half."

Badger simply walked over to his father's horses and chose the four horses closest to him. He did not choose the large horse; he was afraid. Black Cloud did the same and chose two other horses, his half. Lark chose his half, one horse, but perhaps the best of his father's horses. The division of Yellow Bird's horses had been carried out according to Kangee's orders. Only the large, oddly painted horse was left.

It slowly dawned on the three boys what had just happened; the three sons now had their father's seven horses. Badger slowly turned to face Mouse. He placed his right hand on his chest and said, "Hau Kola. You have saved my life! I have made your life miserable for years with my bullying and now you have repaid me by giving me my life. How can I repay this debt?"

Mouse replied, "All I have ever wanted was to be treated as an equal."

Two Gods
1874

Kangee was born in 1824 as measured by the whites, the same year the U. S. Secretary of War established the Bureau of Indian Affairs. It wouldn't be until 1934 that Congress would ratify The Indian Reorganization Act. In the intervening 110 years, the administration of the Indian "problem" was shuttled back and forth between governmental agencies with little or no oversight.

In 1830, when Kangee was only six, Congress passed the Indian Removal Act. All Indians living east of the Mississippi River were ordered to relocate in the "West." The Cherokee Tribe resisted and sued the U.S. Government in the Supreme Court twice. In both cases, the Cherokee prevailed. President Andrew Jackson, however, ignored the court order and sent troops to remove the Cherokee.

Kangee, by tribal standards, was an old man in 1874. The Sioux didn't keep track of time like the whites, but the Shaman knew he was, or was about to be, 50 years old. Old age and perspective were advantages of being a tribal elder. Kangee was often asked to sit in on disputes between families or individuals. His knowledge of the Sioux spiritual customs made his advice on many matters a necessity. In return, tribal members brought food or other items of need to him in payment for his advice and sometimes to garner his favor as well. He always remained true to the principals of Wakan Tanka, the Great Spirit. For that, his people recognized his integrity and trusted him.

Even as an aging man of fifty with graying hair, Kangee remained physically active. He was still able to ride most of his horses, hunt and help erect tipis, although the latter was considered women's work. His aches and pains were minimal and he still had many of his teeth.

Kangee had always loved Mouse. At first he loved her like a daughter or more like an indulged granddaughter. But as

Itunkala was nearing ten winters, she often challenged him beyond his ability to answer her questions.

Itunkala came to him quite often. When she was younger, from the time she walked, she often asked him challenging questions. Intensely curious from the moment she began to speak, Mouse came to Kangee for answers because most of the women feared her. The women feared her because there were disturbing stories told about her and she had a way that made her seem able to look inside them. The men were mostly irritated by her questions. They tended to hide behind the excuse of their tribal tradition that women are inferior, when in truth, this little girl simply made them feel uncomfortable. As she grew older, the questions Mouse asked were unanswerable by most men.

When Mouse was just beginning to talk, her questions were fairly straightforward. She wanted the name of this animal or that plant. Much of her amazing vocabulary came from Kangee. He was very knowledgeable, patient and, secretly, he enjoyed her attention.

Soon simple answers were no longer enough and Mouse began to challenge Kangee's answers with, "Why?" Unlike many bright and precocious children, she didn't ask "Why?" a second time but instead, became quiet and seemed to ponder his answer. These questions were usually followed up with a deeply insightful conversation about the Shaman's answer. Kangee came to love his time with this unpredictable, intense little girl, whose intelligence challenged and entertained him. But, that was when she was very young. As she grew, Mouse began spending more time with Mary, the white woman.

Kangee had been about 40 when Mouse was born. He had no aches and pains back then. Now, ten years later, he thanked Wakan Tanka for his health. He accepted the twinges of his age and was glad to be alive. What he hadn't counted on were the mental strains he was now beginning to endure. Mouse, no longer a baby, had long ago stopped asking simple concrete questions about nature. Her curiosity now concerned the nature of existence, consciousness, and structures of belief. She often came to him after conversing with the white woman about Christianity. After Mouse and Mary spent an afternoon together, Kangee believed he would prefer the pains of falling off his horse to the headache he developed from attempting to answer Mouse's abstract questions. The more difficult sessions between them often had to do with the similarities between Mary's religion and that of the Sioux.

The tribe had stopped as they often did at the Cheyenne well. They felt safe there. For several years they had ignored their own policy of no contact with whites men when they returned to their spot near the Smoky Hill River.

The tribe was still small with fewer than 200 people and gossip was a way of life. Naturally, Kangee heard that Mouse had left for a visit with the white woman. He considered closing his tent flap or riding off with the hunters. Only an act of will and bravery kept his flap open as he waited for her to return with the inevitable barrage of difficult questions.

As expected, late in the afternoon Mouse walked in. And, as always, Kangee indicated that she should take a seat to his left. Mouse was never one for idle chat about things like the weather or the hunt. Like always, she just plunged in with her usual, "I'm confused!"

Kangee sighed, looked up as if asking for help and said, "What about, little one?"

In her typical eruption of words, Mouse began to churn out comments and questions almost faster than Kangee could follow. "Mary reads to me from her book the Bible. She tells me stories; she explains what the stories mean. They call themselves Christians because they worship a man called Christ who is the son of their God. Mary believes the white God made everything. You tell me Wakan Tanka made everything. She tells me good people go to a place they call Heaven; you tell me we go to The Ghost Road. She tells me that bad people go to a bad place; you tell me that The Old Woman Who Judges send some to a place before they go to the Ghost Road so they can learn to be better and then be judged again."

Kangee looked at this intense little girl for a moment as he gathered his thoughts. "These books, this place where the whites put their thoughts, are another difference between our people. They capture their thoughts and mark them in their books. Then, those thoughts are like prisoners, not free to change or flow among the people. These thoughts on paper are like the fences the whites put up against the world. After things happen, our memories of them change. And when we retell our stories, they change, as they need to change because our world has changed. Writing down ideas is like putting a rock on the wind so that it cannot flow and move. It is like how we tie tatonka hides to our lodge poles. An idea is a living thing. Putting that idea in a book is like thinking the hide is the animal. We use it but it is no longer alive. Our memories change. The ideas the whites fix in their books are no more alive than the hide is the real animal."

Mouse thought for a moment, hoping to defend her experiences with Mary's books. "We write our stories on the skins of our tipis. The stories are there to tell; the pictures are writing."

Kangee reached out and took her hand. "Little one", he smiled, "does your father tell his stories exactly the same way every time?"

She hesitated then shook her head.

"The whites have their book about the son of their God. The story is written and doesn't change. The whites fight among themselves because they can't agree; they want it to change as they change but the words do not. When we tell the legend of the White Buffalo Woman, people's telling is different because their path is different. We allow each other their own path, their own story. For us, that is part of the Great Mystery. Each moment is different and Wakan Tanka is there inside us to guide our steps."

Mouse frowned and looked as if she might cry. "You and my father, everybody talks about how we and the whites are different and that makes us enemies."

Kangee held up his hand. "Please, slow your thoughts. What do you want to know?"

"You speak about Wakan Tanka like he is a real person. Mary tells me of the white's God the same way. You are a real person. I see you. I hear you. You touch me and have fed me. But I have never seen Wakan Tanka. You tell me that he exists because of things I experience or feel. You say that experiencing truth is proof of Him. Would truth be the same if I were a white girl, or a Cheyenne, or even a Pawnee? Do animals know truth or does it exist only when Human Beings live together?"

Kangee thought for a moment but before he could speak, Itunkala spoke again. "You also tell me love is proof of Him but love is just a feeling. When horses mate or a puppy feeds from it's mother, they show love. Is love just something that our bodies make us feel?"

For the first time in many years, Kangee felt anger as he spoke. "We are not animals! We have Nagi'"

Itunkala smiled at her old friend. "Mary said the same thing when we talked today. She called it our "Soul". She told me much of what you told me. She also told me that the beauty we see and hear and feel is proof of Wakan Tanka or the white God. You told me the same thing many years ago. But would I think a sunset or the song of a bird was beautiful if I had not heard that is was beautiful since I was a baby? Is that feeling we get when there is beauty true for all people or do we learn it? Would the whites or the Pawnee think of beauty the same way?"

The old shaman hesitated, as if measuring his thoughts. "It is hard to believe in what you do not see. It is normal to question. Our people have followed these beliefs for many, many winters. It is these beliefs that separate us from the acts of animals. It is very hard to have wičála but it is that belief that has made us Human Beings."

Mouse answered immediately. "Kangee, The white woman Mary said the same thing to me. The white word for wičála is

'Faith'. It seems like the whites believe the same thing we believe. Could Wakan Tanka and the White God be the same?"

Kangee shook his head. "We believe Wakan Tanka is more than the Great Spirit. We also call him The Great Mystery because he is part of all things. He is part of you and part of the rocks. He is in tatonka and the trees. That is why we thank the animals we use for their lives, their spirit. We are thanking the spirit that is in the animal. We thank our horses. We thank the trees for giving us tipis. But, the white man destroys these things. He wastes the animals he takes. He thinks he owns the land. He thinks he can steal the land from Wakan Tanka and sell it to other white men. He is foolish and selfish. These men must not worship the same God."

Mouse thought for a moment then replied, "I told Mary about what we believe. I asked her the same question I asked you. She smiled at me and said it is possible our Wakan Tanka and their God are the same. Then she said a puzzling thing. She said, "God works in mysterious ways."

The Gathering
1875

Civil Rights Act of 1875
18 Stat. Part III, p. 335 (Act of Mar. 1, 1875)

Chap. 114. -- An act to protect all citizens in their civil and legal rights. Whereas, it is essential to just government we recognize the equality of all men before the law, and hold that it is the duty of government in its dealings with the people to mete out equal and exact justice to all, of whatever nativity, race, color, or persuasion, religious or political; and it being the appropriate object of legislation to enact great fundamental principles into law:

(The United States Supreme Court struck down this law in 1883 as unconstitutional.)

Powwows are usually a joyous gathering. They are a time for revisiting friendships, trading, dancing, storytelling and feasting. They are a time when history and rumor are shared with great abandon. Young women who have come of age often find husbands there especially if their fathers are attempting alliances. Politics are always a topic of discussion among the leadership. The children play. The women gossip and a large number of children are born nine moons later.

But in the late summer of 1875, there was a terrible urgency to the discussions among the chiefs at a massive powwow. This powwow was called because of the whites; their influx was beyond a critical stage. The flood of whites and the resulting crisis were exponential and catastrophic to the Sioux way of life. The white promise that their sacred homeland, the Paha Sapa would be theirs for eternity had quickly unraveled.

All seven of the Sioux Council Fires had tribes present at this massive powwow. There were also representatives from the Cheyenne and the Arapahoe. More than seventy-five tribes, as well as many of the survivors of the Sand Creek

Massacre were in attendance. Most tribes at the gathering were larger than Stone Foot's clan. Sitting Bull was there, as was Crazy Horse, Gall and many other feared and respected chiefs: Iron Hawk, Spotted Eagle, Spotted Tail, Red Cloud and Two Moons, to name just a few.

It is said that history is written by the victorious so little is known about this gathering. The 1875 powwow on the plains of Nebraska numbered well over ten thousand souls. The battle of Little Big Horn was looming less than a year in the future.

An enormous village materialized on the plains in the central part of Nebraska, a new American state. The site of this gathering was as beautiful as it was symbolic for the location was a symbol of revolt. The Sioux and their allies camped just outside the boundaries of their reservation on a long, narrow strip of fertile land between two rivers, the North Platte and the South Platte.

* * *

Word of the great upcoming powwow spread throughout the prairies and the scattered tribes like ripples from a stone thrown into a pond. Stone Foot and his small tribe encountered another kindred tribe in their own migration while traveling toward their traditional summer home in Colorado. The two groups had met near a small waterway at the borders of Kansas, the Colorado Territory and Nebraska. The two tribes exchanged food and gossip and their children played together. At this small powwow, Stone Foot learned that the foothills of Colorado were swarming with whites; their summer home for centuries was now infested with white prospectors.

Stone Foot and his leadership and the heads from the visiting tribe counseled together. They talked into the night about the upcoming large gathering of the tribes and the latest white treachery. Later, a lone scout from one of the largest and well-known tribes appeared and confirmed the rumor of the big powwow and gave details of time and location.

While the council conversed about the whites and the upcoming gathering, the remaining Sioux took the opportunity to enjoy the novelty of new acquaintances. Children played. The women shared food, gossip and traded for needed goods. The older, married men either sat around the fire and smoked or danced to the drums; they discussed building a sweat lodge but never quite got around to the actual construction. The young men and women gravitated to each other, flirted and in some cases, drifted off into the surrounding, moonlit prairie.

Mouse and several of the other, older children swam and fished in the river that the whites later would name the Republican River. Aponi openly flirted with several of the young hunters and warriors of both clans. She was fifteen winters and a woman even though her tribe had not held the Coming of Age Ceremony for her and several other girls. Chumani, now thirteen and nearly a woman, was torn between flirting and playing with the other children. Several of the younger men of the other tribe paid Chumani some attention but it was Aponi who got the most.

There was a tense moment when a warrior not of Aponi's clan went beyond flirting and openly asked her to slip onto the prairie and have sex with him. It was at this crystalizing moment that Strong Wolf made his intentions known; he stepped between this young warrior and Aponi and said, "This is my woman!" and gently put the palm of his hand on the other's chest and shoved him. The other warrior immediately responded to the shove and pushed back. Even though not tall, Strong Wolf was thick and very solidly built. He shoved again and the warrior from the other clan found himself on his back. Strong Wolf put his left foot on the other man's chest and made eye contact. The confrontation was over.

The next day, as Stone Foot's clan moved west and northward looking for a new summer home, Aponi rode double with Strong Wolf with her arms around him.

* * *

Their usual summer home in the foothills of Colorado was out of the question for Stone Foot's tribe. Miners were thick in the Colorado Territory but gold and silver had not been found in Wyoming. Stone Foot could see no difference between these two places; the hillsides were covered with aspen and pine. The streams held fish. Deer and elk were plentiful. He had no use for the gold metal the white men seemed to cherish.

These white men were such a mystery. They destroyed hillsides and streams, killed fish and drove away deer and elk, food that the Sioux valued. They seemed obsessed to dig this yellow metal in order to buy food that the Creator freely gave in abundance. They ignored Wakanisha and left their families behind to live in dirty camps in their search for this metal. Stone Foot wondered every day why there were so many of these whites and why they seemed to ruin or kill everything they saw.

Knowing that the Colorado foothills were overrun with white prospectors, the tribe traveled north. It was early summer as Stone Foot led his people out of Kansas, through the flat desert-like eastern Colorado towards the foothills of the Wyoming territory. On their first day of hard travel, scouts spotted a wagon train of whites also moving north. The whites were on the plains while the People were traveling in the foothills. They came to the shore of a small river flowing out of the mountains. It was a decision made on the spot. The People turned west and followed the river upstream, away from the whites. In less than a half-day's journey, they found themselves at the bottom of a snowcapped mountain to the north. This camp turned out to be even better than their traditional spot in Colorado. Game was more plentiful, lodge pole pine was on every hillside and the water was clear and cold. They spent the summer there completely isolated and secure.

Their summer camp in the Wyoming Territory was new and untested. No one in Stone Foot's tribe could remember ever setting up a summer camp this far north, or at such a high elevation. They eventually settled for a tranquil spot on what the whites would later call the North Laramie River.

In the late days of summer, Stone Foot noticed the first yellow aspen leaf and that same morning the air held a slight chill. These subtle clues did not go unnoticed. Before the sun penetrated into their clearing, Kangee, Dull Knife and Broken Knife appeared at his door. They packed their pipe, said a prayer to the Great Spirit for the day and watched the day begin. There was very little to say. It was time.

The tribe followed the small river east. On their first day of travel, the stream they followed joined the much larger North Platte River. More than once a day, scouts reported white settlements along the river that forced them to find ways to skirt these places. They continued east for several days. One day they encountered tatonka tracks so the next day they took on meat. The creator seemed to smile on them.

The morning of their fifth day seemed no different than the one before. They broke camp after a brief breakfast and continued moving east. They were still traveling in shade; the sun was low enough that they could only glimpse shafts of sunlight through the tree cover.

There was little warning. One of the camp dogs barked and suddenly before them, thirty or more riders appeared in their path. The horses were painted clearly in Sioux designs but the riders were armed not with bow and arrow but with rifles. Even before those at the back of the column had stopped, thirty or more riders appeared on each flank. There was a short, tense moment until Stone Foot gracefully slid off his horse and held up his right hand. One older man from the other group held up his hand in greeting and dismounted. The two men met and spoke quietly for a few moments. A murmur passed through the people and the tension dissolved. Members from both groups freely mixed, food was exchanged and conversations were started.

The leader of this welcoming party was Kicking Bear, second in command to Crazy Horse, and powerful chief among the Oglala Sioux. Their language was the same but some of the dialect was unfamiliar. What was made clear was that their encounter was welcome. Unwelcome guests would have received a much different greeting.

It was still morning when the tribe came upon the 'city' that was forming for the powwow. The land opened up between the two rivers. To the north and south, stands of trees paralleled both rivers. East and west was open to the sky. In this vast area, a thousand or more tipis were erected. A haze of cooking fire smoke drifted south, and the laughter of children could be heard. Within minutes, Stone Foot's little tribe was surrounded by a rowdy band of children. There were invitations of play and challenges made between both sides. There were stern orders of "No play till our tipi is up." from many mothers. They had arrived!

Setting up camp was pandemonium, bedlam and totally joyous. Routine tasks that had been done hundreds of times efficiently took hours to complete. Crowds of friendly neighbors surrounded on them even before they had a chance to unpack. Offers of help turned into shared eating and gossip. Children of all ages wandered through, laughing and making friends. Young warriors walked through and flirted with any girl that paid attention. The girls left their tasks to flirt back; mothers yelled. The men were unable to settle in to smoke with the other men because their wives called them to help manage the children. Stone Foot and Dull Knife attempted to direct activities but were interrupted continually by other chiefs asking questions, wanting opinions and establishing a chain of command. There were many knowing smiles when Aponi and Strong Wolf walked off toward the river, hand in hand.

The horses were skittish around the strangers. The noises of other horses near made them hard to handle. A stallion was contained in a makeshift corral nearby which added to the general uproar. The usually docile mares pranced and bucked, making it difficult to offload and manage the lodge poles travois that carried all that they owned. Finally, by mid-afternoon, Stone Foot's camp had managed some semblance of order.

The greater camp, this assemblage of small traveling villages, had grown out from a center of larger tipis, which dominated the central hub of the 'city'. These tipis were almost twice as tall as the most with more than twice the diameter. It was at this center where politics were being discussed and strategies laid out.

Radiating out from this center were four broad open areas like streets. Each pointed in a separate direction, one for each of the four sons of Ite and Tate of ancient Sioux legends. The four quarters of this massive collection of Sioux tipis represented a holy symbol of the four wisdoms. The four sacred colors were not represented by the colors of the tipis themselves (every tipi resembled the next) but many flags were flown from tipi tops in these sacred colors: White for north and the wisdom of winter stories told around the fire, Red for the east and enlightenment, Yellow for south and innocence, Black for west where rain originates and represents the end, finality.

Stone Foot wisely chose a spot to camp near the shore of the South Platte. He was a practical man. Their camp was at the southern fringe of this massive circular gathering. He chose not to be near the center of power and influence. He chose instead for the best interests of his people. His encampment was at the furthest southern point of this massive circle of tents. They had no neighbors to the south, only a copse of trees lining the river. Water and firewood were close at hand.

Mouse and Red Feather were ready to explore. In fact, they were more than ready; they were almost vibrating with excitement. They began to pester both Macawi and Broken Knife for permission to explore the enormous camp. Broken Knife looked at Macawi and said, "You must go with your sister Chumani, and stay together!"

Macawi nodded and added, "Remember, there are many clans here. Pay attention! Their rules may be different than our rules. If you are not sure, ask. It is better to ask than show disrespect out of ignorance." She stepped into her tipi and came out with a small sack of dried buffalo meat. "Take this with you. Eat if you are hungry or give it as a gift. It is respectful to offer a gift if you are invited into another clan's circle." She smiled at the three and said, "Go! Go! Be back by dark."

The three darted out of camp. Instinctively, they began to circle the outside of the immense camp clockwise at a dead run. They were like puppies finally released from a cage into a huge field or young horses without riders on a track. Their hearts were full of joyous abandon and absolute wonder. They ran! They dodged other children, dogs barked and chased, adults were startled as they flashed by. Riders on horses yelled at them but they were moving so fast, they were gone before the curses could register on their overactive minds. It wasn't until they exploded past the fourth great boulevard that they realized they had made a complete circle and their own camp came into view. They yelled "Hello!" to the camp and headed south into the trees. In seconds, the river stopped them. They all took quick drink, splashed water over their heads and headed back.

On their second circuit of the great camp, they turned left onto the first street and slowed to a fast walk. Details began to emerge. All the tipis seemed similar to theirs except the pictograph designs of some were strange or told unfamiliar stories. Halfway to the center of the huge camp they came to a group of tipis that were not covered with buffalo hides but with wide strips of bark. The children stopped and stared in open mouth wonder. The People in the camp were dressed strangely; their hair was very different and the tipi drawings were unrecognizable. Mouse was about to enter this odd and fascinating camp when Red Feather grabbed her and they continued on.

They stopped again at the camp's influential center. The tipis at the heart of this massive village of villages were enormous. The paintings covered almost the entire surface of each tent and told of great events, battles and powwows. Sitting and standing in this central area were many men. They were finely dressed and all wore serious faces. Each carried a rifle and their ceremonial headdresses were like none the children had ever seen. They gawked like young tourists at this collection of massive tents, this center of power. They sensed a potential here and felt a power as they came closer to this center, like the gathering of a storm. One of the warriors got up and was about to shoo the children away when the flap on the largest, center tipi opened. An old man, obviously a warrior of great power stepped out. His eagle feather headdress framed his creased face and reached almost to the ground. The children were awestruck and rooted to the ground. A subtle but very real change rippled through all who were standing there. Someone nearby whispered, "That's Sitting Bull!"

The old man stretched, yawned and began to walk across the commons. He had to pass by Chumani, Mouse and Red Feather. As he did so, he smiled at the children as he began to pass. When he made eye contact with Mouse, he stopped, took a step backwards and stood facing the children. Sitting Bull locked eyes with Mouse and said in a gravelly voice, "You have a large spirit, child. Which clan are you?"

She said, "My father is Broken Knife. Our chief is Stone Foot."

"Your chief is a wise man. He does not fight like the bear. He stays hidden like a fox. You have traveled much child."

Mouse took the package of buffalo meat from Red Feather and handed it to the old man. She said, "You have welcomed us here. Pilamaya."

The old man opened the package, took a bite and said, "We are here to talk of the white men." He gestured to all the men standing around and said, "These men argue. They cannot decide what to do about the whites. What is your advice to us, little one with the strong eyes?" He smiled.

She hesitated for a moment then answered, "I know only one white. But it is not a white man; she is an old woman. She is a good person. She helped us in a bad time. She has taught me to speak some of the white tongue. She thinks we perhaps have the same Wakan Taka. If all whites were like her, they would be our friends."

The old man held her gaze for a moment longer then he said, "We will speak later." He reached behind him and pulled an eagle feather from his headdress and handed it to Mouse. "Pilamaya." he said and smiled.

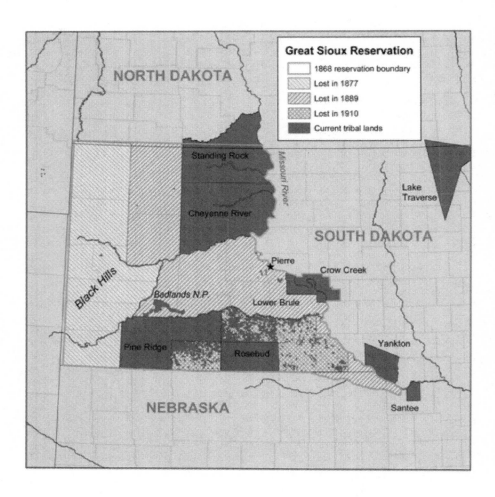

The Gathering - Day Two
1875

The land to the east was unbroken by trees. As the sun rose, its light first touched the banners tied to the top of each tipi as if illustrating the importance of the Four Wisdoms. Slowly, each tipi began to glow with easterly light, awaking the souls within. East, one of the four sacred directions was a symbol for enlightenment. If only the sun held the answer to the white invasion, the reason for this massive gathering.

One by one, cooking fires were lit. Sounds of morning activities slowly spread through the camp. Many pulled their robes over their heads and wished for a little more sleep. Stone Foot and his little band had become minor celebrities. They had arrived with the fresh meat of two buffalos so much of last night's celebration had been centered on their camp. Many men had gathered around to smoke and talk. The women shared gossip long into the night. The children played long after usual bedtimes. Many couples had drifted off into the trees, both young and old, married or not. Aponi and Strong Wolf were one of those couples. It was a long and joyous night.

The gossip quickly turned to Mouse after Red Feather recounted their experience with Sitting Bull. Mouse had tied her eagle feather to the tipi flap because she recognized the rarity of such a feather. To her, it wasn't just a child's treasure, but she didn't fully comprehend the significance of this powwow. She was off playing with new friends as the stories of her spread from mouth to mouth.

Mouse was not the only daughter of Broken Knife that was the subject of gossip. Aponi and Strong Wolf had not returned until morning. They walked into camp and asked to speak to Broken Knife. After they all sat down around the interior of Broken Knife's tipi, Aponi bluntly told her family that Strong Wolf was now her husband. There was a shocked silence for a moment. Then, Chumani and Mouse smiled and began to laugh.

Broken Knife did not laugh. It was hard to read the expression on his face but he was not angry, more confused and hurt. He looked at the faces he knew so well; the younger girls were smiling, Strong Wolf was clearly uncomfortable. Finally, Broken Knife spoke. "What about our customs? The husband usually asked the father, offers gifts."

Aponi looked from her father then to her new husband. "We are committed to each other. We made promises to the Great Spirit. We are married."

"Finally, Strong Wolf spoke. "My family and your family are much the same. We live to help the tribe, not to collect horses and other things of value. Our family is the only thing of worth. What I have to offer you is grandchildren and the promise that I will, like you, serve our tribe and keep our people strong and free." He stood and faced Broken Knife as he touched his heart.

Broken Knife hesitated only for a moment. He stood and gestured for his family to also stand. He said nothing but he pulled his family into an embrace.

* * *

A runner arrived mid-morning. He invited Stone Foot and the rest of their leadership to a meeting with the great chiefs. His little tribe had never seen Stone Foot so nervous, flustered. Perhaps it was only from the late night, but most of his people realized a dilemma was at hand. Much gossip had been devoted to the question of how to deal with the whites. Would there be war? Would there be a consensus that all the People give in to the white's demands for confinement on their reservation, for loss of their tawaiciyan? Even within Stone Foot's little tribe, the divisions were painful. Many of the young warriors wished for battle and glory. The older and wiser wanted life in the past with the freedom to do as they pleased. Even the women were divided. There were many opinions but only two options, war or peace without honor.

Gifts were gathered. Stone Foot, Kangee and their old warrior, Dull Knife carried dried buffalo meat, dried rainbow trout from their mountain camp and a fresh buffalo backstrap. As the men walked toward the center of the huge camp, the divisions within the greater Sioux nation became painfully apparent. Stone Foot and his type of leadership made his little tribe a rarity since there were few tribes that still roamed free. Most of the People now tried to live on the lands assigned to them through agreements made with the whites. Of the few bands that still roamed at will over the plains, many lived by warring on white settlers or attacking small wagon trains. Stone Foot and his group still lived true to their nature but did so by hiding. They were greeted respectfully or jeered at for their cowardice as they walked toward a terrible choice.

There was a short uncomfortable interval after Stone Foot, Kangee and Dull Knife arrived at the camp's center, the location of the power and large tipis. They were not invited in immediately. Instead, they had to stand outside among the other finely dressed men attending the leadership.

These men were not friendly. They exchanged minimal greetings but their demeanor conveyed superiority, annoyance. In his heart at that moment, Stone Foot sensed that a decision had already been made about the whites, and that decision was at odds at how he had led his tribe. The war was real.

Shortly, the tent flap of the greatest tipi opened and many men left, their faces grim and unhappy. Stone Foot and his group were invited in. Directly across from the door, sitting near the wall was the great chief, Sitting Bull. Several other men sat to his left. Introductions were made. Gall, Crazy Horse and Kicking Bear were also present. Stone Foot presented the gifts, a pipe was lit and the men sat to the left in their order of importance.

Sitting Bull began the conversation. "I met children from your camp yesterday. One of them, a very small girl, showed much courage and respect. Please give my thanks to your women for raising such children."

Kangee smiled but old Dull Knife spoke. "We apologize for this girl. She acts as an equal to men at times. She annoys many with her questions. She learns the skills of men and women. The other girls of our camp know their place."

"We will speak of your children later." Sitting Bull said. "I give you a difficult choice. There is much talk of war with the whites. You must ask your people if they will join with us in this war. You have been wise to avoid the whites but a time has come that we cannot avoid. If you decide to continue to hide, that is your choice. But if some of your people wish to join us, then you must allow them their own life choices. We will talk again soon about what your people decide."

Stone Foot, his old warrior and his shaman trudged back to camp pondering their fate. Mouse and Red Feather were off exploring again. Chumani had met a young warrior and the two of them were off by themselves.

As Mouse and Red Feather walked through the western spoke of the great powwow's wheel, they came upon an old woman storyteller. She was telling the legend of the White Buffalo Woman. Many children and a few adults sat quietly listening. Both Mouse and Red Feather had heard this story told many times from Kangee so they almost walked on by. But, when Mouse heard the woman's voice, she recognized a powerful spirit in this woman so they stopped and listened.

"About two thousand winters ago, Wakan Tanka sent her from the stars. She came to many tribes but they called her by a different name.

There was a time of great famine. Two young Sioux warriors were hunting, trying to find food for their hungry tribe. They found nothing and they were very discouraged. Then, in the distance, they saw a figure walking toward them across the plains. When the figure came close, the two braves could see that it was a beautiful maiden walking barefoot, dressed in pure white buckskin. Her buckskin was so white; she seemed to glow like the sun. Her dress was decorated with sacred symbols so finely done in beadwork, it seemed impossible any woman could do work so fine.

These two braves had never seen a woman so beautiful. Her hair was long and blue black, like liquid stone, tied with a single strand of buffalo hide. Her eyes were filled with intelligence and holy light. Her shape was of the perfect woman, a man's every desire. One of the braves was filled with lust to lie with her in the tall prairie grass.

The other brave said, "This woman is sacred. She may be a vision. You must not try to touch her like an immoral woman."

The first warrior, filled with lust, touched the woman where husbands touch their wives in love. Immediately, a black cloud covered the warrior. Lightning struck him and snakes ate his flesh. When the cloud left, his bones fell black on the prairie.

The second brave fell to his knees, cast his eyes to the ground and prayed to Wakan Tanka.

The woman reached out her hand, lifted the man's head so he could look into her eyes and she said, "A man who looks first to a woman's outer beauty will never know her divine beauty for there is dust upon his eyes and he is blind. But a man who sees in a woman the spirit of the Great One and sees her beauty first in spirit and truth, that man will know God in that woman."

The man's eyes filled with tears for love of this woman. She said, "Have no fear, you too shall have what you desire. You and your friend symbolize the two paths that men can take. If first you seek the Great Spirit, you will find what you need from the earth; it will come readily into your hands. But if you first seek to secure your earthly desires and forget the spirit, you will die inside."

Then the young hunter asked who she was. Her gaze pierced him to his soul and she said, "I am the Spirit of Truth and the face of the Great Spirit your people have forgotten. Tell your chief to prepare a tipi tonight that I may come to your people to teach them sacred things that once they knew but no longer remember."

The brave returned to his people and told the chief what had happened. The chief ordered a great lodge built hoping they would receive teaching from one who lived among the stars.

That night she came to their camp. Without speaking, she walked around the central fire seven times in the direction the sun travels across the sky. Each time her feet touched the sand all those there felt her reverence for the Earth. Few dared look into her eyes but those who did saw into the universe and felt naked and revealed, like who they truly were. Her voice was like water in a stream or of birds singing love.

"Seven times I have circled this fire in silence and reverence." she said. "This fire is like the love that burns forever in the heart of the Great Spirit. It is the same fire that warms the heart of every buffalo, every eagle, every rabbit and every human. The spirit of Wakan Tanka is in all things."

She stopped and looked at each person there. Then she continued, "This fire that burns at your center is your love and it is right at times to express this love sexually. This passion, if you do not control it, is like a wildfire that will destroy everything. But with wisdom, this passion will create many generations and warm thousands of lodges through hundreds of snowy winters. With reverence, this passion will give its power to your children's children's children."

She looked at each person again and said, "Remember the brave whose black bones lie in the moonlight. He thought first to show this fire in sex only without thought to the spirit behind it. His way leads to a cycle of illusion and suffering. To follow his way is to weaken your vitality and power."

"Always remember this," she said, "the creative force between a man and a woman is a circle, a sacred hoop. With wisdom and reverence, you gather the power of love in this circle until it explodes outward in new generations. Wakanisha is important in all things!"

She then pulled a burning branch from the fire. "Your people have forgotten the most precious thing, your connection to the Great Spirit. I have come with a fire from heaven to kindle again your memory of what has been and to strengthen you for the times to come."

From a pouch at her side, she took a pipe. The bowl was of red stone and the stem of fine wood. She said, "This sacred pipe represents many things. The bowl is of stone and the stem is from a plant to remind us of the sacredness of the Earth and all living things. The bowl is round and is the symbol of the Sacred Hoop, the cycles of giving and receiving, of breathing out and breathing in, of living and dying."

She held the pipe aloft and addressed the people, "This pipe will help you remember that every breath you take is sacred. Your life is lit from that same fire that burns in the heart of the Great Spirit. Your flame, your individual human life, can light a greater fire ... the flame of love in another's heart and so bring consciousness to the Earth. Keep not the love that burns within you turned towards yourself and your desires but give away that fire that it may burn bright in the helping of each other."

She filled the bowl with the finest herbs, lit it and passed it around the fire seven times. She then taught the People the seven sacred ceremonies.

"The first" she taught them, "is the Keeping of the Soul. At death, they must be purified so they can be reunited with the Great Spirit."

"The second is the Rite of Purification. This must be done in a sweat lodge before any significant undertaking to clean the mind and the spirit."

"The third is Crying for a Vision. You must isolate yourself away from the People and wait for a vision. This vision will help you understand your place in the world."

"The fourth is the Sun Dance. It must be done in the summer on a day with a full moon. You must dance long until you feel the pain of life and the sun's power to renew."

"The fifth is the Making of Relatives. Families come not just by birth or marriage. This ceremony can bring peace between you and another by making you family."

"The sixth is Coming of Age. When a girl first bleeds and then can have children, she must be purified enough to realize that what is happening to her is a sacred thing, becoming a woman."

"The seventh is The Throwing of the Ball. This game represents the course of a person's life and their search for Wakan Tanka. The ball is thrown to the entire tribe only five times during the game, once from each sacred direction and once high into the air to signify as enlightenment coming directly from The Great Spirit. Very few in the tribe will get the ball as very few will experience the Great Mystery. Ignorance makes it nearly impossible to know Wakan Tanka, just as the odds of getting the ball are against you."

After four days of teaching, White Buffalo Woman told the People, "I am leaving but I will return. When I leave, you will see me change four times into four colors. The four colors represent the four colors of men. When you see me return, I will be white and you will know the time of great trouble between men will end.

Then, White Buffalo Woman walked off into the setting sun. The People watched. She lay down on the prairie and rolled and appeared as a black buffalo. The black buffalo then rolled and became a yellow buffalo. She rolled again and became a red buffalo and on the last roll, she became a white buffalo, as white and beautiful as the sun.

To this day, we pray the White Buffalo returns to end these troubles."

* * *

News of the meeting between Sitting Bull and their tribe's leaders spread quickly. Every person in camp knew the question that would be asked. What they didn't know was how each would vote. Bitter arguments broke out among close friends; some wanting war, some wanting to continue avoiding the whites at all costs.

Everyone in camp now knew of the latest white treachery. They knew that many white miners were digging for the yellow metal they loved so much in the Sioux sacred Black Hills. The white treaty signed only seven years before in 1868 gave this land to the Sioux forever and was to be off-limits to all whites. Also, word had spread through the plains Indians of another massacre against their allies, the Cheyenne. The man who led the Washita Massacre, Colonel George Armstrong Custer was the same man who brought the miners to their sacred Paha Sapa.

That evening after the meal, Stone Foot's tribe gathered in a circle around their central fire. They prayed and passed their sacred peace pipe. After all had settled and the People were attentive, Stone Foot spoke. "We must decide what we will do. You know our choices. We can stay here and join our forces with those of our people to rid the land of these whites. Or, we can continue as we have done and try to live in peace by avoiding the whites. We will not vote here because there has been too much arguing. I will speak with each family in private to know what we will do. Even if we decide to continue our way, you are free to take your family or by yourself stay and fight. Other tribes will welcome you. Do what is in your heart."

Stone Foot paused to partake of the pipe as it passed. "If you wish to speak, I will sit."

Slowly, Dull Knife stood. "I am an old warrior, much too old to fight like a young man but these whites must be stopped. I am staying to do what I can. You may join me if it is in your heart." He looked around for another that wished to speak.

A shower of sparks from the fire flew into the air. No one stirred. It seemed that the moment had come for families to return to their tipis. Stone Foot began to get up slowly when Mouse stood.

Dull Knife pointed at the girl and said angrily, "Sit down child! This talk is for adults!"

Broken Knife jumped to his feet furiously. "This is an open council! Any who wishes may speak! These talks concern not just the adults but also our children! We must not ever forget Wakanisha!" He looked at Mouse and touched his heart.

"We have a third choice," she said. "We believe in the White Buffalo Woman." She paused. "The whites believe that their Jesus will return to make things right between all people. We believe the White Buffalo Woman will return to end the troubles between the four colors of men. Tonight, I will pray for them both to return."

Families left the council fire quietly. Broken Knife, Chumani and Mouse said goodnight to Aponi and Strong Wolf. The three entered their tipi and closed the flap, signaling privacy. Many other tipis of their clan also settled in for discussions, deciding their fate.

Broken Knife began by telling his girls as simply as possible the two viable options available to them as a family. They could stay and wage war. Or they could live a traditional nomadic life with the constant threat of white brutality. He smiled grimly at the knowledge that his youngest daughter had more experience with the whites than he did. He took his girls' hands and said, "Our prayers are important but the whites will not stop. What should we do?"

Chumani's response was predictable. She said, "What do you think we should do, Papa?"

He responded, "I want my family to be safe. There seems to be no good choice. If we join with the great chiefs, I will be expected to go to battle. If I should not return, you would be without a mother or a father." As a minor chief of his little clan, Broken Knife was expected to project an aura of confidence and strength. This he did without fail while hunting and interacting with members of his tribe. But at home, with his family, it was another story. He suffered as almost all fathers suffered. He wanted his children to have a better life, to be safe and happy and live full lives of reverence and love. Everything the whites brought to the People were at odds with that wish. At this moment with his family, there were only bad choices. He did what any sane person would do; he wept. He pulled his two daughters close and wished that he could dig a hole in the prairie, crawl in with his family and pull the soil over them and just disappear. They sat on the skin of a buffalo whose spirit he had released to feed and protect his family. He sat with his daughters in his arms as his tears fell into their hair. Elsewhere in the camp, similar scenes were being played out, the sound of weeping, bitter arguments; wails of anguish could be heard as other families faced their own heartbreaking choices.

It was at this moment of despair and anguish that a soft voice outside asked, "Papa, Chumani, can we come in?"

Broken Knife released one last gulping sob and looked at his two daughters. As he wiped his eyes, he softly said to Chumani, "You are the woman of this house now. It is your decision to ask them in or to say no."

Chumani went to the flap and opened it. "How Coula. Come in."

Aponi and her new husband Strong Wolf entered. Aponi sensed the tension and sadness in her family. She knew her father well.   Broken Knife immediately assumed his air of authority and manliness as he shook the hand of his new son-in-law. The new son-in-law pretended not to notice the older man's puffy, red eyes. The family embraced, the men shook hands again and they all sat down around the small cooking fire.

There was a short, uncomfortable silence. Strong Wolf looked directly at Broken Knife and said, "These whites must be stopped! We are staying to fight."

The Gathering – Day Three
1875

Wakan Tanka the Great Spirit created the universe and yet *was* the universe, a paradox of much debate. The sun, a creation of The Great Mystery, rose over the People and the whites alike. To the People sleeping below this rising sun, The Great Spirit seemed indifferent to the clash of these two very different cultures.

Like the morning before, the sun warmed the air and illuminated the sleeping tipis. From the tent city to the east, there were no obstructions to block the light. Morning came early. Like the morning before, the People pulled their robes over their faces and wished for more sleep. Their restless night was not due to joyous fellowship and sharing. Instead of lovemaking and feasting with neighbors and old friends, family disagreements, arguments, bitter crying and separation hindered sleep. The harsh decisions they had to make tore the fabric of every family, their Wakanisha.

Slowly, the camp came to life. Ironically, the first ones up and functioning were those who had the least to lose. Macawi and Spoon Woman had both lost their men long ago and Red Feather was too young for battle so their evening discussion had been much less stressful. Mouse was up early and joined Red Feather for fresh corn cakes baked with berries gathered the day before. The smells of their cooking fire and breakfast began to attract children.

Macawi fully understood the dynamics of the evening before. She had heard the cries and arguments long into the night. What she didn't predict was this gathering of children.

More and more children gathered around until Macawi and Spoon Woman realized that the children were coming from other camps, from other families in crisis. Instead of shooing these hungry children away as she would normally have done, she simply told them to return with food from their own homes and that she would cook for them.

Soon, Chumani and Mouse had a second cooking fire going. By the time adults from their camp were up and about, there was a small tribe of children around their camp's central area. Quickly, there were fewer jobs to do than children to do them. Those who had been fed began to play and, like children all over the world, their behavior became more and more exuberant.

Kangee stepped out of his tent with some urgency. He had overslept and was considering an undignified jog to the communal latrine when he was nearly bowled over by two boys playing tag. His initial reaction was to tongue lash the boys but when he saw the dynamics transpiring in the village, he immediately understood.

When he returned, he found a place in the early morning sun, sat down and said loudly in the deep voice he used for making pronouncements, "The first to bring me a corn cake gets a magic stone!"

The effect was immediate. The children froze momentarily, and then made a mad dash to bring him a cake. One small boy who had just been handed a fresh cake was the first one there. Kangee gravely accepted the cake, reached into his pouch and produced a shiny black stone he had picked up at the river the day before. With a simple sleight of hand, he had the boy choose one of his closed fists, and then made the stone 'appear' from the boy's ear. Having drawn the attention of a small crowd of curious children, Kangee calmly took a bite of his cake as he gestured for them to sit. In a deep and resonant voice, he began a story.

"A woman was once gathering corn from the field to store away for winter use. She passed from stalk to stalk, tearing off the ears and dropping them into her folded robe. When all was gathered she started to go, when she heard a faint voice, like a child's, weeping and calling:

"Oh, do not leave me! Do not go away without me."

The woman was amazed. "What child can that be?" she asked herself. "What child can be lost in the cornfield?"

She set down her robe in which she had tied up her corn, and went back to search; but she found nothing.

As she started away she heard the voice again:

"Oh, do not leave me. Do not go away without me."

She searched for a long time. At last in one corner of the field, hidden under the leaves of the stalks, she found one little ear of corn. It was the hidden ear of corn that had been crying. This is why all Indian women have since gathered their corn crop very carefully, so that food to the last small nubbin should not be neglected or wasted, and displease the Great Mystery."

By now, the crowd in front of Kangee included almost all of the children. More were arriving and, as each was given some breakfast, joined the crowd. Kangee very theatrically gestured as if he were going to get up and leave.

The reaction from the audience was almost unanimous; "Tell another!"

Kangee stroked his chin and seemed to be considering what to do. There was a loud, "PLEASE!" So he began again,

Once upon a time a prairie mouse busied herself all fall storing away beans. Every morning she was out early with her empty cast-off snake skin, which she filled with ground beans and dragged home with her teeth.

The little mouse had a cousin who was fond of dancing and talk but who did not like to work.

This lazy cousin played all summer and most of the fall. When she realized she had no food for the winter, she found she had no packing bag. So she went to her hardworking cousin and said, "Cousin, I have no beans stored for winter and the season is nearly gone. I have no snakeskin to gather the beans in. Will you lend me one?"

"But why have you no packing bag? Where were you in the moon when the snakes cast off their skins?"

"I was here."

"What were you doing?"

"I was busy talking and dancing."

"And now you are punished," said the other. "It is always so with lazy, careless people. But I will let you borrow my snakeskin. Now go, and by hard work, try to recover your wasted time."

Kangee could tell that his audience was beginning to squirm just a little, so he started in on the story of Rabbit Trapping Elk.

"Rabbit was out hunting and laid down his bow in the path while he looked at his snares. An elk coming by saw the bow.

"I will play a joke on the rabbit," said the elk to himself. He stuck his hoof –"

"We've heard this story", yelled the children. Some of them were getting up and wandering off.

"Well", he said and paused for effect, "We'll have to have a contest for prizes. How many of you have bows and arrows?" Many of the boys held up their hands noisily. "Return to your homes and respectfully ask your parents if you can be in our contest. Bring your bows and arrows if you have them. We will find out who can run the fastest and the longest. We will see who is best with a bow and arrow. We will find out who is the Red Hand champion. One of you will be the Tag Chief. But most important of all, you must choose a partner to work with. If you cannot work with others, you will fail. We will meet on the east side of camp very soon."

The children dispersed almost as if by magic. Kangee smiled to himself as he walked back to the river to collect a pouch full of the polished, black stones.

By the time Kangee had collected his rocks and walked to the east side of camp there was only a small gathering of fewer than twenty children. One thing distracting them was the horse racing on the west end of camp. Horse races were an almost daily occurrence among the younger braves. Many horses were won and lost there. It was not a safe place for children but they were drawn to the area by the excitement.

Kangee noticed another reason for the smaller-than-expected crowd of returning children. Except for Mouse, there were only boys. Kangee was accustomed to Mouse taking part in every part of boys training, and had forgotten that most tribes firmly discouraged girls from men's activities.

Kangee whistled loudly between his fingers and said, "Everybody, sit."   After a moment of shuffling and maneuvering the young crowd sat quietly. "There will be five games to start.", he said, 'two races, Red Hand, tag, and bow and arrow accuracy."

"First, you must choose a partner. If you do not have a partner, you cannot be in the games. If you are not chosen, it means the others believe you do not have the skills to make them successful. This is fair, because this is how we choose our chiefs. We choose men we feel have the best skills to lead us. If you are not chosen, you may stay and help me or watch. It is your choice. Do not be disappointed if you are not chosen. You must learn skills to earn respect. Now, stand and choose a partner. When you have a partner, sit down quietly."

Several of the older larger boys quickly paired off. After some quick negotiations, there were finally seven pairs of boys. Only a few small boys and Mouse were left without partners. Red Feather and another boy from their own tribe had paired up. As hard as Mouse tried, no one would be her partner. She sat down with the small group of dejected little boys and bit her lip.

Kangee looked around at the group. "This is how we will score. The winner of each game will get two stones and the second place winner will get one stone. If your partner wins a game and you don't, you will still get the same number of stones that he does. At the end of all five games, the partners with the most stones win. Questions?"

A boy of about twelve had been standing to the side. He was dressed much more nicely than the rest of the boys. The bead work on his shirt, leggings and moccasins, all made of beautiful elk skin made it obvious he was a son of one of the major chiefs. He said, "Is it too late to join?"

"No. But you must have a partner." He pointed to the group of rejects and said, "Choose from one of these."

The new boy looked over and made eye contact with Mouse. He walked over to her and said, "How Coula. My name is Black Elk, are you Itunkala?"

Mouse stood and said, "How Coula. How did you know my name?"

Black Elk said, "My mother gossips with the other women. There are stories about you. A girl who pulled a rattle snake out of a hole should make a good partner!"

She looked at him for a moment then asked, "Why should I choose *you* for a partner?"

He held her gaze for a moment and said, "Because I do not have dust in my eyes."

Mouse and Black Elk didn't win the contest. But they won something more important. They won friendship.

During the first short race where everybody ran as fast as they could, Mouse and Black Elk fell. The two of them were so intent on beating each other; they lost sight of the race. They were both very competitive and began to elbow each other out of the way. Eventually, they got tangled up and fell in a twisted heap. They jumped up with fists raised, angry and ready to fight. Then a moment later, the two of them collapsed, laughing at each other. They shook hands and agreed to try to work together in the second race.

During the second race, the children had to circle the whole camp twice. Mouse and Black Elk ran together and cheered each other on. Halfway through the second lap, Black Elk was completely winded and told Mouse to go on. Mouse might have won this one if she hadn't chosen to run side by side with Black Elk for the first lap. She stayed with Black Elk because she realized that the prize was not the shiny black rocks, it was teamwork and partnership.

There was simply no one who could beat Mouse at Red Hand, the hand slapping game. It might have been that being the shortest there gave her an advantage. But most of the children who lost to her said they just couldn't concentrate when she looked at their eyes. Mouse also won the tag game. Small and very quick, no one could out-maneuver her.

In spite of their crash during the short race, Mouse and Black Elk might have won if it hadn't been for the archery accident. Kangee had found a huge rotten tree to hold the target. He tied a piece of buckskin up with a black circle painted on it. A number of the children couldn't even hit the tree. Many could hit the tree, but not the target. Black Elk and two other boys consistently managed to hit the target but Mouse's arrows hit the circle in about half of her shots. Finally, it was down to Black Elk, Mouse and another older boy. Black Elk hit the target almost in the center and it would have been a winning shot. The other boy's arrow was near center but not as well placed as Black Elk's. When Mouse took her turn, her arrow knocked Black Elk's off the target and their arrows fell to the ground. She laughed until she saw his face. First there was surprise, then anger, naked hatred for an instant, then a questioning wonder.

Mouse held his gaze as she said, "I'm sorry. I also wanted to win." She walked over to Black Elk and handed him her four stones.

He began, "But–"

She held up her hand and said, "Your face tells me we are on different paths. Winning these stones was important to you. My prize was the laughter and friendship we shared. We both have our reward." She turned and walked away.

That night, Black Elk and his father spoke. The boy told his father everything, about the contest, his own arrogance, the little girl with the powerful eyes and the more powerful will, everything. He even confessed that he thought he would win because he was the son of a powerful medicine man with more wealth and power than the common children.

"My son, the Great Spirit has spoken to you." his father said, "At first, we see with our eyes. You saw a child and judged yourself superior. Then you saw a female and judged as many of our men do. A child's heart is pure and a woman is part of the sacred hoop. See with your heart and you will see the spark in each person that is the Great Mystery. Listen to what the Great Spirit has spoken to you. It is what you learn from the Great Spirit that will make you a man and a true Human Being."

The Gathering – Day Four
1875

"Hear me, four quarters of the world--a relative I am! Give me the strength to walk the soft earth, a relative to all that is! Give me the eyes to see and the strength to understand, that I may be like you. With your power only can I face the winds. Great Spirit, my Grandfather, all over the earth the faces of living things are all alike. With tenderness have these come up out of the ground. Look upon these faces of children without number and with children in their arms, that they may face the wind and walk the good road to the day of quiet. This is my prayer; hear me!"

> *Black Elk's Prayer for All Life*

"Papa, I know it is our tradition that boys hunt when they are ten winters." said Mouse. "What is the truth? I ride well, better than Red Feather and I am better with bow and arrow. Why don't our women hunt?"

"If we were alone, I would take you." Broken Knife answered. "Today, we ride with hunters from other clans. Many believe that a woman will make the animals act differently or make arrows go wrong. It is not truth, it is belief."

"Papa, you and I have hunted together. Did the rabbits or deer I killed act differently? Did your arrows fly away?"

"No little one. I have taught many boys to hunt. You are the best I've seen at this age, boy or not."

Mouse frowned at her father as she opened the flap of their tipi. "You know I want to hunt with you today but I will stay with the women instead. I do not understand why we must act as if another's beliefs are true when we do not believe them."

"Truth is hard to understand. What we believe may not be truth to others. We must try to see The Great Mystery in others instead of being ruled by our own beliefs. Differences make enemies. Understanding makes friends."

The men and boys rode south and west toward a shallow ford in the river. Scouts had reported a herd of elk lazing in the shade of the cottonwoods several miles west of the big camp. They planned to approach the herd from upwind and allow the boys to shoot from tree cover because elk are difficult to take from horseback.

Chumani and Mouse finished their morning chores early. There were no fresh skins that needed scraping and drying. Since they had been eating mostly dried meat and fish from the river, there was little food preparation to do. They decided to walk to the river for firewood and a swim. They were about to leave when Aponi joined them.

It was a rare day for the daughters of Broken Knife. The men were hunting and had not taken any animals yet. Since they were hunting far from camp, the men would probably quarter any animals they killed before returning with them to camp. That meant the three sisters had a day to themselves.

Mouse slung her bow and quiver over her shoulders and the three picked up their gear. They all carried rawhide rope, packs with shoulder straps and water bladders. Mouse, as always, carried the big knife the white woman had given Macawi years ago. It was another perfect, prairie morning when the girls headed into the copse of trees near their camp. The river was not far.

The girls walked in silence for a while, then Chumani asked, "Do you like having a man? What is it like?"

Aponi walked on for a moment, then stopped and smiled. "I like being with Strong Wolf. Nobody told me what to expect but I'm learning."

"Tell us. You know. What is it like being with a man?"

Aponi stopped and looked at her sisters. "You don't mean cooking and cleaning, do you? You want to know about kichi yungka, to lie with a man, to have sex?"

"I know how to clean and cook." said Chumani "but we didn't have a mother to tell us about these things."

"The first time he hurt me. But you know that. You have talked to other girls. For a while, he was so fast and kept hurting me. I tried to talk to him but we could not find words. It got better."

"How better?" asked Chumani.

"You have seen the horses and dogs mate. You know what happens. When the horses are mating, they change; you cannot control them. When you see a boy or a man, sometimes you feel this urge, this feeling. It draws you to them. When I am with my Strong Wolf, that feeling is so strong that we lose control; we are like animals that cannot stop. It is a gift from the Great Spirit and it can be joyous. But then I felt something was missing. The story of the White Buffalo Woman talks about having dust on our eyes. We were sharing our bodies but not our spirits. Again, I tried to talk to my man but we didn't have the words. Then I talked to Macawi."

"What did Coonshi say?" both girls asked.

"She helped. She told me that we had to learn. She told me that I am the chief in my lodge and I had to be the one to change. She gave me advice about this, also. At first I was to just talk to him of simple things. Then I gave him compliments, like how good a hunter he was, how nice and handsome he looked. But the best advice Coonshi gave me was for me to take control of the sex. Often, I now make the first move and tell him what I want. I choose how we lie so I can talk to him and make him go slow. I tell him that we must connect our spirits as well as our bodies. We practice. It is getting better. We are learning each other and we are now connecting our spirits. We were both children when we married but we are growing together. We have become friends. Sometimes, we just lie together and talk. He is a blessing to me and now I am very happy."

The girls came to a fallen tree. The limbs were dry and many broken branches lay on the ground. They quickly thanked the Great Spirit for this unexpected bounty as they bound their fuel into bundles. Leaving their bundles hanging from branches, they walked south to the bank of the river and found a spot with little brush and a natural, sandy beach.

Quickly, the three removed their buckskin skirts and leggings and waded into the water.

Mouse looked at her sisters. They both looked like women; they both had nicely formed breasts and wide hips. Chumani was beginning to grow hair between her legs. She had bled the first time while still in their mountain camp and was waiting for their clan to perform the Coming of Age ceremony for her and the other girls who were ready for men. Mouse looked down at herself and saw, except between her legs, the body of a boy. She was still very small and her chest was flat. Her sisters were almost plump, desirable women, but her body was thin and muscular, like that of a young camp dog.

The girls swam for a while then sat on the bank drying. Mouse asked, "When will I be a woman? When will my feeling for boys change?"

Aponi said, "Your time is coming soon little sister. I had my first blood when I was thirteen winters. The boys were looking at my body before that. It will happen. Enjoy this time. It is one of the four stages of life and when you pass to the next, you will wish to have this time back."

"Right now I wish I was a boy, and I hate them at the same time. They get to hunt and practice with weapons. We must clean and cook and make babies. It's not fair." said Mouse.

"Do you think you are a berdache, a two-spirit?" asked Aponi. "They become very important in a tribe."

"I'm not sure, I don't think so.", said Mouse. I swim with Red Feather all the time and I see other boys. Sometimes, when I see a young warrior swimming, I feel sort of interested, that is the only way I can say it. Naked girls I see don't make me feel the same but I do look at their bodies and compare theirs to mine. Mouse is a good name for me. I mostly annoy people and I think I will never make a man happy."

Aponi hugged her and said, "Mouse, your spirit is very big! Someday, you will marry a man with a spirit as big as yours and we will sing songs about you."

Instead of walking directly back to camp, the girls explored east along the river. Not far from where they swam, they found a thicket of ripe sand hill plums. The girls yipped and yelled thanks to the Great Spirit and ate their fill. They carried as many as they could hold in their folded buckskin shirttails and headed back to camp singing the Song of Happiness.

As they entered camp, Spoon Woman rushed up to them frantically. "Where have you been? We have searched the entire city for you. Mouse, Stone Foot is waiting for you in his tent. We have visitors!"

"Has something happened to my father?"

"This has nothing to do with your father." Spoon Woman replied. "Some important men came and asked to talk to you. There is a big white man with them! Do you know what they want?"

Mouse answered, "I have no idea! I wish my father was here!"

Mouse quickly returned to her tent and stored her fuel and plums. She inspected her clothing and hair then walked to Stone Foot's tipi. "It is Itunkala, may I enter?" she said to the closed flap.

The tent flap opened slowly and Stone Foot motioned her to enter. She stepped nervously into the old chief's tipi. Several men were seated around the wall. In the middle of the group sat the white man. She immediately recognized Kangee and Dull Knife but the white man and the other two Human Beings were strangers to her.

As Mouse stepped into the tipi, the white man began to get to his feet. When he realized that none of the other men were getting up, he sheepishly sat down again.

Mouse was initially frightened both by the situation and being confronted by this unexpected visitor. But when she saw his completely human discomfort at being in an unfamiliar situation, her fear turned first to wonder then to curiosity. He was dressed in a dirty U. S. Cavalry uniform.

Stone Foot was the first to speak. "Your father is away hunting. I would have had him here but Kangee will act as your parent." Stone Foot pointed to his left. "Next to me is Ten Bears. He is the chief of another clan."

Mouse stepped up and shook the man's hand.

"The next man is Kicking Bird, the Medicine Man of their clan." Kicking Bird smiled at Mouse warmly as he shook her hand.

"Please sit and talk with us." Said Stone Foot. Kangee, furthest left, patted the ground next to him and motioned for Mouse to sit.

Instead, Mouse stood in front of Stone Foot. "I am a girl and was told women do not talk at council. I will find a man to speak to you with your permission."

The old chief's face reddened but he managed to say, "You speak the white man's talk. We need you to talk to this Wasican. Please join us."

Mouse looked from face to face then approached the white man. *"My name is Mouse in your talk."* She held out her hand.

The white man jumped up, smiled broadly and shook her hand almost violently. *"My name is John Dunn. I am very glad to meet you."*

Stone Foot broke in. "As he speaks, tell us what he says. We will have questions. Tell him that."

Mouse removed her hand from the hand of the white man's and indicated that he should sit. She walked around and sat next to Kangee who gave her a knowing smile. After she sat, she said, *"These men want me to talk to you and tell them what you say. They say they will have questions. Will you talk to them?"*

The white man said, *"Yes, I will speak to them. Please tell them my name and that I come in peace."*

Mouse translated then said, "I will tell this man your names. Am I right to believe we are to respect our customs and be polite?" The men Sioux around the circle all nodded their heads "Yes!" She stood up and said to John Dunn, *"I will tell you these men's names. It is polite for you to shake their hand."*

The white man stood and asked, *"How did you learn English?"*

"First, we will talk to these men, and then I will answer your questions." answered Mouse. She translated to the Sioux.

Immediately, Dull Knife said, "Do not tell this man the places we camp!" Mouse shook her head in agreement.

Mouse pointed to the first man in the circle and said, "*This is the chief of our clan. His name is Stone Foot.*" The white man shook hands and nodded at the old chief. "*You came with this man; he is the chief of his clan. His name is Ten Bears.*" Again, the white man shook hands. Next, Mouse introduced Kicking Bird. She said, "*He is a religious leader, like a pastor in your language.*"

The white man shook hands with Kicking Bird then asked, "*How do you know about a pastor?*"

Mouse translated to the Sioux men then answered, "*We will speak later. Now, we speak to these men.*"

Mouse also introduced Dull Knife, the old warrior but did not have the word for dull so she called him Knife that will not cut. She also did not have the word raven in her English vocabulary so she introduced Kangee as Large Black Bird.

After the introductions were made, Mouse sat, again on Kangee's left. Stone Foot spoke to Mouse and said, "Ask this man why he is here." Mouse translated.

The man hesitated for a moment. "*I am here because I broke the law of my country. I am a soldier but I refused to kill another man. I am here because I tried to obey the law of my God.*"

The Sioux men looked at each other for a moment then Kicking Bird asked, "Why are the laws of your country and your God different? Our people live the law of Wakan Tanka. That is our law."

Mouse translated. John Dunn looked at the men gathered there and said, "*I wish to live like you. That is why I am here. I wish to live in peace.*"

As Mouse translated, old Stone Foot slowly rose to his feet. He walked across the floor and stood above the white man. The old chief extended his hand to the white man and as the two men clasped hands, Stone Foot pulled the white man to his feet. For what seemed like a very long time, the older man stared into the eyes of the younger white man. Finally, the old chief shook the other man's hand, smiled and let him go. Still looking into the white man's eyes, Stone Foot said, "You may learn to become a Human Being. If you want, you may stay and live with us. We believe the same; we want peace. We will not fight in the war to come and will try to live in peace. You may be helpful when the Wasican find us." The old man continued to look into the white man's eyes while Mouse translated.

There was a shocked silence among the circle of men. There had been much debate at council and around the fire. It wasn't until that moment that Stone Foot had given his opinion about their clan's future

Stone Foot sat down again and spoke to Mouse. "You have shown me that I have been mistaken about you. I am sorry. When I looked at you, I saw a child and a girl. Now I see a strong spirit. When you look at me, please don't see an old, bad tempered man. Try to see my spirit. We must not have sand in our eyes. We must do the work of the Great Spirit."

Mouse nodded. "In my heart, you are my Thunkashila." "I will work with you."

"You give me joy, child." He gave her a sly smile. "There is work for you; teach this white man to be a Human Being."

Jondunn
1875

Mouse stood and said to their guest, *"My name is Itunkala, Mouse in your language. Our chief has asked me to be your guide because I speak your language."*

The big cavalry officer scrambled to his feet and held out his hand again. Mouse hesitated a moment then stepped up and shook the man's hand again. She was barely half the man's height but to all present, it was obvious that the huge man deferred to this child.

"I'm pleased to meet you Mouse. May I call you that? My name is John Dunn. I'd be much obliged if you can get me situated here."

Mouse looked up at the man. *"First, we will walk around the floor this way; follow me to show respect to the home of Stone Foot. You have much to learn."* She led John Dunn clockwise around the floor to the tipi flap and stepped outside.

Problems started almost immediately as Mouse and John Dunn stepped out of Stone Foot's tipi. As they walked across the common area, a woman stepped out of her tipi. Seeing the uniform, she screamed and fell backward with a small child in her arms. Dogs barked; the child cried. A very nervous crowd gathered.

Moments later, the white man was surrounded by several young warriors. Mouse began to step into the center of this tense situation when Kangee's hand gripped her shoulder and stopped her. "This is his first lesson. We will watch."

Both Kangee and Mouse knew the young men were as frightened as the woman but they were bound by tribal honor to not show fear. One by one, the warriors shouted at the white man, pushing him front and back. No weapons appeared. It was a typical reaction for these young men to display more bravado than good sense. They were counting coup, impressing themselves and one another.

The big cavalry officer just stood there, almost impassively. Some fear shown in his eyes but he kept his hands at his sides and said nothing. Initially, he made eye contact with these young men but quickly, he dropped his eyes to the ground. Finally, he looked at Mouse as if to say, "Now what?"

The shoving stopped but the verbal abuse began escalating. Kangee stepped through this ring of insults and stood beside the white man. "This man is our guest. His name is John Dunn."

Immediately, Kangee, himself, became the focus of this negative energy. Calmly, the old Shaman stood there and said nothing with the white man until the curses and insults subsided. Again he said, "This man is our guest. His name is John Dunn."

The impasse was finally broken when Dull Knife stepped into the circle. He simply shouldered a young warrior to the side and shook hands with the white man. "Welcome Jondunn. We will learn from you and you will learn from us."

The little drama was over almost as quickly as it started. The young warriors left gesturing, flipping their hair, attempting to be as nonchalant as possible while maintaining their manliness. Jondunn gossip spread like wildfire.

* * *

The next several days were incredibly busy. Soon after Dull Knife announced his opinion that their tribe would not join the war, a long council was held. In the end, it was decided that they would leave but anyone that wished to stay and make war on the whites could stay. Stone Foot announced that many of the other tribes would gladly accept any that wished to stay and fight.

Mouse's new pupil took almost every minute of her time. Kangee gave her advice and she often intruded on Dull Knife for his opinion, but for the most part, she was on her own as she worked to integrate this large white man into their daily life.

Broken Knife was initially angry at having to share his tipi and his family with this man. But he quickly saw the wisdom of having this white as a source of intelligence. It was, in fact,

Broken Knife's suggestion that the white man wear something other than the uniform of their enemy. He loaned Jondunn some of his buckskin clothing.

The gossip within the tribe was nonstop. When Jondunn stepped out of Broken Knife's tipi for the first time wearing buckskins much too small, he had to endure yet another round of abuse. He looked ridiculous. Inches of his ankles and wrists were exposed and the buckskin barely fit his frame. He took all this in stride. He simply followed Mouse around like a large puppy and did as he was told. When word got around that this huge man blushed deep red and refused to change into his borrowed buckskin in front of Mouse and Chumani, even the women began to tease him.

Another incident was the source of much tongue wagging when Mouse led Jondunn to the river to bathe. Many in camp, mostly the women, had complained about the man's smell. A small crowd followed them to the river. When he realized what was next he blushed, much to the delight and cheers from the gathered crowd. It wasn't until many of the others stripped down and swam that Jondunn finally relented. A fresh round of gossip swept through the camp the next morning.

Mouse took her student to Macawi and Spoon Woman's to have clothing made. The two women had agreed to make buckskin breeches and a shirt if Broken Knife would supply the skins. It was painfully obvious to every person present that Jondunn and Spoon Woman were attracted to each other. While she was measuring the skins by holding them up to him, her touches were obviously intimate. Even with the language difference, the way he looked at her left no doubt. When Mouse came to collect him for a hunting lesson, she nearly had to drag him away.

Mouse's small bow looked ridiculous in the hands of this man. To his credit, he learned rapidly and was hitting the target within an hour of Mouse's instructions. When Broken Knife came to check on Jondunn's progress, he reported spotting some small deer upwind from the camp. Broken Knife lent a bow to Jondunn and the three set out to kill a deer.

Mouse and her father chatted as they walked. The two laughed about the gossip. Mouse smiled up at her father. "He looked like a thirteen year old when Spoon Woman was fitting his breeches."

Her father laughed out loud. "The women say Spoon Woman was singing and asking lots of questions about him."

"What are you two talking about?" the white man asked.

"I told my father how well you shot with the bow." Mouse translated what she said. She and her father laughed again.

They spotted the deer in a clearing. Using hand signals and whispering, Mouse had Jondunn hide behind a large cottonwood tree. She joined him. He looked down with a frown on his face. *"How do we get close?"*

"Make this arrow smell." She handed him a poorly made arrow.

He shook his head. *"Smell? I don't know what you mean."*

"Pee on it. Or put it under your arm. That smells." She smiled at him and held her nose.

He opened his shirt and rubbed the arrow under his armpit. She sniffed it and nodded her head. She crawled to some brush and, without showing herself to the deer, shot the arrow high into the air. It flew over the deer and landed on the upwind side of them. One by one, the deer began moving in their direction, away from the smell on the arrow.

Mouse signaled him to nock an arrow into his bow, and stand ready behind a tree. A few moments later, the deer walked within feet of them.

Jondunn did a surprisingly good job gutting the deer but refused to even taste the liver. Mouse and Broken Knife made a quick travois to transport the deer, and they all returned to camp.

The big white man insisted on towing the deer. *"It was my kill. I will do the work."* Mouse and her father smiled at each other. They were both glad to let Jondunn do the work. He was, after all, their student.

When they arrived back at camp, Jondunn towed the deer straight to Spoon Woman. Again, Mouse was glad to be relieved of the job of cutting up the deer. The looks between Spoon Woman and Jondunn needed no translation. That night, Spoon Woman cooked for both families but she only had eyes for the big white man. The translations Mouse made that night taxed her limited vocabulary. The words were simple; the unspoken words were the most difficult.

* * *

Gossip that night around the fires and the next morning spread throughout the camp. Half of the gossip, mostly from the women, approved of the match between Spoon Woman and the white. She had, after all, been without a man for many years. The older men were ambivalent but not the young. To the young warriors and hunters, Jondunn was still the enemy and should be killed.

It was one of those young, unmarried hunters who brought about a major shift in the approval rating of this naïve white man. Black Cloud, son of Yellow Bird, arrived at Spoon Woman's tipi about midday. He dropped a deer, uncleaned but freshly killed at the door to Spoon Woman's tipi. When she stepped out of her tipi, he informed her, "You will cook for me and make the hide into a fine shirt."

Spoon Woman smiled at this impetuous young man. "There are many willing girls who will do this work." She turned and stepped back into her tipi.

Black Cloud became insistent, then loudly incensed. The resulting shift in the camp's tranquility triggered the usual crowd of on-lookers, including Jondunn.

With only a few days with this tribe as his large extended family, Jondunn had no way of knowing that this exceptional woman could easily deal with this brash young man. To Jondunn, a person he cared for was being abused and, on some level, he realized he had caused this problem. Jondunn stepped into the skirmish.

The dispute between Spoon Woman and the younger Black Cloud had escalated to the point where the two were kicking the carcass back and forth, telling each other what needed to happen to the unlucky deer.

At one particularly loud and intense outburst from Black Cloud, Jondunn stepped between the two combatants. He held his hand up, palm out toward Black Cloud. *"Take it easy young man!"* He stood there like a bear.

The young hunter attempted to slap the white man's hand to the side, to pivot him away from Spoon Woman.

Immediately, Jondunn put up his fists in a classic boxer's stance.

One moment, Black Cloud came at the larger man in an attempt to shove him out of the way. The next, he was on the ground only semiconscious.

Jondunn kneeled beside the young man who was rubbing his jaw. *"Are you alright? I'm sorry!"* The big white man looked around, worried what the others might do but to his surprise, instead of hostility, the crowd around smiled and laughed. Many came up and patted his back or shook hands.

Mouse arrived at about the same time Black Cloud managed to sit up and rub his chin. "How did you do that? How did you knock me down?" Mouse translated.

"It's called boxing. I hit you with a left hook." The big man stood and took the stance again, demonstrated the move. Jondunn extended his hand and pulled the younger man to his feet. *"Left hook."*

Black Cloud shook hands with Jondunn and said, "Leftook!" Many in the crowd repeated, "Leftook!"

Spoon Woman pulled Jondunn around so they were face to face. "Leftook" she said softly. The two stared into each other's eyes. Slowly, she reached behind her and untied the strap holding her hair. As her hair cascaded around her face softening her look, she reached out shyly and took the big man's hand. He responded by reaching out with his free hand and gently placed his palm on her cheek, his fingers behind her neck. The two stood there for a moment and as he began to pull her into an embrace, she pulled him into the tipi with her. The tipi door softly closed; it was two days before anyone saw them again.

Oh, What a Friend We Have in Leftook
1875

Mouse was the first to awaken to an unfamiliar noise. It was a tapping noise, like a woodpecker but muted, soft. Then she realized it was coming from the tent flap. She got up, opened the flap, and standing there with a smile on his face was John Dunn.

For moment, Mouse was startled and did not recognize him. A three-day beard made the bottom half of his face almost black, which offset his sheepish grin. He looked more bear than human. Spoon Woman had made him a buckskin shirt and breeches. Her work was always good, but this outfit was truly a masterpiece. The shirt hung just below his waist, unlike most that came down to mid-thigh. The breeches were almost tight, but the overall look seemed a cross between traditional Sioux clothing and the cavalry uniform he wore. Spoon Woman had done only minimal beadwork, but the work was fine and vaguely mimicked the markings on his uniform.

Mouse slowly returned his smile. "How coula? *You look almost like a Human Being. What was this noise you made?"*

"I was knocking on your door."

"What is knocking? I do not know this word?"

"It is our custom to knock on the door of a person we visit." He demonstrated on a lodge pole. *"It is not respectful to walk in until invited."*

"It is good to know the whites are respectful to each other. Our tradition is different. If the flap is open, all are welcome. If the flap is closed, you must speak your name and ask to come in."

The big man handed Mouse a bundle, her father's borrowed clothes. "Pilamaya." He smiled. *"I'm learning."*

Chumani and Broken Knife bid Leftook a good morning as they left the tipi together. As they walked away, Leftook told them, *"I've come for my old clothes. I'm going to burn them."*

Mouse fetched the bundle of dirty clothing from near the wood pile and handed them to 'Leftook.' They talked for a few minutes then the big man walked toward the center of camp.

The communal central fire was burning nicely. Several men including Dull Knife were sitting, visiting and eating breakfast around the fire. The men smiled at each other. Leftook held up his hand. "How coula." The other men grunted their replies and continued talking together.

Leftook dropped his bundle on the ground near the fire. He removed the belt from his trousers and went through the pockets. He set his boots aside and began removing the buttons and metal insignias.

By now, the other men around the fire were curious. When it became obvious what 'Leftook' planned to do, Dull Knife roared, "Aphe!" He stood and walked to the fire. "Aphe! Aphe!" He put his hand on the clothes and said, "Aphe."

Mouse arrived moments later and translated. *Our chief says wait, these things may have value. Do as you wish but if they become smoke, we have lost chance."*

"They are dirty and torn. They scare the People."

The old chief listened to Mouse translate. "A warrior cares for his weapons." was his answer. The old chief smiled and returned to his seat by the fire.

After breakfast, Mouse and Spoon Woman invited John for a walk to the river. They had discussed a lesson for him. All three stopped near a clump of yucca. Mouse held out her hands. *"Show me your torns."*

The big man laughed and handed Mouse the shirt from his old uniform. There were small holes in both elbows and a seam around one sleeve was gaping. The pants had a long seam tearing out just above the area of the knee.

Mouse and Spoon Woman smiled at each other. Spoon Woman took the man's hand and led him to the yucca. She kissed him briefly, and then pointed to his eyes, then to her eyes. "Watch and learn!" She selected a long strand from the plant, gripped the sharp, needle-like end and tore it from the plant. The needle came away with a long strand of fiber. Spoon Woman used this needle and thread to repair his uniform.

Mouse, using a stout cottonwood branch, dug out a large root from the same plant. She used her knife to cut the root into smaller pieces. When they got to the river, Spoon Woman dunked the soiled clothing in the water. She rubbed the yucca root over the fabric, twice and three times over the really dirty areas. She turned the garments inside out and repeated the process. Rubbing the wet material together caused suds to appear. After a vigorous washing, she rinsed out the clothing. Leftook's uniform was as clean as it had ever been.

As Spoon Woman held up the uniform, looking for tears and dirt, Mouse said, *"Spoon Woman calls this plant watho haipajajablu, soap weed in your language. It is very useful. We also eat parts of it. The seeds and flowers are good."*

The three walked back to camp, the two adults hand in hand. While Leftook's clothing dried, he moved the remainder of his belonging to the lodge of his new friend.

* * *

Late that afternoon, Stone Foot called a council. Leftook was invited, as well as Mouse. The first order of business was the move. A majority of their little tribe wanted to continue their life of tawaiciyan, the freedom to live their lives in the age-old traditional manner. There was some discussion of logistics, where they planned to winter, their route and, of course, how to avoid contact with the whites.

Mouse translated for Leftook as well as she could. As the discussion continued, Leftook became more and more agitated as he listened to incidents of the whites atrocities. Finally, he broke into the conversation. *"I must speak!"* Mouse translated and he continued. *"One hundred years ago, leaders of my people wrote laws that give every person the right to life, liberty and the pursuit of happiness. Our laws are made to give people liberty. But, as you say, the whites speak with forked tongue. These laws do not give the red man, the yellow man or the black man liberty."*

Everyone began talking at once. Stone Foot had no gavel to quiet them. He bellowed loudly enough that the men finally quieted. Mouse looked at Leftook questioningly. He shrugged his shoulders as if to say, "Sorry!"

Stone Foot addressed the white man. "These laws, are they the laws of your God?"

After Mouse translated, he answered. *"The whites have two laws. We have the laws of the God we worship and the laws of men. These laws often work against each other."*

Everyone began talking again. Stone Foot held up his hand and scowled. "We live because Wakan Tonka gives us this land and our spirits. Does the white man with his laws think he is God?"

There was a long silence. John Dunn, now called Leftook, looked at the ground as he spoke. *"Our Bible says all men are equal in His eyes. But the whites make laws that only apply to them. Their laws make those with different colored skin less than men."*

After Mouse translated, it was Kangee that had to yell above the outraged voices. "Then why are you here? Why do you want to walk the Red Road with us?"

Leftook looked from man to man, making eye contact with each. *"I am a Friend, a Quaker. That is my church, one of many the white man has. The whites have many different beliefs but we worship the same God. We Quakers believe that there are two great evils; one is to kill another man and the other to make him a slave. The war the whites fought with each other tore our church in half. Some believed we should join the war to help free the black men in the south. I was one of those men. I killed men for this belief. When I spoke out against the war, they sent me here to kill you. The men I came here with had no honor. That's why I came to walk the Red Road with you."*

Kangee spoke again. "If the whites have one God but many different beliefs, how do they live together?"

Leftook shook his head sadly and said, *"We whites are much the same as you. You and the Cheyenne have different beliefs and language yet you are friends. You are also friends with the Arapaho but the Pawnee are your enemies. We all believe in a Great Spirit that favors us."*

Mouse stood and faced the council. "We must have wakanisha in all things."

* * *

The next morning farewells exchanged were muted and brief considering the immense changes to come. Several older warriors from neighboring camps quietly told Stone Foot of their respect for his bravery in his decision not to fight but to live free. The old chief invited them to join him. They sadly declined, saying it was too painful to leave family and old friends.

A few war chiefs from other tribes actively tried recruiting young warriors from Stone Foot's tribe to join the war. These war chiefs were referred to Broken Knife. Some were not respectful. They openly called both Broken Knife and Stone Foot cowards, and accused them of hiding in the prairie like rabbits. The old chief met these taunts with stoicism and grace. Broken Knife's famous temper was sorely tested.

Sitting Bull, Gall and Kicking Bird arrived and asked for a council. The women were quickly and efficiently dismantling the camp so the men sat around the central fire. Kangee summoned Broken Knife and Badger. The old war chief, Dull Knife was the last to arrive. Sitting Bull solemnly lit a pipe and passed it. Each man said a brief prayer.

When the pipe arrived back at Sitting Bull, the old chief spoke. "Each of us has chosen our path to tawaiciyan. We will meet again." He stood, signaling the end of the council. The rest of the men stood and shook hands somberly. As Sitting Bull shook hands with Stone Foot, he handed his new Model 73 Winchester repeating lever action rifle to him. "To Freedom."

Kicking Bird gave his rifle to Kangee and Gaul gave his to Badger, along with several boxes of the .44-40 cartridges. The men nodded to each other and then were gone. Old Dull Knife, the tribe's war chief for decades, simply stood, placed his hand over his heart and walked away.

The tipis were dismantled and attached to the travois, the horses secured, food stored and packed for travel, and goodbyes exchanged. Several families were being split apart. Mothers leaving sons were wailing, their fathers standing stoically. Brothers leaving brothers shook hands while sisters sobbed. Aponi approached her father. She said, "Papa –"then couldn't finish. She held him and wept into his chest. Chumani and Mouse joined the hug. Aponi's new husband Strong Wolf stood quietly to the side. Broken Knife sat there on the prairie and pulled his daughters to him. He bitterly remembered an earlier time holding his daughters, wishing the moment would never end. Broken Knife looked at each in turn and said, "We will be together again."

The first day of travel, the tribe moved south and east. Stone Foot wanted to get them close to their traditional winter camp in southwest Kansas. The area was still virgin prairie with few white settlements. It was early fall; they hoped to find buffalo there and prepare for winter.

By mid-afternoon, the tribe reached the headwaters of a tiny stream the whites would later call the Red Willow River. The land was dry and almost barren. It had been a very hot day. When they spotted the tree line, they headed for the shade. Crossing the stream, they found a suitable spot on the bank with welcome shade from the setting sun. Scouts were sent out in all four directions; a few hunters and trackers scouted for game as the women set up camp. Fires were lit and dinner preparations were underway. The tranquility and privacy of the place was something of a relief after the massive "city" where they'd been staying for almost a week.

The stillness and serenity of the tribe's new spot was shattered as a scout rode into camp, frantic. "Soldiers are coming!"

Broken Knife quickly called the warriors together who began preparing horses and weapons. Stone Foot conferred with the scout and Broken Knife. "There are two groups, about twenty men in each group."

The old chief looked at Broken Knife for a moment then said, "Aphe!" He called Leftook over to him and whispered in his ear. The big man turned pale then nodded his head. "Mouse! I need you!" he yelled.

When she arrived, he asked, "*How long do we have?*"

Mouse asked the scout and he said, "One fist of the sun, maybe more. They are not riding hard."

Leftook ran to the tipi he shared with Spoon Woman. Minutes later, John Dunn reappeared in uniform wearing his sidearm and carrying his saddle and saddlebags. He ran to his horse, and saddled him up. He opened his saddlebag, took out his razor and ran to the river. By the time he had finished shaving, a small crowd had gathered. The drama being played out by this man was as fascinating as the fear the tribe felt for the oncoming soldiers. He loaded his rifle and placed it in the scabbard on his horse. And then, through Mouse, he called the entire tribe to him.

"*When the soldiers arrive, do not show fear. You will not know what they say but everything Mouse tells you to do, you must do without anger. I will tell them that I am taking you to a white man's fort. Do not show any anger. If they do not believe me, you will know by how they act. Then, and only then, defend yourselves. When the soldiers are here, I am your chief. You must obey! If you have questions, you must ask now.*"

Stone Foot stood stiffly as he alternately listened as Itunkala translated and closely watched the white man's body language. He paused for a moment then made eye contact with his other chiefs. The old chief nodded briefly and almost instantly, the tribe began to prepare.

The warriors readied their weapons and hid them within easy reach. Each woman had a knife or hatchet ready. They waited. When the soldiers finally appeared on the ridge above their camp, tension in the tribe had almost reached a breaking point. Lt. John Dunn mounted his horse and before he rode out to meet the oncoming cavalry, he repeated to the people, "*Show no fear. You belong here.*"

Lieutenant John Dunn rode tall as he approached the man at the head of the column. Not one person in camp could hear what was said even if they could have understood. They watched as the soldier at the head of the column saluted Lt. Dunn. The men proceeded to talk for a while. Lt. Dunn pointed once to the west. The soldier at the head of the column pointed to the north, in their direction. They appeared to talk some more, the man saluted again and Lt. Dunn returned the salute. The soldiers began to ride toward the camp but circled then to the east and continued on their northward journey. Lt. Dunn rode back to camp, dismounted, waved and smiled as the soldiers rode past. As the last soldier passed over the hill to the north, Leftook vomited into the fire.

Spoon Woman rushed out, took him by the hand and the two of them disappeared into their tipi.

* * *

As the sun set on this extraordinary day, Leftook emerged from the tipi with Spoon Woman at his side. He was completely unprepared for what he saw. The women's faces were painted red. The men's faces were painted red with a blue circle around the face and blue lines on the chin, forehead and cheeks. The sacred Making of a Relative ceremony had started shortly after the white threat had ridden over the hills to the north.

Mouse and Stone Foot appeared at his side with huge smiles on their faces. Leftook could only stare. She said, "*You are family, Leftook. We welcome you as a Human Being. Our White Buffalo Woman taught us to make a relative of any man who makes peace. We welcome you into our family, my brother.*" One by one, each member of his new tribe touched his heart and welcomed him home.

Hate is a Verb, Love is a Choice
1875 -1876

In time we often hate what we fear.
  William Shakespeare

Animals don't hate, and we're supposed to be better than them.
  Elvis Presley

At ten winters, Itunkala began to fully understand that the freedom her people lived came at a price. That price was an irony. They were free to hide like rabbits.

The winter of 1875 and 1876 was one of contrasts. There were weeks of fair, warm weather followed by the coldest nights any in Stone Foot's tribe could ever remember. Howling blizzards were followed by mild, spring like days. The game was strangely docile all winter, easy to harvest and always available. The tatonka herd roamed freely around their Kansas winter camp, almost as if the Great Spirit was sustaining them for the trials to come. Little Big Horn was less than half a year away.

When they arrived in their traditional wintering area in southwest Kansas, Stone Foot ordered them to temporarily set up camp near Dry Lake. The land in that area of Kansas is semi arid, covered by buffalo grass, sage and prickly pear cactus. In rare years with a wet spring, wild flowers bloomed in abandon. There were no trees for thirty miles in any direction.

The old chief sent scouts out in all directions looking for two things, whites and a shallow bowl of land deep enough to conceal the tops of their tipis when seen from a distance. Two days later, two young scouts returned and led the tribe to a spot south of Dry Lake in what was then called Sequoyah County and later, Finney County. The land there contained a series of ponds, buffalo wallows and low spots that would comfortably fit three to ten tipis. It was an unusual arrangement for them. Instead of being all-together, the tipis were spread out in little, isolated neighborhoods. Many in the tribe were uncomfortable with the arrangement until they climbed onto one of many high spots with views in all directions. In reality, it was an ideal hiding spot. Game was plentiful, sage and dried buffalo chips for fuel were there in abundance and intruders could be seen easily.

The blizzards, when they came, created some problems and solved others. The earthen bowls tended to drift deeply with snow while shielding them from the wind. Often, the drifts were deep enough to cover the tent flaps and make entry difficult. But the snow packed around the base of the tipis kept out the wind and acted as insulation. With plenty of fuel and food, the families stayed snug and warm during some of the coldest nights their old ones could remember.

Neither Stone Foot nor any other person in the tribe knew or cared about the presidential order reissued on January 31. In their minds, they were part of a sovereign nation, the great Sioux Nation. They clung to their sovereignty without acknowledging that a new nation existed that did not recognize the Sioux right to exist unless they gave up and occupied the pitiful land given them by the whites. The Unites States ordered all Native Americans to report to the reservation assigned to them by law. The United State was aware of the upcoming conflict; federal troops moved continually onto the northern plains during the spring and summer.

The spring of 1876 arrived early. The cool rainy nights gave way to warm, humid days. The prairie grasses and sage greened up and the yucca sent up stalks. The children began to take rabbits and a few of the older boys took a few antelope. The horses were fat from little work and plenty of grasses. The tribe's food supply was almost overabundant. The tribe had had fresh meat all winter and the excess was almost a problem; it was nearly too humid to dry the meat into jerky.

There had been no contact with any whites all winter. The tribe thanked the Great Spirit for the easy winter and at the same time felt the old uneasiness. They knew white men surrounded them. When the wind was from the north, they sometimes could hear the screeching of the white man's metal monster that followed the metal road. Scouts came back with stories of many cattle being put on the traveling boxes going west. Other scouts told of many wagons following the river way to the south. Wagon trails following the Arkansas River were becoming roads.

Then, this feeling of complacency and security disappeared instantly. One gunshot after another rang out to the north. Within minutes, one of the three scouts assigned to observe their northern flank rode in breathlessly. "There are two white men taking tatonka. They have a large wagon with two horses. They also have a horse with the leather place to sit. They are taking skins."

Stone Foot thought for a moment. "Take Broken Knife, Leftook and a few more men with rifles. Watch these Wasicans but do not show yourselves. Kill them only if they find our camp." He thought for another moment then said, "Bring Leftook and Mouse to me."

Moments later, the big white man and Mouse arrived where Stone Foot was sitting near the central cooking fire. "Leftook, I believe it is important that no white man see you living as we live. You must always be in your white man's clothing when you talk to these people. If the whites know there is a white man with us, we may lose our make-believe. We may need to act as if you are leading us again." He smiled at Mouse as he said, "I want you to go and see these men." The old chief held her gaze for a moment then nodded to her. "Talk the white talk to these men only if your father advises it."

The scout led Broken Knife and Mouse back to near Dry Lake where the white hunters were killing buffalo. Leftook and several other young warriors went along with strict instructions; do not confront the whites unless seen. Then, the white hunters were to be killed and their bodies hidden.

The Sioux approached these dangerous men from the south. The wind was blowing briskly from the north so their sound and smell were much less of a problem. The scout led them to a low spot near at the base of a small outcropping of sandstone. The other scouts' ponies were tied to the sage at the bottom of the hill. The lookouts waved, and then pointed in the direction of the white men they were watching. Broken Knife and the rest of them dismounted, tied their horses, and joined the two scouts.

Sun Hawk, the oldest lookout, angrily told them of his observations. "These Wasicans killed ten tatonka with a big rifle. They killed bulls and cows; they don't care. Then they drove their wagon from kill to kill, taking only the skin and the tongue. They leave the rest for the coyotes."

"What are these men doing now?" Broken Knife asked.

"They just finished taking the skin of the last tatonka. They were putting the skin on their wagon when you arrived."

As the group peered over the rise, in the background, they could see Dry Lake. The wet winter had nearly filled the three-mile's length. There was a small salt flat surrounding the lake, which the buffalo, deer and elk loved. Near the west end of the lake, the Sioux could see the wagon and horses of the white hunters. The men seemed to be talking but were too far away to make out any details.

Broken Knife led his little party quietly around several small hillocks until they were only about twenty yards south from the white men. The Sioux were lying on their stomachs, each behind a scrubby stand of sage.

Both white men were sitting on the end of the wagon, passing a bottle and talking. Both were wearing side arms and each had a rifle leaning against the wagon. The younger man's rifle was a Sharps 50 caliber. In the wagon were the hides of the buffalo they had killed. Of the two Human Beings hiding there that knew some English, Leftook's was the best but his Sioux was the worst. He did his best to translate.

At first, the conversation was mundane at times, embarrassing at others. The younger man bragged about his conquests with women in some detail. The older man laughed but didn't respond when asked about his sex life. With each pass of the bottle, the conversation became more erratic and animated. The old man farted loudly and the men laughed uproariously. The bottle passed again and this time around, both men took long draws on it instead of sips. The younger man slid to the ground and lost his footing and nearly fell. The men laughed again until the older man nearly fell out of the wagon. The younger man staggered away from the wagon a few steps, unbuttoned his trousers and urinated into a prairie dog hole.

"*Three bucks apiece! Not bad for an afternoon's work.*" The younger man said. "*Ten hides, thirty greenbacks. Shit, that's a month's wages.*"

"*Yea, maybe if you're helpin some damn sodbuster. I gotta pay to feed ma team, make this wagon pay for itself.*" the older man answered.

"*Still, fifteen bucks ain't bad. I can stay drunk for a week on that.*"

The older man stood up straight as he could and said, "*Ya lickfinger! Who says ya get fifteen bucks?*"

"*We's splittin it ain't we?*"

"*Hell no we ain't splittin! Where'd ya git that ideer?*" the old man yelled.

"*I jus thought –*"

"*Touch my raw, ya asswipe!*" the older man yelled again. "*It's my team, my wagon that's haulin these some-bitches. And shit, I did almost all the skinnin! You just sat on your quim and shot that fancy rifle. You didn't do shit!*"

"*Pay me you old whoremonger or I'll use that rifle on your sorry ass!*" the younger yelled.

The older man drew his pistol and said, "*Git your lazy prick out a here. You try to slash my hide and you'll be buzzard bait. Git! Git on your horse before you die of lead poisoning.*"

The younger man scowled at the older man, put his rifle in the scabbard attached to his saddle and mounted. "See ya in the lower town, ya old cherry!"

The older man stood in the back of his wagon and kept his pistol aimed at the younger man's chest. "Yeah, well just keep your squatter streaks in your nether garments and git back to your strumpets!"

The younger man swung his horse around and began riding north. He turned in his saddle and said, *"You cheap Nancy boy, you better watch your back!"*

"Keep ridin you gol-dern boat licker or you'll have a hole in your back." The older man let out a cackling laugh and then spit a wad of yellow phlegm toward the departing man. As the young man rode off, the older man, while keeping his pistol aimed, reached down and pulled his lever action rifle up beside him. He quickly holstered his pistol, cocked the rifle and aimed it at the departing horseman. He kept that stance until the rider disappeared over a hill to the north.

The older man kept watch, thinking that the young man with the rifle would appear on the next hill. Seconds later, the back support of the wagon seat exploded into a shower of splinters followed by the crack of a rifle. *"Holy shit!"* the older man yelled as he dove for the reins. He began to urge his horses to pull the wagon but changed his mind. He dropped his rifle on the mound of buffalo hides and ran around to the front of his wagon. He wanted to have the wagon and his horses between himself and the shooter. He began to lead his team in the opposite direction to the south, directly into the sights of Broken Knife.

Broken Knife and his warriors stood as the man and his wagon was less than ten yards away; multiple rifles were pointed directly at the man. The warriors waited for the order to shoot.

The white man blanched and put his hands in the air.

Broken Knife held up his hand. "Aphe. We wait. Mouse, talk to this man. Tell him to put his gun on the ground."

Mouse stood and looked questioningly at her father. She turned to the man and said, *"My name is Mouse in your language. What is your name?"*

The man gawked for a moment then found his voice. *"Bill. Bill Moore. Why do you Injuns have your guns on me?"*

Mouse translated after her father said, "Tell this Wasican that he is wasting our sacred Tatonka."

"Put your gun on the ground and we'll talk."

The man unbuckled his belt and the gun and his holster fell to the ground.

Mouse said, *"My people don't understand why you take only the skins of our buffalo and leave the meat to rot. To us, it's a sin against God."*

"You can have the cussed meat. Hell, you can have the skins too!" Bill Moore dropped his hands, walked quickly to the back of the wagon as if he was going to unload the skins. He leaned into the wagon and instead of grabbing the skins he grabbed his rifle where he had dropped it. He pulled it out of the wagon by the barrel and when he did, the trigger caught on something and it fired into his stomach. For a moment, he had a surprised look on his face then he collapsed onto the prairie in agony.

The entire group of Sioux gathered around the white man, not sure of what to do for him. Broken Knife picked up the man's revolver and threw it in the back of the wagon with the rifle.

"You dratted heathens! Look what you've done to me!" screamed the white man. He lay on the ground and writhed in pain.

Mouse kneeled down and asked, "What *can I do for you?"*

"Leave me alone! You God damn Injuns, worthless bastards! We'll kill you all! You all should be Sam Hill dead! Finished! Go to bell fired Hell!"

She stood up and looked at her father. "We should take him back to camp, maybe Kangee or Macawi can help him."

Leftook shook his head. "Soldiers in the war with a wound like this never survived. We should just leave him to die or put him out of his misery."

Broken Knife was about to agree when Mouse said, "We are Human Beings. We are not murderers. We must hold to our beliefs or The Great Spirit will leave us."

The men looked at each other then Leftook and one of the warriors started to pick up the wounded man. *"Keep your randy hands off me you bastards!"* he shrieked.

Broken Knife nodded and the warriors picked up the man and placed him gently on top of the buffalo skins. The white man screamed obscenities at them over and over.

Leftook tied his horse to the wagon as did Mouse. She rode with the injured man and Leftook drove. She tried to talk to him, to calm him, to give him some comfort. He did nothing but hurl curses at her, at all Indians, at women. Finally, he lapsed into unconsciousness.

* * *

In camp, Macawi and Kangee tried to tend to him. When conscious, he cursed them. Macawi made a drink of powdered tree bark for the man's pain but he refused and threw it in her face.

Finally, Macawi told Mouse and the rest to leave, that she would stay with him, be with him when he died.

Hours later, Macawi came and found Mouse. "His spirit is gone. He is not in pain. At the end, he called for his mother."

Mouse looked at Macawi sadly. "The whites are all so different. Mary is so full of love. Leftook is gentle and honorable. How could this man be so full of hate?"

"I think we fear what we do not understand. We fear the whites; maybe they also fear us."

Love is a Verb, Hate is a State of Mind
1876

The Americans combine the notions of religion and liberty so intimately in their minds that it is impossible to make them conceive of one without the other.
    Alexis de Tocqueville

All the ways of a man are pure in his own eyes, but the Lord weighs the spirit.
    Proverbs 16 – 2

In death, the body of William Moore was more frightening than it was in life. While alive, it was easy to hate him, to see him as all that was wrong with the whites. Now he lay there peacefully as an indictment for some crime the Sioux must have committed but couldn't comprehend. His presence in their midst generated terror in all that looked at his body. He seemed like a magnet drawing revenge in from all points of the sacred directions to punish them for their simple desire to just exist.

The body of Bill Moore had just begun to cool when Stone Foot called a hurried council. "We must leave today. We will go to our summer home early."

Those gathered around the central cooking fire on that warm spring afternoon all began speaking at once.

Stone Foot held up his hand. "I will give you my reasons, then we will talk. The other white man may return. He may bring other whites with him to find this dead wasican. If these men come, they will find us with this man's body and his wagon and horses. We must return this man and his belongings to where you found him. That is where the other whites will look first."

Broken Knife spoke. "We did not kill this wasican. We tried to help him. That is not a crime."

The old chief shook his head and shrugged. "These white need no reason to hate us. We will use this man's wagon to bring back one or two of the dead tatonka to use the meat for our journey. We will leave the same number of skins as bodies we leave on the prairie to rot. We will leave the wagon, the horses and the man's weapons. We must not be found at all, but to be found with this wasican's possessions will make us look like his murderer."

The discussion was short. Kangee made a suggestion that altered their planning and speeded up their move. He proposed that Leftook, some warriors and several women leave immediately in the wagon with the white man's body. They were to take the tools needed to butcher the meat they needed for their move. The rest of the tribe was to follow as soon as they were packed. They planned to meet at Dry Lake, take on the meat and travel through the night north and west toward their mountain camp. Food was plentiful; there was no reason to delay.

Stone Foot spoke again. "We need Leftook in his soldier's clothing. Who else can drive this wagon?" Badger stepped forward and agreed to take the wagon. Macawi took two other women and rode in the wagon; their job was to butcher enough meat for the journey to the mountains. Several younger warriors followed on their ponies for protection.

While the camp was being disassembled and readied for travel, Leftook shaved, rubbed buffalo fat on his boots and once again became Lt. John Dunn.

Shortly before sunset, the entire tribe reunited on the shore of Dry Lake. They left Bill Moore's body in the back of his wagon with eight buffalo skins, his side arm and rifle at his side. Taking two of the slain buffalo as travel provisions, they also made sure to take two skins.

Stone Foot gave strict instructions that no Indian ponies were to leave tracks in or near the lakeshore. Sage branches were used to brush away the wagon tracks leading to their old encampment. Badger and Stone Foot had a brief disagreement over the white man's horses. Badger wanted the horses freed from their traces; Stone Foot disagreed. The horses were left hooked to the wagon, to survive or not, depending on the will of the Great Spirit.

The tribe followed the fresh tracks of the small herd of buffalo for several miles directly north to complete the illusion that they had never been there.

As the sun set on this solemn day, the tribe made their way north and west into the fading light.

* * *

The glow of a gibbous moon and clear skies made night travel possible. As they traveled, lookouts kept watch in all directions. They kept a minimum of eight riders scanning the perimeter of their travels. Only once did they have to detour around a small pasture surrounded by barbed wire. A small cabin near what is now called Scott City, Kansas sat on the banks of Ladder Creek. The scouts traveling on the north side of the tribe reported in about the cabin and wire. Stone Foot detoured slightly to the south. They stopped briefly when they finally came to the tree line of the creek to rest and take on water.

Mouse was bitterly disappointed and argued briefly with Stone Foot when he announced they would not stop or even travel close to Cheyenne Wells. "Whites like you saw at Dry Lake are everywhere. We cannot chance meeting any wasicans who would report us. It is just too risky."

They traveled all that night and part of the next day. Stone Foot pushed them hard. His goal for their first day was a little known spot, a tiny valley. It was ringed by worn sandstone cliffs with pools of standing water, trees and visual safety from the totally flat prairie surrounding them. Ladder Creek fell into this oasis as it flowed east to join the Smoky Hill River.

By early afternoon, the tipis were erected, cooking fires started and children wandered off to explore and play in the water. After the hard night's travel, the young warriors grumbled when assigned sentry duty. Stone Foot held up his hand and explained. "Yes, we are well hidden in this low spot but we cannot see who approaches. Do you want the whites to find your families without warning?"

A rock formation the whites would later name 'The Devil's Backbone' cast shadows onto the floor of this lovely little valley. The women of the tribe were preparing an evening meal. The children had gathered hundreds of crayfish to add to the meal. The men relaxed and smoked their pipes. Stone Foot, Kangee, Lt. John Dunn and Broken Knife quietly discussed the next day's route. Once again, their sense of calm was interrupted with the arrival of two scouts.

Broken Knife stopped what he was saying and approached these two visibly upset young men. "Many whites are coming in wagons. They have six white soldiers with them. They also have Pawnee scouts. They may already know where we are. Many men with rifles are riding in front of the wagons."

Leftook, still in uniform as Lt. John Dunn, looked at his friends around the fire. "I will ride out to meet them. What is your wisdom, Stone Foot? Should some of you ride with me to show that we are not hostile?"

Stone Foot thought for a moment. "All of us here around the fire will follow you at a distance. Itunkala should come also to talk to these whites, to show them we are not bad people. You should only talk the white talk to them. Signal us to ride forward after you have talked, and let them know they are safe from us, the Human Being animals.", he added bitterly.

As they rode up the slope to the flat prairie above, Mouse asked, "Do you think there will be children with them? I have never seen a white child. I wonder what they are like."

Kangee rode up beside her and smiled. "The whites are much like us. They have families and love their children. We are different in what we believe. Our fear and anger make us enemies. But, in their own way, they practice Wakanisha."

The moment that Lt. Dunn and his little band appeared on the prairie, there was extreme tension. The riders from the wagon train, including the six soldiers, immediately dismounted and took a defensive stance behind what little cover they could find. Rifles were aimed, hammers cocked. The wagons began to form into a circle.

Leftook held up his arm and his group stopped. He stood in his saddle and waved, rode forward to half the distance and waved again. He was well within range of their rifles. Finally, one of the men in uniform waved back so Leftook rode forward, again halving the distance between him and the whites. He shouted his name to the formation and was waved forward.

Watching from a distance, the Sioux saw Leftook dismount and return the salutes of the soldiers there. He then shook hands with several of the men. They appeared to talk for a while. He then disappeared among the wagons long enough that Stone Foot thought they might have to return to camp and mount an attack. It was a very stressful few minutes. Just as Stone Foot was ordering his warriors to return to camp, Leftook walked out onto the prairie and signaled them to join him.

By the time introductions were made, a small crowd of whites had gathered at the fringe of their wagon train. They were all very curious, but fearful of these Indians. When they heard Itunkala speaking English, the children of the wagon train were unable to contain themselves. They moved forward a step at a time with their parents in tow. Mouse was just as curious. At one point, she waved to the white children. After a second of stunned silence the children rushed forward and surrounded her horse.

Stone Foot smiled at her and said, "Be careful little one. Give no locations or names. It is better for these people to think you learned the white talk at a school or at a fort." She nodded her understanding and continued to translate.

Leftook did not speak any Sioux while talking to the whites. But he did give her a lengthy message to translate to Stone Foot and the rest of the Sioux. "*I have told these people that when you learned of the White Leader's order, you surrendered to the soldiers at Ft. Larned. I was ordered to escort you to Ft. Laramie because that is near the Sioux reservation.*"

Stone Foot listened then thought for a moment. He smiled at Mouse as he said, "Tell these wasicans that we are camped in a good spot with water. Tell them we have much fresh meat that we will share with them. Ask them if they wish to camp near us and share our food."

* * *

The wagons appeared at the rim of the little canyon and ponderously made their way down to the creek. Continuing on, the wagon train bypassed the tribe's encampment and moved upstream several hundred yards.

The Indian children stood at the edge of their camp and watched as the wagons rolled by. White children in the wagons waved shyly; a few of the Indian children ran along beside the wagons. The children of both camps seemed ready to interact and play, but the adults were tense and distrustful.

The white men and women seated at the front of the wagons frowned and seemed very unfriendly. The soldiers and other men on horseback did nothing to mask the naked hostility on their faces. The parents of the Sioux children stared fearfully at the whites.

The sun began to drop behind the canyon wall and a shadow passed slowly over the two dissimilar, untrusting camps. Smoke from the Sioux cooking fires rose around the tipis but no cooking seemed to be coming from the wagon camp. Mouse was nearly vibrating with curiosity. When she could stand it no longer, she got Red Feather and approached Macawi and Spoon Woman. "If you will come with us, our children can gather firewood for the whites. If we help them, maybe they will be friendlier."

Macawi spoke briefly with Leftook. Broken Knife told Mouse to gather the children. There was a cheer as the Indian children gathered around. Macawi said, "Bring a rawhide strap and gather as much firewood as you can carry. When we are ready, we will offer this gift to these whites. But you must remember; the rules of our camp may be different than of the camp we will visit. This is true of any place you visit. If you have a question, ask. Do not show bad manners."

Minutes later, the small pack of Sioux children with their loads of firewood arrived at the outskirts of the circled wagons. With them were two Sioux women and Leftook dressed as a cavalry officer. They were met by several armed men with a small pack of white children behind them. Both groups of children stared bashfully at each other and smiled. The men seemed unsure of how to proceed. Finally, Mouse said, *"My name is Mouse in your language. We bring you a gift."* Almost simultaneously, the children held out their bundles. One little boy's bundle came untied and tumbled to the ground. The children on both sides burst into giggles.

The white men stood there, scratching their heads, unsure of how to proceed. An older, gray haired man stepped from behind a wagon and spoke. *"We have no need of firewood. Our food does not need cooking."*

"We have fresh buffalo meat and there is much food to be harvested near here." Mouse said.

"We have salt pork and hardtack. We have no need of your food." the man replied.

"I wouldn't mind some fresh meat," one of the men said. There was a chorus of agreement from the others, and from the growing crowd of whites that had gathered to watch this interesting exchange.

The gray haired man smiled benignly at the others and said, *"Abstain from food polluted by idols, from sexual immorality, from the meat of strangled animals and from blood. From the Acts of the Apostles, brothers."* He walked away.

Mouse looked from face to face. *"We bring gifts. I am hearing yes and no. We do not wish to make problem. We will leave if you do not want us here."*

A man and woman of about thirty came forward with two children, a boy of about ten and a girl around six. *"We accept your gifts. We would love to have some fresh meat. My name is Frank and this is my wife Abigail. These are our children, Luke and Stella."* The two children looked out from behind their parent's legs and smiled.

Lt. John Dunn stepped forward and shook the young couple's hand. *"There is fear and mistrust on both sides. I understand, but you are safe here. These people are friendly and want to live in peace. They will share their food with you or, if you feel comfortable, they will share a meal with you."*

Nearly all the people from the wagon train were now gathered near listening to Lt. Dunn and Mouse. After some discussion, the Indians were invited to bring their food to the wagon encampment because night was coming and the whites had kerosene lamps; but most of them knew it was simply fear of the unknown that made the whites prefer their familiar surroundings.

Macawi sent Red Feather with strict instructions to bring half the fresh meat, cooking stones and any people in the tribe who wished to mix with the whites. With Mouse's help, she organized a food-gathering party inviting anyone who wanted to join in.

Macawi took half of the crowd and Mouse with her and began gathering yucca blossoms. Spoon Woman led the other half down to the stream. Lt. Dunn went with Spoon Woman and her group, explaining, *"I speak a small amount of Sioux. I'll do my best to translate."*

Mouse made small talk while Macawi led her group up a hillside where the yucca was thick. The warm spring weather had encouraged the hearty plants to cover their stalks with blossoms. Mouse began heaping these blossoms into her shirttail as the whites stood watching, slack-jawed. *"You eat cactus?"* one of the women asked. Without saying a word, Mouse picked a flower and ate it, then another.

The woman tentatively tried a bite and said, "Why, they're amazing!" Soon all the whites in the group were eating more flowers than they were saving. Mouse just watched, and her heart smiled.

Spoon Woman led her group to the edge of Ladder Creek. She looked for several moments and found a spot where the water was very shallow and the stream seemed choked with weeds. Reaching in, she began pulling large handfuls of greens out onto the bank. She put a few of the leaves in her mouth as if testing them, then smiled and gestured that everyone should begin harvesting. The Indian children began without question. The whites, children and adults alike, seemed repulsed by what they thought were some kind of moss. One of the older white women picked up a small amount of the greenery and looked carefully at it. *"This is watercress!"* she cried. *"This is a delicacy in St. Louis. Taste it!"* She put a small amount in her mouth and said, *"Delicious, absolutely delicious!"* Smiling at Spoon Woman, the white woman said, *"Watercress, we call it watercress."*

The rest of the tribe arrived with huge slabs of meat at as Spoon Woman and her group returned to the wagons with baskets and buckets full of watercress. Mouse arrived with mounds of yucca flowers and a happy band of followers.

The travois was loaded with the meat, cooking stones and several sprigs of fresh sage. Kangee called the clan to the side of the travois and said, "We thank you Wakan Tanka for the spirit of this animal and the meat that will feed us. Thank you for leading us to this place of understanding."

The white men had used almost all of the firewood to make an enormous fire at the center of their circle of wagons. Uneasily, the white men and the red men sat around the fire as the women began to cook. Stone Foot lit a pipe and started it around the fire. The children, white and red, began to play games older than language. When Mouse started to join them, Stone Foot called her back. "We need your white talk." Mouse disappointedly sat in the circle with the men.

"Why do you make such a large fire?" Stone Foot asked Mouse to ask the whites.

With Mouse translating, the older white man with the gray hair answered, *"A big fire keeps the wild animals away."*

With Mouse's help, Stone Foot responded, "A small fire will also keep animals away."

Hearing this, the gray-haired man smirked, *"You have a lot to learn about living in the wilderness."*

Mouse looked at the white man for a moment then turned to Stone Foot. "He says there is a lot we could learn from each other."

The Last Supper
1876

He who corrects a scoffer gets himself abuse, and he who reproves a wicked man incurs injury. Do not reprove a scoffer, or he will hate you; reprove a wise man, and he will love you. Give instruction to a wise man, and he will be still wiser; teach a righteous man and he will increase in learning.

Proverbs 9: 7-9

I do not serve what you worship; nor do you serve what I worship. You have your own religion and I have mine.

The Koran

As this unusual meal was prepared, the people there formed into three very distinct groups. Mouse would liked to have been playing with the other children or helping the women cook, but her ability to speak the white talk put her in the position of the only female sitting among the group of edgy, aggressive men.

She could hear the children playing happily together, laughing and learning to play Red Hand. The women of the tribe quickly began cutting meat and starting small cooking fires. The white women could see how easy it was to fry the meat on hot stones and cheerfully joined in to help where they could. Smiles and hand signals were the only communication the children and women needed.

The men of the tribe as well as the white men gathered in a circle. Stone Foot started this process and took his place facing east. Broken Knife and Kangee did their usual polite but awkward gestures as they tried to decide who would sit on the chief's left. Finally, Kangee sat first followed by Broken Knife and Leftook. Badger and a few of the younger warriors stayed with the horses and continued to act as lookouts. Mouse sat at the left of Lt. John Dunn.

As soon as Stone Foot sat, the rest of the Sioux men quieted and sat respectfully. The white men around the circle noticed the cue and also became quiet. Stone Foot looked around the circle from man to man. He nodded to Mouse for her help, and then said, "I am called Stone Foot and we welcome you to this beautiful land."

Mouse translated his greeting. The older, gray-haired man stood and said to Stone Foot, "*My name is Dr. Cyrus Bartol. It is I who should extend a welcome to you as you pass through our land.*" He was not a large man but projected some sense of force that was vaguely unpleasant. When he spoke, there was no emotion, no inflection; no facial expression or body language illustrated the significance of his words.

Mouse swallowed hard, looked at Leftook for a moment, then translated, "This man welcomes us and thanks us for this food."

Dr. Bartol looked at those around him then spoke to Mouse. "*My job, my God given solemn duty is to lead my people across this land but also to lead them on the one true path. My conscience also tells me to lead all you non-believers to the one true God. Jesus saith unto him, I am the way, the truth and the life: no man cometh unto the Father, but by me.*"

As Mouse translated these words, Kangee and Stone Foot exchanged a look, a glance that spoke volumes. Then Kangee smiled at Mouse and said, "Tell this man what I say." The Shaman turned and attempted to make eye contact with Dr. Bartol. Kangee felt that even though he was looking into the man's eyes, there was no contact, no sharing. "Brother", Kangee began, "you say there is only one way to worship the Great Spirit. If there is only one religion, why do you white people argue so much about it? Why not agree as you all read the same book, your Bible?"

Kangee paused, looked at Mouse then continued, "Brother, like you, our religion has been handed down from father to son. Our forefathers taught us to love one another, give thanks for all the creation that the Great Spirit has given us and be united as a people. We never quarrel about religion because it is a matter between each man and our Creator.

Kangee reached out to shake Dr. Bartol's hand again but the man did not respond in kind; the white man seemed to be there only in body. Kangee dropped his hand to his side. "We want to enjoy our own religion for now. We will watch you whites and see what effect your preaching has on your people. If it make them more honest and makes them treat the People more fairly, we will consider what you preach."

Mouse swallowed hard and began to consider what she would say to this strange white man when a sudden loud clanging startled the Indians.

Dr. Bartol laughed. The white man smiled and looked expectantly toward the wagons. *"That's the dinner bell. It's a signal that food is ready. Please join us in prayer."*

When Mouse didn't translate his prayer, Dr. Bartol asked, *"Why did you not pass my prayer on to your people?"*

She replied, "We always give thanks to Him as we release the spirit of an animal we take, but this animal was killed by a white hunter. We thanked God, the Great Spirit, earlier."

"There is only one true God," Cyrus Bartol exclaimed as they made their way to the meal that was laid out.

Mouse looked at the man as she walked behind him. "Yes, *I believe that too!"* she said quietly to his back.

* * *

Dinner highlighted the contrast of two very different cultures. White etiquette dictated that guests be served first. Mouse grasped and explained that custom to her people, but again, she had to speak up when she learned that the whites served *women* first. Sadly, she overheard more sarcasm in both languages than good-natured laughter and forgiveness over their differences.

All gathered there agreed that the meal was wonderful. It was the first fresh food the whites had had in weeks and many of them thanked the Indians profusely. True to form, the good

Reverend Dr. Cyrus Bartol caused discomfort in the group when he refused the fresh game and greens, eating only hardtack and salt pork.

Other than a knife, few of the Indians had ever used utensils for eating. When handed a plate and fork, they watched and learned to eat "white style'. While whites were accustomed to sitting for their meals, the Indians walked about as they ate, conversing with each other.

The Sioux were intensely curious about the whites' wagons. To them, the wagons vaguely resembled tipis and, because the flaps were open, it appeared there was an open invitation to investigate. The overly protective response to this snooping from the white wagon owners reflected their fears that all "Injuns" were thieves and murderers.

For Mouse the meal was far from relaxing. As the only translator, she was a lightning rod for many minor encounters that, without her language skills, could have quickly become lethal.

When dinner was over the people broke into predictable groups; whites talking to whites, reds talking to reds. Mouse sought out Kangee for some relief and reality. They had just begun to speak; Kangee was asking her for her impressions of the whites and some of the more interesting encounters when Dr. Bartol approached.

"You are an amazing little girl. Where did you learn to speak our language?"

"We trade much with the white men." she lied. *"I learned from a woman who often visited our camp. I also talk for my people when we stay near the forts. The white soldiers have taught me much."*

"That is a lot of responsibility for a little girl. Are you even seven yet?"

"I am very small but I am eleven winters, years. That is why my name is Mouse."

Interrupting, Kangee asked Mouse, "Does this white man ever smile?" as he smiled kindly at Dr. Bartol. Mouse introduced Kangee. *"Dr. Bartol, "This man's name is large black bird; I do not know the white word for it. He is our spiritual leader."*

She turned to Kangee and in Sioux said, "This man's name is Bartol and he is their Medicine Man, their Shaman."

With his face turned toward the white man, Kangee said, "May the Great Spirit be with you always," and he held out his hand to shake.

Dr. Bartol did not respond. He did not smile or react to Kangee's gesture in any way. He stared at Kangee devoid of any expression at all, almost as if this Sioux holy man did not exist. He turned to Mouse. *"I do not know what this man's beliefs are. Some in my church believe the Indians are without a soul; are nothing but animals."*

Mouse translated to Kangee precisely what the man had said. Facing the white man and looking directly into his eyes, Kangee instructed Mouse, "Tell this white man that animals do not sit around a fire and discuss The Great Mystery. Animals do not share their food with others. Tell this white man that animals do not teach their children of a Great Spirit that loves and teaches love."

After Mouse finished translating Kangee's remarks, Rev. Bartol again quoted scripture. *"Jesus saith unto him, I am the way, the truth, and the life: no man cometh unto the Father, but by me."* He looked at Mouse coldly then said, *"Do you know Jesus?"*

"Yes, I know much of Jesus. My friend Mary read the Bible to me and we discussed many things. Jesus and his friends seem much like the stories of my people. The man Peter from the Bible often said that we are to love one another because love takes care of many things. He said that we should not be angry with each other because each person has different abilities. He said that we should take care of each other and when we do, we make God happy."

A small crowd of whites had formed near them to listen. Had Reverend Bartol raised his voice or his body language become aggressive, Mouse's people would have swiftly surrounded her in defense. But outwardly, the man's demeanor was benign, almost as if he were discussing the weather or the meal they had just shared. *"The wages of sin is death. You and your people do not know Jesus therefore you will all burn in Hell."*

Mouse looked around her. The white faces she saw reflected the same earnest feelings and emotions she saw in her own people when they discussed the meanings of their beliefs. She recognized the similarities, not the differences.

"Our teachings speak of one who will come to end the troubles between men, much as the teachings of Jesus. The woman who taught me your Bible believes that we all have the same God."

In that instant Bartol's demeanor changed from laconic to furious and aggressive. *"That's blasphemy!"* Bartol roared, "You people are Godless heathens! You will rot in Hell!"

Naturally, the sound of Bartol's outburst brought many people running, including Stone Foot, Mouse's father and Leftook, as well as many whites from the wagon train. All were aware of the tensions that existed, especially with Bartol. Lt. Dunn took one look at the faces of those present and said in Sioux to Stone Foot, "We should leave!"

From the edge of the crowd, a large white man spoke up. *"I ain't no Bible scholar Reverend, but I'm a good judge of character. These Injuns are childlike and honorable. I was ascared when they showed up but they seem like good people to me."*

"Take heed to yourselves: If thy brother trespass against thee, rebuke him; and if he repents, forgive him" Rev. Bartol bellowed this at his own people. *"Have these red niggers repented? No! They try to bring their heathen teachings to God's people!"*

The young white woman Abigail stepped into the circle. *"Reverend, I'm not speaking against you but I want to talk. I was terrified of these Indians. I heard stories about them all my life but they are not like the stories. They are very polite. At every fort or trading post where we stopped, most white men made me uncomfortable, made me feel dirty in the way they looked at me, the little comments they made among themselves. When these Indians came through the food line, I felt I could trust them. They were very respectful. And their children are wonderful. Rowdy maybe, but I felt their love."*

"They are non-believers. They bring their heathen teachings among us."

Inserting himself into this exchange, Lt. Dunn spoke, *"Thank you for your hospitality. We need to try to get to Fort Wallace tomorrow. Good night to all and thank you."* In Sioux he said, "Unj ya!"

One by one, each Sioux picked out one white to approach and said, "Pilamaya." No one spoke to Reverend Bartol.

The two groups parted. Arguments among the whites became less distinct as the distance between these groups of people became greater and greater.

Isnati Awicalowanpi

Coming of Age - Day One

1878

In 1878, a constitutional amendment was proposed that provided "The right of citizens to vote shall not be abridged by the United States or by any State on account of sex." This same amendment would be introduced in every session of Congress for the next 41 years.

In July 1890, the Territory of Wyoming, which allowed women to vote, was admitted as a state. Wyoming became the first state to grant women suffrage.

Gunfire shattered the afternoon calm. The distinctive long-lasting crack of rifle fire came from the south. Women swiftly gathered their children. The men of the tribe gathered near Stone Foot's tipi, weapons in hand. Cooking fires were quickly extinguished as the younger men gathered the horses.

Moments later, a scout rode hard into camp with news. He reported that at least six white men on horseback with rifles were taking buffalo and two or more men with a large wagon were with them.

Stone Foot silently cursed the whites yet again. Because of the recent new white towns and ranches springing up in southern Kansas, he had made his people's winter camp in the rolling hills between Dry Lake and the headwaters of the Pawnee River. Their camp was nestled in between a ring of hills with a natural opening to the south. Gentle spring rains and warm days had greened up the prairie and life had been pleasant. The choice of where the tribe would winter was dictated by the whites intrusion but hunting had been easy and their stores of food increased.

Stone Foot looked around at those who gathered there; they looked to him, waiting for direction. Turning to Dull Knife he said, "The whites, if they come, will approach between the hills to the south. Put five men with rifles in hiding behind each hill. Hide more with rifles in the brush along their path. Do not fire on them unless you're seen. Then gather the council!"

Broken Knife was the last to arrive. He and a small group of young hunters had heard the gunfire and had ridden hard back to camp. As he entered Stone Foot's tipi, he heard Leftook saying, "These whites must be from their new town to the south. They will take the hides, tongues and backstraps and go back to their town."

Broken Knife looked from face to face. Kangee simply said, "There are many whites to the south taking tatonka. They have rifles and a wagon." Broken Knife nodded and sat down.

The council was short. Stone Foot did not ask for opinions. "The whites are too close. We will move our camp to the mountains tomorrow. Today, we prepare. Leftook, we may need your pretend; become our white soldier that leads us to the white man fort." He looked from man to man, nodded and stepped outside to smoke.

* * *

As Itunkala and Chumani dismantled their tipi, they heard the older women talking about dream walking, a term the girls had heard for years but didn't really understand. Other women complained about the upcoming move to the summer home in the mountains.

Horse Woman was especially vocal. She seemed to be talking to everyone and no one in particular. She repeated over and over, "The women never get a say. When will our women decide how our people live?" Many of the other women listened and nodded as they worked, while the men standing nearby, glared at her. Stone Foot either ignored her or didn't hear her, no one was sure.

Broken Knife's two daughters quickly and efficiently removed the skins covering the cone-shaped frame of their shelter. They stacked the skins nearby and, one-by-one, lowered the lodge poles that were free standing. The rawhide lashings were untied and unwound and the last three poles were carefully lowered.

Two older boys brought two of Broken Knife's three horses. The boys flirted with Chumani but refused to help the girls build and hitch the travois to the horses or load the family's possessions. Chumani made last minute adjustments to the loads as Mouse trekked to the spring to fill the water bladders.

* * *

The sun was almost directly overhead when Mouse snapped to consciousness. She had walked since midmorning leading one of the horses. She remembered talking to Chumani and a few of the other women as they walked. Then for several miles, she had not been aware of her surroundings; she had been dream walking. The tribe was nearing a small stream lined on both sides with ancient cottonwoods.

She realized someone had spoken to her. There, next to her, Leftook was riding his big cavalry horse dressed in his uniform. "The map your friend Mary gave us shows this creek. They call it White Woman Creek."

"I am sorry." she said. "I was lost in thoughts."

"I said the map Mary gave us shows this creek. I think many things may be missing but there is also good detail. Here, let me show you." Leftook dismounted and showed Mouse the map. He showed her the drawings of the mountains to the west and pointed out several other waterways they would cross before arriving in the Wyoming Territory.

The map fascinated Mouse. "Where did we start?"

Leftook pointed to a spot on the map. "This is Dry Lake. Here is the river the whites call the Pawnee River and this was our winter home." He moved his finger over the map indicating the route they had taken. "We are near here." He pointed to a spot on the map that was clearly a waterway.

* * *

Stone Foot did not need to tell his people; he simply stopped, dismounted and began to eat. The women unpacked dried meats and the water bladders. The men led the horses to the creek for water. The children played in the water and more than several of them asked to fish.

Some of the women led by Horse Woman loudly voiced their opinion that they would like to stop for the night in this lovely place. Stone Foot ignored this talk. When he finished eating and watering his horse, he remounted and began to ride west across the stream.

Horse Woman stood, placed her hands on her hips defiantly and yelled across the stream, "We want to stay! We travel tomorrow!"

Stone Foot stopped his horse midstream, turned and frowned. "The men decide. It is our tradition." He turned his horse and rode on.

* * *

Itunkala and Chumani were the first of the women to cross the stream with their horses in tow. The scouts rotated in and out with news of the surrounding countryside. Broken Knife and a few of his young hunters readied their weapons and rode upstream, into the prevailing north wind, hoping for fresh meat to take on their travels. The remaining women grumbled among themselves but crossed the stream and followed the staggered column of Human Beings. The conversations, the chores, the grumbling and complaints were as old as the centuries of migrations the First People took. The very real threat of the whites discovering them was much more recent.

Leftook stayed behind to help Spoon Women ready their possessions for travel. When they were ready for travel, he kissed her affectionately and rode over the stream to join the men at the front of the column. As he approached Chumani and Itunkala, he smiled and greeted them. Chumani's question literally stopped him in his tracks. "Leftook, tell us of white women."

Leftook looked every bit the cavalry officer as he looked down on these young women. He cleared his throat uncomfortably. "What do you want to know?"

Chumani smiled at him coyly and said, "Walk with us. We want to know how it is between white men and women."

Leftook climbed off his horse and began walking beside the two young women. Both Chumani and Mouse smiled as they sensed the big white man's discomfort; he was beginning to blush.

"You have a woman. Spoon Woman is a good woman." said Chumani. "Did you have a white woman before you walked the Red Road with us?"

"Yes. I was to marry and girl I knew from my church."

"Was it the same to lie with her as it is with Spoon Woman?"

The big man blushed a deep red. "I did not lie with her. We were not married."

Mouse asked, "Why not? You lie with Spoon Woman and you are not married. My sister has many men lie with her. She is a woman now and to be with a man is natural."

Leftook thought for a moment. "The whites believe that a man and a woman must be married to be together or it is a sin."

Kangee had been walking behind listening. He stepped into the conversation. "The People had no word for awahtani; sin is a word we learned from white teachers of your Jesus."

Leftook, in an attempt to turn the conversation said, "Is there no sin for Human Beings?"

The old shaman smiled and made eye contact with Leftook. "Our sin is not against Wakan Tanka. We sin when we act against our own conscience."

Chumani frowned at the Shaman because the conversation had taken a turn away from the subject of her curiosity. "Was Spoon Woman the first woman you had sex with?"

The big man blushed an even deeper red. "No."

"I want to know what it is like to lie with a white woman?" Chumani asked.

"Well, there are white women who lie with men for money. Those women stay near the forts and make money from soldiers. I have been with that kind of woman a few times."

Kangee and the two young women looked at each other then Kangee asked, "If you lie with a woman you are not married to, you believe it is a sin. Is lying with these women who take money a sin?"

"Yes, I suppose it is." the big white man said. "Women who have sex for money, they are treated like they are less than human, much like how many whites feel about the Human Beings." He hung his head and said, "That way, when you pay them, it is like the sin is theirs."

Chumani was unrelenting. "Is it the same to lie with a white woman and Spoon Woman?"

"No!" Leftook said forcefully. "No. When I was with the white women, I felt shame. With Spoon Woman, I feel joy."

* * *

When they finally arrived at their summer home, the tribe breathed a collective sigh of relief. Stone Foot continued to post scouts at the eastern edge of the foothills to spot any intruders who might follow the river into the mountains.

Nearly a moon had passed without incident so the tribe settled into a comfortable daily routine. The men hunted when needed and nearly always returned with deer and an occasional elk. Daily, the boys and young hunters' trapped cottontail rabbits, smaller but much better tasting than the jackrabbits from the plains. The women fashioned rabbit fur into excellent winter clothing and the elk and deer hides were turned into functional and sturdy garments.

Broken Knife, unhappily, had assumed the role of head warrior. Already in charge of all hunting, he was now in charge of the security of their little clan as well. Dull Knife and a few of the tribe's young warriors had stayed on for the battle of Little Big Horn leaving Broken Knife in charge.

The clan desperately waited for news of the battle and of their warriors who had stayed behind to fight. Communication among the various tribes was now almost non-existent because the whites had very nearly contained all of the People on reservations. Federal soldiers had not encountered any other free roaming tribes in almost a year.

Mouse continued to learn English from John Dunn, Leftook, while Broken Knife learned some American military tactics from him. The maps that Mouse and Leftook had borrowed from the white woman at the Cheyenne well helped Broken Knife understand geographically how this vast land was transforming into a predominantly white nation. Broken Knife was now relying ever more heavily on this Wasican information to ensure the tribe's survival. In their hearts, the clan knew it was just a matter of time before they would be forced to join their captive brethren on the reservation in the Black Hills. In the meantime, they were fiercely proud to live a free life and practice Wakanisha.

* * *

Traditionally, when a young Indian woman had her first moon, or menses, her tribe would hold a celebration and ceremony. The Coming of Age Ceremony was exceedingly important in a young woman's life. It signaled her ascension into adulthood and her readiness to marry. For her family, especially for her father, it meant receiving gifts of horses and other things of great value in exchange for the hand of a daughter.

The clan's evasive and at times, erratic travels had made their important religious observances difficult. So, after these several weeks of tranquility in the mountains, the women began to plan. Several of the girls had bled for the first time since their winter stay on the Kansas prairies. Chumani and another girl had been waiting for more than a year. So the women of the tribe demanded the ceremony and celebration.

One afternoon after Chumani had finished her chores, she met with a young warrior and the two of them were walking out of camp toward the stream. Macawi stepped up to the two and asked to speak to Chumani alone. "You have no mother to stand with you. I will stand with you; I will help you through this important time."

Instead of withering under the powerful will of this woman, Chumani squared her shoulders, looked into Macawi's eyes and said. "I thank you for this honor but I am already a woman. My mother has been with me always. Help my little sister when her time comes." She touched her heart then placed her palm over Macawi's heart. "You were my teacher, my guide; my mother spoke through you many times. Pilamaya Coonshi."

Macawi tenderly placed her hand over Chumani's and held the girl's hand over her heart. "Yes, you are a woman and make your own choices. I hope you choose to join us and learn the women's wisdom that has passed from mother to daughter since the First People. I want one last chance to be Coonshi to you." Macawi raised her hand and held her palm on the girl's cheek.

The two women looked into each other's eyes until Chumani smiled and nodded.

* * *

The planning, began to take on a life of its' own. The men, usually apathetic about this particular celebration, actually joined in the preparation. They planned an extravagant hunt to provide a feast. Even old Stone Foot could be heard singing snatches of song and adding his ideas about the upcoming party. The tribe needed this. The pace and content of their lives had been dictated by the white man for too long. This celebration was going to be more than a typical Sioux Coming of Age Ceremony; it would give these proud and still-free people a chance to celebrate their very existence.

A custom in many early cultures was to separate women from the group during their monthly periods and the Sioux were no different. During the Coming of Age Ceremony, the first phase required the young women to build their own tipi away from the rest of the clan.

The first day of this important ceremony finally arrived. As part of their rite of passage, the girls had to construct their own tipi without any help whatsoever from her mothers. This traditional ritual served a practical purpose. It symbolized the girls' preparation for having their own home away from their mothers, as well as providing the opportunity to practice their tipi building skills.

Other women of the village were not allowed to physically help the girls with their project but a ring of mothers and "aunties" formed around the perimeter for support. Shouts of advice from the women were offered as the girls worked to erect the thirteen poles that supported their ceremonial tipi. For the men, this was a humorous time. A loosely formed ring of men and boys stood behind the watchful women, and enjoyed a good laugh while they watched the inexperienced girls grapple with poles and hides. The thirteen poles represented the thirteen moons of a woman's year.

* * *

It was on this same day that Red Feather approached his mother and grandmother to inform them that he felt called to a Vision Quest. Spoon Woman and Macawi stoically accepted this but asked that he inform Kangee and Broken Knife and solicit their advice. The two men wished him success and gave their sage counsel. Red Feather prepared for his quest.

Red Feather was almost across the river heading up the mountain when Mouse stopped him.

"Please, tell me where you plan to go." Mouse pleaded.

Red Feather pointed the direction he intended to travel. "We explored there many summers, Mouse. Do you remember the ridge of rock that looks into this valley near the lake? I will be there."

"Red Feather, you are my only close friend. You are my brother. Do not lose your way."

Isnati Awicalowanpi

Coming of Age - Day Two

1878

That night, Mouse had nightmares about two men. Their faces never quite came into focus. At times in her dream, the two were reassuring. At other times, they were evil, demonic. In one moment they seemed familiar and protective, but then they changed and frightened her terribly. Throughout the dream she continuously saw Red Feather's face but she could never quite reach him. She held out her hands to him and he seemed to look over his shoulder and smile at her. But then he would look away and he seemed afraid. He was always just out of her reach, receding into some danger she could not see. Mouse awoke in the middle of the night soaked in sweat, convinced that Red Feather needed help. She could not get back to sleep and the feeling of impending danger would not leave her.

By dawn, she was convinced that Red Feather was in some trouble. She went to Kangee's tipi. "You are up early little one," he said. "Come in, let's talk."

In her usual manner Mouse rushed through telling the story of her dream to the old Shaman. She explained the compulsion she felt to follow Red Feather's path onto the mountain to be able help him if he needed it. The more she talked the more frantic and animated she became. Finally, without really thinking about what she was saying, she blurted out, "I'm going to find him!"

"Sit down now little one." Kangee said softly, "Is your dream still with you? Do you feel the spirit of it on this side of your sleep?"

"Yes, it is very strong! I see the dream clearly now while I'm awake. Can you tell me what this means?" She sat, but was nearly vibrating with stress.

Mouse was as visibly distraught as Kangee had ever seen her. He said, "Girl, it is not uncommon for a young woman to feel the call of a Vision Quest. All young men are expected to hear the call, but many do not. It is the quest that helps define our lives. I am not surprised you have a call. Your spirit is too large to sit in a tipi and be tended by women."

Mouse leapt up and was about to leave when Kangee caught her hand. "I have to go!" She said this with a question in her voice.

Kangee stood and hugged her. "Prepare first, girl. Think! Take the things with you that you may need. Tell your father of your call and tell him where you are going. He will understand. He will not like it but he will understand."

Mouse was already out of the tent and running to get her things when the old man yelled after her, "I will pray to Wakan Tanka for your quest!"

* * *

The same night of Itunkala's dream of men, the girls in their ceremonial tipi also thought of men. Their teenage energy kept them awake long into the night.

No wild animals attacked the girls during the night. No Pawnee warrior rapists snuck into their tent and ravished them. But from outside, it sounded like that and more. Even though the ceremonial tipi was in a separate location, the girls' mothers heard every squeal, every giggle. The three girls finally fell asleep a few hours before dawn. Their mothers, like mothers everywhere, lay awake in a state as old as mankind, concerned for their children.

One very bittersweet part of the Sioux Coming of Age Ceremony involves food. For the entire four days, the girls are not allowed to feed themselves or drink unassisted. Their mothers tend their daughters as if they were babies.

At first, the girls react to this restriction with anger. Every bite of food the mother feeds her daughter, every drink of water is at odds with the adolescent rebellion the girls feel. This age-old conflict between mothers and daughter is brought into sharp focus. For the mothers, it is a return to the natural nurturing of motherhood. For the daughters, they are forced for the last time to be dependent. Like their funeral ceremony where the dead are released from their earthly responsibilities, mother and daughter face up to their feelings for each other.

The second day, mothers and daughters gather herbs and flowers used in healing. This day is an intense and pleasurable day for teaching and learning. On this day, the girls become connected to knowledge passed from mother to daughter for millennium.

* * *

By midmorning, Mouse had crossed the river and was climbing steadily. She was carrying a small amount of water and food, enough for two days. She had packed a lightweight elk hide, her bow and arrows and the large knife she always carried. The images from her dream increased in urgency as she exerted herself climbing.

As she traveled, the terrain varied greatly from moment to moment. There were stretches where the ground was almost flat with wildflowers and rich mountain grasses underfoot. Sunlight filtered through the pines; grasshoppers jumped from near her feet and flew away snapping like cedar in a fire. It was from these meadows she could see her objective far above her on the slope. The rock outcropping overlooking the alpine lake was still very much in the distance.

As Mouse walked briskly through dense stands of yellow pine and lodge pole, she smelled the tangy, crisp mountain air. Her path was never straight; she had to sidestep huge pink boulders covered in lime green moss. Avoiding slopes covered in loose stone she chose paths through fields of rock outcroppings, at times gingerly scaling rock faces that were almost vertical.

The thin air made breathing more of a challenge but nothing erased the frightening dream from her mind. The single mindedness of reaching her friend clouded her judgment. She didn't notice how treacherous her journey was proving to be.

Late morning, Mouse crossed a small stream. She knelt down, cupped her hands and scooped a drink of the icy water to her mouth. Immediately, her thirst almost overpowered her. She dropped to her stomach and stuck her face into the water and drank deeply. The cold water snapped her back to reality. She realized she had been walking as if in a tunnel without her usual acute sense of her surroundings; dream walking without a sense of her surroundings.

With wet hair and face, she sat down on a fallen tree and took out a small piece of elk jerky, thinking deeply as she ate.

For the first time since awaking from her nightmare, its power was beginning to burn away, partially because of the physical intensity of her climb. "What am I doing here?" she thought. Suddenly she realized she had no plan, no objective other than to find Red Feather. She felt foolish and flat, strangely indifferent. It was unlike her to be lethargic but sleeping seemed like it would make the most sense. It occurred to her that she didn't feel very well. Her stomach hurt; her abdomen was cramping.

She stood up, unsure of what to do. Continue up? Go back? The sound of the stream finally intruded into her consciousness. She realized she was close to the south shore of the lake that she and Red Feather had visited so many times. So, Mouse picked up her gear and continued uphill, following the stream.

After another half hour of walking her stomach cramped violently, almost doubling her over. She stopped long enough for the cramp to subside then began walking again. She was now within sight of the lake. Just around a bend the lake emptied between a rock outcropping, forming the creek. She had another strong cramp and with a queasy feeling, realized there was something warm and sticky running between her legs. She was about to pull down her breeches when she saw blood staining the buckskin she was wearing. "I'm a woman!"

she thought with some apprehension. "Nobody told me it would hurt so much."

Mouse walked over to a stand of trees near the shore and hung up her pack and her bow and arrows. As she walked to the shore, she wanted nothing more than to clean herself up and wash out her clothing. She would look later for some of the moss the older girls used during their time and try to remember how they arranged leather straps to hold the moss in place.

A stone clicked behind her; it was a sound that was out of place. Mouse whirled around. Staring at her from less than twenty yards was a large cougar. Two things registered immediately; the cat smelled her blood and it was standing between her and her weapon.

Mouse pulled her knife and screamed at the cat. She attempted to make herself as large as possible but she was a tiny person, less half the size of this mountain lion. The cat hesitated for a moment then continued walking slowly in her direction, flipping its tail back and forth aggressively.

Lying nearly at her feet was a stout branch as long as she was tall. She picked it up, swung it around while yelling at the lion. The cat hesitated again then continued openly stalking her.

Mouse looked around frantically. About twenty yards away, a small ridge of rock jutted out of the shoreline that formed an alcove deeper than she was tall. At ground level, two large boulders touched each other and made a small cave-like opening that offered some protection. Mouse picked up a rock, threw it as hard as she could at the cat, and ran flat out for the rock opening. Her aim was good and the rock struck the cat. Without that diversion, Mouse would have never made it.

The lion and Mouse reached the rock opening at nearly the same time. She had her back to the wall of the small cave when the cat attacked, coming at her with its front claws. She managed to poke the lion in its snout with the branch. The lion shrieked and backed off. She flattened herself against the back wall and had just enough room to sit cross-legged on the floor with her back to the rock when the lion came at her again. Again, she tried to stab the lion in the face but it batted the limb aside, nearly pulling it out of her grasp.

The lion crawled into the opening, its body holding the limb against the side. Mouse dropped the limb, pulled her knife and when the cat reached for her, she stabbed through its forearm. The cat screamed again and backed out. The beast paced back and forth in front of the opening, flicking its tail from side to side. It came at her again. Mouse stabbed it again.

The lion lay down several yards in front of the opening and glared. Mouse quickly pulled the rawhide strips she carried and pulled the limb to her. She lashed her knife to its end to create a longer weapon. Slowly, she crawled out but just as she began to stand up the lion attacked. The speed of the animal was astonishing. One moment it was lying on the sand and the next, it was nearly on her. Mouse managed to slash the lion's shoulder and it retreated again.

Mouse was unable to leave the cave; she was trapped. She crawled to the back of the cave and waited.

The shadows became long as late afternoon crept over the lake. The lion lingered close by but only showed itself if Mouse tried to stand up to retrieve her bow and quiver of arrows. Each time, she was driven back by the threatening snarls.

Mouse realized that whatever small advantage she might have would disappear with the daylight. She decided that live or die, now was the time to make her move. In darkness, she would have no chance at all. She crawled out, stood up, and immediately the cat attacked again. But this time, Mouse did not retreat into the cave. She poked and slashed, screamed and yelled and tried to work her way over to her bow and arrows.

There was a moment when time seemed to stop. The lion was crouched ready to spring; Mouse was poised to defend. The two stared at each other. Suddenly, the lion leapt, but not at Mouse. It leapt sideways and landed on all fours, thrashing around, biting at its side. Mouse saw an arrow protruding from the Lion's chest. Then, another arrow found its mark. The cat fell on its side and emitted a loud, unearthly howl. It shuddered twice then was still.

Mouse held her stance unable to believe her ordeal was over. The lion still did not move. She took one tentative step toward the cat, then another. She picked up a stone and threw it at the beast. Her aim was true but the cat did not move. Out of the corner of her eye she saw movement and at the same time heard a footstep. She whirled around holding her makeshift spear in front of her.

Red Feather stepped out from behind a small rock outcropping about thirty feet away. He was pale and trembling, still holding his bow. The two stared at each other for a few moments. Slowly, they both lowered their weapons and walked toward each other.

"Pilamaya" Mouse said softly. She took his hand in hers and looked into his eyes. He was trembling and when Mouse touched his hand, he began to cry. Red Feather was more than a head taller but when Mouse pulled him into a hug, he put his head on her shoulder and wept. She held him like a parent for several minutes until he cried himself out. Finally, Mouse lifted his chin and said, "You always were a terrible shot," and smiled.

Red Feather wiped his face and said, "I was so afraid. I was going to run until I saw that it was you."

She looked at him for a moment. "I may have died here. Instead, we have found something. We will talk to Kangee and he will tell us what we found."

"I found that I am a coward." Red Feather said bitterly.

Mouse punched him lightly on the chest and said, "You found something in yourself that killed that huge igmu taka and saved my life. You are no coward! You had fear but you still acted. Thank you for my life!" She placed the flat of her hand on her chest then touched his chest the same way. "Pilamaya!"

Red Feather helped Mouse skin the big cat. They used the hide to wrap the meat they carved off the carcass. They gathered their belongings and set out. As they walked around the lake to the north side, they said little. The short walk helped bleed off the fear left they both had felt. By the time they reached the sandy beach, their moods had lightened. Red Feather gave her a playful shove and Mouse ended up stepping in the water to keep from falling. She recovered and ran up behind him, kicked one of his feet so that it locked on the other ankle. He fell flat on the sand. They laughed together like children.

The camp was a familiar place where the two of them had been many times. It was now in shade as the sun having dropped below the tree line, but the air was still warm; the colors of the sky beautiful. In the past, Mouse and Red Feather had camped there together alone, as well as with other children. They had come to this place every year since the tribe had designated the area its summer home. They had swum together in the lake like otters.

The north end of the lake formed a natural cove. The shore was sandy with few rocks and the sand extended up into a shallow cave. The cave floor was flat and a fire smoldered at the opening. The space inside the cave was somewhat circular, about the size of a small tipi. Red Feather had arranged the space like any Sioux would do. Near the left side of the opening, he had spread pine boughs and spread his elk robe for sleep. There he had stored ample fuel for a fire stored on the right and his food was buried and covered by stones. To the north, there was an amazing view of the lake and a part of the valley below.

Mouse said, "I will cook but first, I need to clean my clothing and swim." She stripped off her bloodied buckskins and rinsed them vigorously in the water. She hung them up near the fire to dry and pulled off her top. As she waded into the water, Red Feather undressed and joined her.

She dove deep and shook out her hair. She then swam toward shore till she was waist deep and cleaned herself; she rubbed sand between her legs to loosen her dried blood. Red Feather swam up behind her as she was rubbing water off herself. He gently took her shoulder and turned her to face him.

He looked at her body and said, "You have changed since we were here last year. You are a woman now." He reached out and touched one of her small breasts. "You are becoming a beautiful woman," he said.

"You have changed too." Mouse said as she looked at his body. "Last year, you were a boy. This year, you are a man."

He pulled her closer and placed the flat of his hand below her navel on her flat stomach. "This place is the most beautiful." he said breathing hard. "This is the place you will carry a baby." He pulled her closer and he looked into her eyes. "Itunkala, I ---" The rest of his words were lost and he pulled her fiercely to him. He buried his face in her hair, her neck.

She responded to him, to the powerful emotions that were overpowering them both. She pulled him close and moaned into his chest. She felt his hands explore her body. She felt her reason leave as her body reacted to age-old animal desire. Hand in hand, they walked to the cave.

Red Feather put his arms around her again as they entered the cave. He began to lower her onto the bedding when she placed her hand on his chest.

"We must wait," she said. "We have forgotten that we are not animals. We are Human Beings. The Great Spirit has given us these feelings but we must also think of him. Remember the story; we have dust in our eyes."

Red Feather's eyes shone with love for her but his lust was in control of his body. He pulled her again and was about to use his size and strength when he saw her eyes. He saw the depth of her soul, a spark of the Great Mystery looking at him. It wasn't the strength of her hand on his chest that changed him; it was the force of her eyes and the potency of her heart. His lust melted into a desire to protect and nurture their relationship.

The two stood facing each other, hands clasped, looking at each other as their breathing slowed. "Now what?" he asked.

"I will cook for you," she said. "Then we will sleep. But first, we must thank Wakan Tanka for our meat. We took a spirit today. We must never forget to thank The Great Spirit for our lives."

That night, they slept nestled together like they had slept since they were children.

Isnati Awicalowanpi

Coming of Age - Day Three

1878

The second night in their isolated tipi was much different. But being fed by their mothers had been the same. The feelings of anger and rebellion had been there as well. The difference was that the girls were feeling a distinct shift in the way they were feeling about themselves.

Instead of sitting up giggling about fantasy sex with warriors or gossiping, the girls began to discuss their feelings. One by one, they confessed to each other that being fed like a baby was beginning to feel comforting. The girls felt like a door was opening again between them and their mothers; a door they had slammed shut as they began to experience puberty. They discussed at length something one of their aunties had said. "All creatures leave their home. Bears leave their cubs. Birds push the young out of the nest. Humans create conflict to mask the pain of separation."

One by one, they confessed to each other that they wished they could stay young a while longer; adult life scared them. They went to bed earlier and slept better.

Early the next morning, a soft call came from outside the tipi asking for permission to enter. The young initiates looked at each other not really knowing who was in charge. Finally, the girl closest to the door whispered, "Please come in."

When the flap opened, a large number of women crowded in. The mothers were there as well as many "Aunties". Macawi and Spoon Woman were there for Chumani; all the women were carrying packages.

The girls got their breakfast, visited the communal latrine and took a morning stroll through the camp. When they returned to their tipi, the mothers and "Aunties" had spread out their packages. Each package contained a lesson.

Through the day, the girls learned to cook several meals. One of the women had brought buffalo meat and berries; the girls learned to prepare a special holiday feast.

The girls each made their own medicine bag out of the finest deer hide and practiced bead work using strips of strong animal gut as thread. The girls learned and practiced the proper way to scrape and preserve animal hides. Learning and doing traditional woman's tasks with the older women felt warm and comfortable. The conversation felt like talk among equals. The young girls were relaxed and happy.

About mid morning, the young girls began to realize that the real lessons being taught were not the crafts but the conversation. The mothers and aunties began talking about the realities of family life, sex and pregnancy, childbirth. Slowly and gently, these young girls were drawn into frank conversations about their bodies, what to expect with men and their first sexual experience, and modesty. The girls heard real stories about childbirth, sexual abuse, and incest. They heard about the pain and joy of relationships from their mothers and their aunties, women they knew well.

Macawi and Spoon Woman spoke reverently saying that a woman's experience is an important part of The Great Mystery. Then just before dinner, Macawi formed all the women in a circle. They held hands as Macawi told them, "You are the master of the house, in charge of the man and the children inside your home. You must do this with the strength of your will. You must be strong and equal to your man. It is you who has the most sacred task of all; you must live Wakanisha."

* * *

The sun had not cleared the tree line when Mouse awoke. She carefully removed herself from the warmth of Red Feather's body and dressed. The air was cool but with no wind, the lake reflected the beauty of this spot. The trees and rocks were reflected perfectly. When an eagle flew over, it was an omen or blessing seen and enjoyed twice.

She rekindled the fire and began to prepare a stew of fresh cougar and elk jerky. She had brought sage with her from the prairie and she added this to the stew. Growing near the stream that entered the north side of the lake were little patches of wild asparagus. She thanked the Creator for this blessing and added a handful to their breakfast. There were still a few wild strawberries growing at this altitude and she picked two handfuls of these as well. She was pleased that Red Feather would arise to a pleasant meal.

A combination of pleasant smells and soft singing finally got Red Feather up and out. He stood there smiling at Mouse, completely naked like they had slept. She smiled at him and said, "Its cold. Get dressed before a bird sits on that thing."

He laughed and walked just out of sight and relieved himself. He came back moments later and wrapped himself in his elk robe and sat next to her by the fire. "Smells good." he said.

They ate a comfortable breakfast together. They sat and talked about inconsequential things, shared childhood memories, laughed at each other's stories. They let ground squirrels interrupt their thoughts, watched fish jump. Mouse added fuel to the fire and the two of them just stared at the fire for a while. A slight breeze came up and the lake lost its luster as a mirror. The sun was still not over the tree line and the breeze was cold. Mouse leaned into Red Feather so he pulled her under his elk wrap with him.

They sat there contentedly as the fire warmed their faces. He draped his arm over her shoulder and pulled her tight. "Thank you," he said. "I was like the first warrior in the story of White Buffalo Woman. I didn't see your spirit. My body wanted sex with you. I'm sorry"

"I felt the same," she said.

They sat there for a few moments, enjoying the warmth of the fire and each other. Finally, he said, "I think this is the first moment I have ever been a Human Being. I am in this beautiful place. I am with you, a person I know better than anyone and a person I love. This is the first time that I really feel the Great Spirit touching my heart. I have known what it means to be happy but this moment, I feel joy for the first time. I think I am feeling this because I am sharing this with you. Our spirits connects us. I give thanks."

The sun cleared the trees to the east and shown on the two of them. The elk robe began to warm from the sun and the warmth spread to the two inside.

Mouse placed her hand on Red Feather's chest and said, "I give thanks also." She rose up, turned his face to hers and she smiled at him. She looked into his eyes and saw his spirit.

They spent the day as they had for years; they were children together. They fished, explored the area around the lake, but mostly, they laughed and played and enjoyed the very last days of childhood.

* * *

Late in the evening, as they lay under his robe, they talked for hours. He said, "Pilamaya for this day. I feel the joy of being with Wakan Tanka in this perfect place. I now know what it means to be a Human Being."

Mouse stared into his eyes for a moment then said, "I fear that we must learn to keep this feeling when our lives are not perfect. Then, we will be Human Beings."

Isnati Awicalowanpi

Coming of Age – Day Four

1 8 7 8

Many human cultures celebrate the emergence of their young into adulthood. A common theme in recognizing this transition is religion. In some cultures, the arrival of adulthood is tied to physical maturity, the ability to have sex and reproduce. In others, an arbitrary age predicts spiritual accountability where the child must demonstrate knowledge of their beliefs.

To the Sioux, religion was not separate from everyday life, but was woven through all phases of living. They believed that Human Beings, like the buffalo and other animals, were created from the Mother Earth, that humans and nature are one. For them, there was no clear distinction between the natural and the spirit.

On the third and last night of their isolation, the girls felt sad that the wonderful day spent with their mothers and aunties was over. Any natural feelings of rebellion and friction between mother and daughter that had arisen during puberty were now replaced with a sense of belonging, of true kinship.

The girls talked among themselves late into that night of their aspirations and plans, wishes for the future with realistic goals. As they drifted off to sleep, they realized that they were now young adults, not just girls. Their childhood fantasies of being grown-ups had been replaced with sensible, pragmatic concepts. Their mothers and aunties had given them the tools to begin their own lives.

The fourth day started early. The mothers, Spoon Woman and Macawi waited outside the ceremonial tipi. As the sun peeked over the horizon to the east, the older women asked for permission to enter.

There were tearful, happy hugs and warm greetings as the older women stepped inside. Each mother had brought her daughter's favorite food. Each pair isolated themselves as well as they could for this intensely private moment when mothers would feed their daughters for the last time. This would be the last meal they would have together as mother and child, an intensely tearful and poignant event for both. As Macawi and Spoon Woman fed Aponi, they softly told her stories of her mother.

After breakfast, each mother or surrogate bathed their daughter in sage water and talked to her about her birth, her young days and her future. When the last words were said, the last embraces shared, the girls dressed in their ribbon dresses, moccasins and beaded regalia.

As the girls stepped out of their tipi, a loud cheer went through the camp. Many more aunties, relatives and friends rushed over to congratulate and compliment the girls. One by one, the girls were introduced to the tribe as women. The feast started immediately.

* * *

The fire burned fitfully outside the cave. The wind gusted for seconds then the air was still. Shadows flickered on the roof over their heads but Mouse was the only one watching. Once he lay down for the night, Red Feather had fallen asleep almost instantly. Mouse felt restless, unsettled. There was something just out of her grasp, something she couldn't quite concentrate on, something bothering her

As she drifted toward sleep next to Red Feather and watched the firelight shimmer above her, memories came: dancing to the drums with her Ate, her feet on his, her sisterly love for Red Feather, blood gushing out of a neck she had just cut, discussions with Kangee about life, the cougar, a distant memory of being underwater and being saved by her father, the kind white woman. She thought about her frenzied climb up to this beautiful spot as if it had happened centuries before; she felt like she had always been here. Then, with a jolt, she realized this was the second night she and Red Feather had been absent from camp. And with that thought came the reality that they should have returned earlier. Guilt troubled her as she fell asleep. "Our families must be worried."

Finally, Itunkala slept. Her dreams seemed to meld with the firelight. One moment, she was warm and secure and the next, she stood in places familiar and frightening. She stood on the banks of a creek, looking into the water. Behind her, a figure appeared on a ridge in the distance, a woman. Mouse recognized the mother she had never known. With a rattlesnake wrapped around her arm, the woman slowly raised her eyes and pointed toward the horizon. Mouse's eyes looked in that direction and saw that horse soldiers were coming. She turned to run but suddenly found herself on a vast open prairie. Behind her, the thunder of hoof beats came closer. She ran, as dreamers do, as if mired in mud. In the distance, thousands of tipis appeared to her arranged in a circle. At the center of the circle stood a tipi, impossibly tall. Inside it, a man was calling to her, offering safety, happiness and contentment. One moment, she was looking down on this city of tipis; the next moment she was on the ground running through the passages that led to the man who beckoned to her. Behind her, she could hear obscene laughter. Snow began to fall. The harder she ran, the deeper the snow grew. She finally reached a huge open area where a fire was burning. She finally saw the tipi offering safety and the man was beckoning to her, urging her to come to him. Suddenly, Red Feather stepped in front of her wearing the hide and head of a huge cougar. He looked at her through the eyes of the cat and held the palm of one hand toward her, telling her to stop. Then, in slow motion, she watched Red Feather pull an arrow, nock it in his bow and release the arrow directly toward her man. The sound the arrow made as it pierced him woke her with a start.

The fire had collapsed upon itself; the moon was high overhead. The faintest light seeped across the horizon to the east.

Mouse knew that more sleep was impossible. She got up, dressed and rekindled the fire. She sat staring into the fire until the sky turned from black to shades of pink and salmon. When the sun's rays peeked through the trees to the east, Red Feather stirred. She snuggled up to him for warmth, enjoying the easy contentment she felt with her closest friend, her brother in spirit.

Mouse slipped into a place between sleep and awake. "I don't think we should marry." he said.

"Did you ever want that?" she asked.

"There has never been a time I haven't known you. You are my closest friend. I love you. When I was little, I always pictured us together but now my heart tells me we are not right for each other. Your spirit is so big. It continues to grow. Mine will fall behind."

She put a finger to his lips as if to silence him and whispered, "I also had the same thoughts when I was little. When I made you play husband, you always hated it. I knew then we would be friends but not be together."

"I dreamed last night." Red Feather smiled at the memory. "A woman is coming that needs me. She and I will soon have a child. I dreamed this woman is the mate of my heart. I think the Great Spirit gave me this vision."

Mouse smiled. "I also dreamed last night but my vision was not so happy. There was a man searching for me, calling for me. His spirit is very big and," she hesitated, "I am afraid."

Mouse cooked a quick breakfast. She and Red Feather picked a large bundle of wild asparagus to take back and collected as many strawberries as they could find. They wrapped their treasures carefully and started for home.

As they passed the carcass of the lion, they both shuddered at the memory of the terror they felt. Mouse had an idea. "Gifts are given at Isnati Awicalowanpi." She smiled at Red Feather. We should take gifts."

She put down her pack and took out her knife. One by one, she removed the claws from the cat.

Red Feather said, "I will make necklaces for my mother and Coonshi with the teeth." With a stone and his knife, he removed the lion's enormous fangs as well as many of the sharp front teeth."

With their trophies wrapped and tied to their packs, the two trudged back down the mountainside in a contented silence.

They stopped to drink from the stream in the same spot where Mouse had stopped on her frenzied climb. As she shouldered her pack, she said, "Do you remember when we had the contest at the big powwow? We had to have a partner. You hurt me when you chose somebody else."

"I know, I'm sorry. I didn't want the other boys to laugh at me." He answered. "You hurt me too. Coonshi and Kangee talk to you for hours. You know the white talk. You make me feel stupid."

She reached out and took his hand. "You will always be my brother."

* * *

It was late afternoon when they crossed the river and walked into camp. Both of them were nervous about explaining their recent absence to their parents but no one took much notice of them. A huge fire was burning at the center of camp. Smells of roasting meat and singing filled the air. Several men were dancing around the fire; a celebration was in full swing.

Broken Knife eventually noticed them and said, "Welcome back. I see Red Feather is fine. You almost missed the feast." Spoon Woman waved to them from across camp but continued talking and eating.

Mouse and Red Feather smiled at each other. They dumped their packs near their respective tipis and joined the festivities.

Just before sunset, Kangee got up and called for attention. Many ignored him and continued to eat and dance, laugh and talk. He went to his tent and returned moments later. He stood near the fire and bellowed in his deep voice for attention.

Then, he threw a small amount of gunpowder into the fire. The resulting flash of light quieted down the crowd.

He began, "The Isnati Awicalowanpi is one of our sacred ceremonies. Their four days away from our tribe represents the death of these girls. It is a symbolic death. They die as children and are reborn as women, able to make children. This cycle is part of the sacred hoop, part of Wakanisha. We welcome these women to our fire!"

There was much cheering and congratulation. Several young men were flirting with the 'new' women. Their parents began the traditional giveaway, presenting of gifts to significant adults that influenced the lives of their daughters.

Red Feather smiled at Mouse. "You are also a woman but maybe we should wait until tomorrow to give our gifts."

Gifts
1878

Mouse closed her eyes to the familiar sounds and smells of her home. The raspy snores of her father and soft breathing of her sister comforted her. For all of her thirteen winters home was the same, reassuring place. Mouse snuggled in with Chumani under her buffalo robe, something she hadn't done in years. The intimate surroundings of her childhood cradled her, yet this night she felt apart, alone. Sleep would just not come.

She let her mind drift back to swimming with her sisters, admiring their woman's bodies and wanting to grow up. Aponi had said, "Enjoy being a child. You'll miss it when it's gone." And it was true - now that Mouse had become a woman, she did miss the uncomplicated ease of childhood.

She was exhausted yet images from the past days thrilled her, terrified her; the cougar, her frenzied hike in search of Red Feather. The memory of those tormenting dreams was the most troubling to her mind. The man who seemed to be calling out and searching for her still seemed to stir her heart. She yearned to find this man.

Finally, as she drifted off to sleep her dreams began again. This time Red Feather seemed older, more of a man. He was on a horse, a weapon in his hand, waiting with her father. Red Feather wore the cloak of a cougar but her father was nearly naked and seemed vulnerable. The other man, the one searching for her, was holding her and comforting her. Behind her was an infant who was silently watching with deep soulful, eyes. Then, the three men rode away on their horses toward a sea of white soldiers.

Mouse awoke with a start. Her dream and wakefulness were tied to the sound she at first thought was a baby crying. She lay there waiting, when she recognized the call of the ever-present camp robber bird, halhata.

Her father was not in their tipi and Chumani was still asleep. Mouse placed the strawberries and the asparagus on their mother's cooking stone, picked up the rolled cougar skin with the teeth and claws inside, and stepped out into the light of a new day.

Mouse walked across the common area to Kangee's tipi. His flap was open so she stepped in. The old Shaman at first smiled, then saw her face. He looked at the bundle she carried then back at her face. "Sit down little one. Tell me everything."

"You prayed for my quest the last time we talked. Much has happened!" She unwrapped the cougar pelt and laid it on the ground between them. "This is my Isnati gift to you."

The old Shaman sat quietly for a moment then rubbed his hand across the pelt of this fierce beast. He looked into her eyes and said, "I dreamed of you. You were standing before a great many Human Beings. You held a child. In this dream, you gave a great gift. I could not see this gift and the place was very strange. There were no tipis and the People lived in boxes like the whites. It was a sad place."

"It was my dream that sent me up the mountain to see Red Feather. When I left, you said you prayed for my quest. I, too, dreamed every night. I also dreamed of a baby, but there were men, always two of them. One was Red Feather and I did recognize him but the other is a man calling for me, searching for me. I am very drawn to this man. Other times, I dream of another two men but they are terrible. They frighten me. What do these dreams mean?"

"Tell me everything. Start at your first dream and tell me everything."

Red Feather appeared at the tipi opening. "I also had dreams. May I join you?"

Kangee motioned the young man in and had him sit next to Mouse.

"I also dreamed of a baby. A woman came to me and together we had a child. Please talk to me about my dream"

The old Shaman sat quietly for a moment then began to speak. His voice was blotted out by the sound of a horse ridden hard into camp.

Red Feather jumped up to see a scout running to Broken Knife's tipi. A crowd gathered almost immediately behind Broken Knife. The scout, one of three watching the approach from the east reported. "There are six to eight riders with a small herd of ponies approaching. They look like us, like Human Beings. They were too far away to see if we knew any of them.

Broken Knife asked the scout, "How long?"

"One or two sun fists; they ride slow. They ride openly, not trying to hide."

Broken Knife yelled to the crowd. "Every man with a rifle, come with me. Those with good bows follow. We will melt into the forest on either side of the stream. Stay hidden. We will hide on both sides of the stream twenty paces apart. Be sure you can see the man on either side of you. Do nothing unless you hear a rifle. We will walk downstream quietly and wait for these people."

Then, he spoke to the women and older men. "If you are caring for a child or wish not to fight, hide in the trees above the camp with some food and water. When you hear the call of the owl, all will be safe. If you hear fighting and we do not come back, gather at the lake on the mountain to the north."

Within minutes, the camp was deserted, silent. Kangee took his bow and arrows and found a spot uphill with a view to the entrance of the east side of their camp. Mouse and Red Feather took a spot downstream looking down onto the path. They had cover from both a rock outcropping and trees.

The only sound was the gentle lapping of water on stone. No birds sang, no dogs barked. Mouse checked and rechecked her bow, rearranged her arrows several times. Red Feather did the same. From time to time, they saw Kangee peer around his tree. They desperately wanted to hear Broken Knife's owl call; even a gunshot would have been better than the waiting.

Gradually, Mouse became aware of two sounds. One was the plodding of horses; the other, a baby crying.

It took all of her self-control to remain hidden. There had been no signal, no owl call, no gunshot, only the sound of horses coming up the path and the baby. Then, she heard happy voices, laughter. Around a bend in the path came her father with his arm around a woman and he was carrying a baby. The happiness radiating from her father could be seen and felt from far away. Mouse stood and showed herself. Her father noticed her first; he pointed. The woman looked up. It was Aponi! Mouse leapt down the hillside and ran to her sister. The two wept and hugged and laughed. Broken Knife showed the baby to Mouse and said, "I have a new name. I am Kaka!" He almost wept with joy as he handed the baby to Mouse.

By now, the procession had stopped and figures were appearing from the trees. There were happy conversations, some laughing and some soft crying. One woman was wailing. These other sounds began to intrude into Mouse's consciousness. She turned to look and the others that had arrived were a handful of those of their tribe that had stayed to fight two years before. Many had not returned including Strong Wolf.

Around the bend came a man leading the horses. He stopped and made eye contact with her. Her recognition was complete and profound. This was the man searching for her; the man she felt calling to her from her dreams.

Eight Horses, Eight Stones
1 8 7 8

I could see that the white man did not care for each other the way our people did. They would take everything from each other if they could. Some had more of everything than they could use, while crowds of people had nothing at all. This could not be better than the old ways of my people.

Black Elk – 1863 - 1950

Black Elk stood for several minutes outside the tipi of Broken Knife and listened. Inside, he heard the happy conversation, the laughter. He heard the baby cooing and fussing. He heard them all talking over each other, sharing stories. Aponi, the woman who led him here, mentioned his name. There was an audible gasp then silence. Nervously, he stepped up to the open tent flap and said, "May I enter?"

Broken Knife looked up, startled. He had been so intent on being with his three daughters and his grandchild that he had not heard the stranger arrive. He stood and as Black Elk entered and shook his hand. "How Coula? You are the young man that led my daughter back to me. Pilamaya!"

Black Elk, at 15, seemed much older. He was not a big man but projected the power and confidence of an elder. He looked boyish yet radiated an intensity of purpose that seemed at odds with his handsomeness. The power of his will shown in his eyes, a gaze that took courage not to look away from. Broken Knife immediately felt that power as Black Elk spoke. "My name is Black Elk, son of the Shaman of Crazy Horse. It was Aponi who led *me* here and I am thankful. My tribe and what is left of my family have lived under the thumb of the white man. You have lived free with honor." He touched his heart in a salute.

Black Elk then turned and made eye contact with Mouse. The two were so focused on each other that the others in that small space felt invisible. All there sensed a change in the air like just before a storm or a lightning strike. Even the baby looked from face to face, trying to understand. Mouse stood, returned the baby to his mother and took Black Elk's hand. There was a moment when time seemed to stop. Then, they both spoke to each other at the same time. "I dreamed of-" They both stopped speaking with their voices but their eyes continued to communicate.

He intimately placed his other hand on her handshake and she did the same. "Your sister has told me many stories of you. You and I only had one afternoon together but I know about you. I have been dreaming of you also. Sometimes dreams are wiser than waking."

"In my dreams" she said, "you search for me, call to me. Today, I finally see your face."

"When I dream, part of me is missing. I look for that part to make myself complete, whole. My dreams have not been happy because I could never find what I was looking for."

Mouse nodded. "My dreams have been troubled also. Bad things happen to keep me from finding you."

Broken Knife stood. "Daughter" he said, "You have not offered our guest food."

Black Elk turned to Broken Knife. "Pilamaya. I will take your offer of a meal later but now, with your permission, I would like to talk to you alone."

Broken Knife shrugged and looked at his family. One by one, they made eye contact, smiled and left the tipi, taking the baby along. Broken Knife closed his tipi flap, sat opposite the door and indicated that Black Elk sit to his left.

The older man solemnly prepared his pipe, got it lit and tried to steer the conversation. "Tell me of the battle at Greasy Grass."

"If invited, I will talk of the battle and our people at council. I came here hoping to find a wife. I wish to talk to you about your daughter."

Broken Knife thought for a moment. "I have three daughters. My oldest lost her husband in the battle as you know. She has a child and needs a man. My second daughter,

Chumani, is about your age and would also make a fine wife. She is very strong and a very good cook."

"My heart longs for Itunkala."

Broken Knife sat quietly for a few moments gathering his thoughts. "My little Mouse has a big spirit but she can be very, uh, challenging. She seems to feel equal to men. I have indulged my children but Itunkala has never taken her place as a woman. My older daughters will obey a husband."

Black Elk took a puff of the pipe and passed it back. "Our traditions are for a man to offer a father a gift in exchange for his blessing to marry a daughter. I brought some horses with me as a gift. With your permission, I want to give you eight of my horses for your permission to have Itunkala join my life."

A look of utter astonishment crossed Broken Knife's face. He sputtered for a moment then said, "I will accept your gift but you must understand; her spirit is too big for her body. She must also choose you. Then, I will accept your gift and you as a son. They both stood and shook hands.

Black Elk said, "I will find her and ask her."

Moments later, he found Mouse and her two sisters sitting around the central fire. He nodded to Aponi, smiled at Chumani and the baby and held out his hand to Mouse. She stood and took his hand.

He led her away from the camp to the edge of the stream. When they were alone, he had her sit on a large rock overlooking the water. He took her hand, looked into her eyes. He began to speak, stopped, started again then seemed unable to continue.

"Yes!" Mouse stood and looked into his eyes. "Our spirits have been searching for each other in our dreams. You are here and I want to be with you." She leaned into him, put her arms around his waist and rested her head on his chest.

He lifted her chin and looked at her with a sorrowful look. "I am carrying a burden that I must give you. The day I took this burden is the day I began to love you. It is the day you made me see myself. Pilamaya!" He opened a pouch that he wore and took out eight shiny black stones. "These have been very heavy to carry. They have reminded me every day that I was a selfish boy. It was you that made me see the Red Road I needed to walk."

Mouse smiled, took her four stones from his hand and threw them into the creek. He laughed, threw his four into the water and hand in hand, they returned to camp.

* * *

The next morning, a joyous crowd gathered at the center of their summer village. Black Elk, followed by four warriors, entered the clearing from the west wrapped in a blue blanket. Mouse walked in from the east also wrapped in a blue blanket. Four women, two of whom were her happy sisters, followed her. Kangee, Red Feather and the proud father waited near the central fire, holding a white blanket.

The two smiled at each other as they met at the center of the camp then faced the crowd. Red Feather and Broken Knife held the white blanket over the two as Kangee said:

"From the east you receive the gift of a new beginning with the rising of each morning Sun, the dawn wind breathing into you both open of heart and purity of mind and body."

"In the south we see the earth that will feed and enrich you, helping you to build a stable home to which you may always return."

"In the west we see the storm clouds and the oceans, the mystery of water teaching you the capacity to feel emotion through tears of sadness and of joy."

"In the north we see the northern lights, teaching us the importance of energy, passion, creativity and the warmth of a loving home."

"White Buffalo woman brought us the fire of passion. May you seek and share with one another the light that comes from the fire within, and may it guide you through the darkness; for there is no darkness without light and there is no light without darkness."

"Walk gently on our Mother the Earth and know her beauty before, beauty behind, beauty above, beauty below and beauty all around."

Then the old Shaman smiled. He reached out, took Mouse's hand and looked into her eyes and said softly, "Wakanisha in all things little Mouse." He then placed her hand in the hand of her husband to be and touched their hands with his ancient bodark walking stick. In his deep baritone he announced, "The sacred hoop is complete in these two Human Beings."

The blue blankets were pulled from them and with help from their loved ones; Itunkala and Black Elk were wrapped together in the white blanket of their new life together.

Dreams Explained
1878

The second day the wedding feast was well under way when Mouse and Black Elk returned from the woods to the small assemblage of tipis. Kangee sat near the central fire with a few of the men and when he saw the newlyweds, he smiled and indicated they join him. Their walk across camp was interrupted many times as the two were stopped and given small gifts and congratulations.

The couple dropped the buffalo robes they were carrying near the fire and sat near the old Shaman. "As a people, we have many traditions, ways of doing things." He smiled and took her hand in his. "You have always done things your way; that is why I love you. A married couple should always spend their first night in the tipi with her family. A girl should never learn to hunt. And nobody should pull a rattlesnake out of a hole." They laughed together.

"Another tradition we have is to never speak of the dead." The old Shaman twisted around so he could speak with Mouse face to face. He was not smiling as he said, "You are much like your mother, and her mother. As young girls, they were very strong like you are strong, in the heart. They made men mad by asking questions, doing things that were against the traditions for women, just like you. Your grandmother's husband was very strict with her, her life was not always happy because she was made to obey. Your mother was luckier. Your father is a gentle man and loved your mother very much. She returned that love by hiding her will and being a good wife to him, a good mother. Your mother gave her strength to your father and now he is a man of respect, a chief."

Kangee then looked at Black Elk then back to Mouse. "Now here you are, a woman with a new husband. And this man is here beside you because he sees your strength and wisdom; he sees an equal, not a thing he owns. You must work very hard to balance the strong hearts you both have, you must not own each other but listen to the wisdom of each other. You will share your deepest thoughts, feelings and fears, as you must to praise the Great Spirit. And there will be times when you disagree, when you are angry. You must never use what you know of the soul of your mate to wound them to win an argument. You can never take those words back because your trust will be broken. You must have Wakanisha in all things." Kangee pulled Mouse to him and kissed her forehead then pulled both of them into a tearful embrace.

"When we last talked", the Shaman continued, "we were speaking of your dreams." He reached out and touched Black Elk near his heart, saying to Mouse, "Now, your dream is obvious." He chuckled. "While you have been in the woods and not sleeping with your family, Red Feather is also not following tradition. He and your sister Aponi have been together constantly. Your sister's baby may have a new father."

Their conversation was cut short by a loud pack of children running through the center of camp. They were playing a game they had invented that involved pine cones, sticks and a lot of yelling. There appeared to be two teams but who was on what team wasn't any clearer than the object of the game. The children were obviously having fun even though the game involved throwing the pinecones at each other.

Mouse noticed that only boys were playing and the camp girls were on the sideline, looking wistful. "Do you remember the big powwow three winters ago?" she asked Kangee. "You organized some games for the children who came to our camp to eat." She smiled at Black Elk and said, "It was at those games that I met this man, but he was a spoiled little boy then!" She poked Black Elk in the ribs and laughed.

"And you were this little girl mouse who thought she could beat all the boys." He put his arm around Mouse's shoulders and gave her a rough hug.

She leapt up and taunted her husband. "You want to play some Red Hand, spoiled boy?"

He took a playful swing at her that she easily dodged then rapped him on the top of his head with her knuckles. He jumped up and grabbed her in a bear hug. "You did beat all the boys, little mouse with the heart of a bear!" They stood there hugging each other affectionately. He whispered in her ear, "But you didn't beat the men."

She shoved him so hard and so quickly on his chest he nearly fell. "You think men are better than women?" she uttered sarcastically. "I think we should find out."

Black Elk smiled slowly. "You choose the contest!"

She stood there for a moment with her hands on her hips. "My sisters and I challenge you. Find two others and we will see who will win."

While Black Elk walked through the camp looking for men to take the challenge, Mouse and her sisters disassembled their two tipis. They stacked the lodge poles in identical piles and heaped the buffalo skins in similar piles.

Word spread quickly. Black Elk recruited Red Feather but had trouble finding a third. Broken Knife refused, saying he wanted to keep his honor. Kangee just shook his head and smiled. Finally Lark agreed to be part of the competition.

About mid morning, the tribe gathered at the center of camp, men on one side and women on the other. When Black Elk realized what the competition actually was, he said, "This is not a game, this is women's work."

"You said for me to pick. This is what I pick. And since this is women's work and you men are so much better, you should have no problem. Do you give up little boy?"

The three young men looked at each other. "How hard can this be?" Red Feather asked, "The women do it quickly." There was easy laughter from the women's side of camp; the male side began to mutter nervously.

Chumani stepped to the center of camp near the communal fire. "Smoke from a cooking fire inside a completed tipi will signal the winner. Questions?" she said loudly. There were no questions.

"Begin!"

Each of the men quickly grabbed a pole and began to stand them. Then, Lark said, "No, one of you tie them." Both Red

Feather and Black Elk dropped their poles at the same time. The women began to snicker.

The three sisters quickly selected three poles, laid them parallel with the small ends facing the fire. Using sturdy rawhide strips, they tightly tied a clove hitch on each pole about three quarters up near the small ends. Using rawhide strips, they tied the ends together leaving some slack and wrapped the leftover strips around the knotted area. One very long strip was tied around the joined poles at the junction. Then, each sister grabbed a pole and lifted it so the poles were all vertical. Aponi was holding the center pole. She nodded, said, "Now!" and the three women backed up until they had made a standing tripod of their poles. Then, without having to speak, each stood another pole, nestling them into place, making a rough circle. They repeated the process until all twelve poles were standing. Mouse quickly grabbed the dangling long rawhide strip and walked around and around the standing poles, whipping the rawhide up and down. As she circled the framework, the rawhide cinched the standing poles at the narrow junction.

By now, the men had three of their poles standing only because they copied what they saw the three sisters doing. The men in camp were shouting at the three men, telling them to hurry up. The rest of the women in camp were laughing and jeering.

Mouse and Aponi dragged over the first buffalo hide. Chumani brought a pole and placed it with its large end butted against one of the tipi poles. The hide had several holes pierced at the perimeter and Chumani tied a long strand of rawhide through one of the holes. She then placed the tip of her pole into the same hole with the pole underneath the hide. Working together, the three stood the pole with the hide until it fell against the tipi. Mouse threw the long rawhide strip over the top and tied it quickly on the other side. Using shorter strips, the sisters quickly tied the edges of the rawhide to the adjacent poles. Efficiently, they repeated the process until their tipi was covered. Mouse and Aponi quickly took the left-over narrow strips of hide and fashioned the tipi skirt, tying them into place underneath the larger hides so if rain came, the skins would shed water. Aponi fashioned the door flap so it faced east. Chumani gathered firewood, kindling and dry grasses and formed the cooking area with stones inside. Mouse neatly arranged firewood on the left side of their completed tipi and moved in the furnishings. With a few strikes of flint, the fire started and smoke began streaming out of the top of the women's completed tipi. There were cheers from the women's side, groans from the men.

Mouse walked over to her husband who had a large knot on his head. A pole had fallen and wounded his pride much to the amusement of the women. "Can we help you little boys with your chores?" Mouse asked. The men finally had the tipi frame standing but the skins were still strewn about with some rawhide strips tied to them.

Black Elk was in no mood for teasing. His head hurt and he felt he had lost face in this new tribe. He put his hands on his hips and using his height over his tiny wife said, "This means nothing! I still am the man in our family."

Mouse quickly ran into her finished tipi and returned with her cooking stone. She dropped it at his feet and by standing on the rock and her tiptoes, looked him straight in the eye. "I am your equal!" There was loud laughter from both the women and the men.

Aponi got a piece of firewood and stood on it and looked into Red Feather's face, eye to eye. "I am your equal." More laughter.

Chumani faced Lark. She jumped up so her eyes were at his level and said, "I." She jumped again. "AM!" On the third jump, she screamed, "YOUR EQUAL!"

By now, the entire tribe was howling with laughter.

A tiny four-year-old girl ran up to Leftook. She literally climbed him, using his buckskin for handles until she was looking into his eyes. In a tiny voice, she said, "I AM your equal."

There was pandemonium. Every female in the camp faced a man perhaps they feared or loved but repeated the words, "I am your equal."

But when Spoon Woman faced Kangee and Macawi faced the old chief Stone Foot, the silence was absolute. Kangee simply shook Spoon Woman's hand and nodded.

Macawi locked her intense gaze onto the old Chief's eyes. She did not attempt to stand on anything to look eye to eye; she simply stood in front of him. "Am I your equal?"

The old chief stood quietly for what seemed like an eternity. Then slowly, he placed the flat of his hand over his heart. As he lowered his hand and said, "Háŋ."

The Destiny Manifest
1878

History never looks like history when you are living through it.
   John W. Gardner

We have it in our power to begin the world over again. A situation, similar to the present, hath not happened since the days of Noah until now. The birthday of a new world is at hand.
   Thomas Paine

History happens during every person's lifetime. Some events are more significant than others and very often those events pass without a person knowing. Stone Foot's life was no different.

Stone Foot was not the name his parents had given him. As a young boy, he was called Spotted Horse because of his fascination with horses. He was called that when the whites forcefully relocated his people to the west side of the Mississippi. His family and tribe had lived in the rich area now called Wisconsin and Minnesota. He grew up as his tribe and family moved from place to place, trying to fit in while his people battled other tribes for land and game. He learned to survive by hunting, trapping and fighting with others when necessary. Even before his teens, other boys of his tribe began to see him as fierce and a natural leader.

Stone Foot earned his name in what is now central Kansas. His tribe and several other Sioux tribes moved into an area already inhabited by a large and brutal group called the Pawnee. Spotted Horse and his tribe were setting up their camp about sunset on an oxbow near what is now called the Smoky Hill River. He was only fourteen winters but considered a warrior. Just as the sun disappeared below the horizon, a group of Pawnee warriors crept across the river and attacked without warning. Spotted Horse was one of the first to respond and gave the warning. Immediately, an older Pawnee warrior attempted to skewer Spotted Horse with a lance. Spotted Horse grabbed the lance, fell on his back and, with his legs, flipped the Pawnee warrior over his head. Spotted Horse simply stood and crushed the Pawnee warrior's skull with his heel. That act, which occurred in a split second, earned Spotted Horse a new name and the credentials that would eventually make him a chief.

During his lifetime, he had always lived as a Human Being, free to practice his people's ancient and holy customs. As he aged, living Tawaiciyan became harder every year as the white man's presence increased. He knew he had led his tribe well. His one wish was to die still a free man unlike all the other tribes that now lived as captives under the control of the white man.

His early knowledge of encounters with the white man began with memories of stories told by his family. White traders had been part of tribal life long before he was born. His father shared stories of white traders speaking a different white language. They called themselves French and had been reasonable men, trustworthy and honorable. Then, a French trader they knew arrived with many white men with canoes. These men had not been traders, and when they refused to give one of their canoes in trade for the right to use the river, they had almost all been killed. But they had a woman with them, a Human Being from a northern tribe. Had it not been for this woman, the whites would never have been allowed to cross Sioux land and go west. But those incidents seemed inconsequential compared with what his people now faced.

* * *

Tonight Stone Foot thanked the Great Spirit for the appearance of Black Elk and his people who had survived Little Big Horn. The wedding feast and celebration had distracted his people from their reality. Winter was not far away which meant another impending move from their secure and happy mountain camp. They would need to move south and east onto the plains, which meant more exposure to the whites.

The whites! They were a curse, a disease. Stone Foot knew that his little tribe was one of the last, if not the last, tribe living free. Their route across the foothills and into Kansas would now be even more infested with white settlers and soldiers.

Stone Foot sat in his tent and wished that all the whites could be like Leftook or the white woman Mary. Every encounter, every powwow, every communication between the many Sioux tribes told of deceit, broken promises, theft and massacres. He was tired; too tired to lead another trip. He wasn't able to get on his horse now without help and his people expected him to lead them to safety on the Kansas plains again for another winter.

He had just stepped outside to call a council when Macawi walked up to him and with her intense eyes asked, "Am I your equal?" He observed the joy around him, the freedom. But he was so tired.

Stone Foot made eye contact with Kangee. No spoken words were needed. There would be a council.

Around sunset, Kangee, Broken Knife, Black Elk and Badger arrived at his tipi. Kangee and Broken Knife did their old, masculine dance to decide who would sit on his left. Black Elk diplomatically sat in the least important position. Little did they know that their maneuvers were almost prophetic.

Stone Foot smiled to himself at the two men. He smiled again as he said, "Now that we know we are equal with women, should we invite them to our council?"

There was a short, uncomfortable silence then Black Elk spoke. "My father talked with my mother about tribal matters. He often took her advice to council."

"I knew your father. He was a wise man." The old chief looked from face to face. "None of you answered my question."

Broken Knife finally spoke. "Women think from their hearts. Men believe we speak from The Great Spirit. Our women should be here!"

"Leftook should be here also," the old chief said. "What we have to discuss concerns us all. Tonight, I am not your chief. I am too old and will soon die."

The men all began to speak at once until Stone Foot held up his hand. "Call the people together and we will decide."

* * *

Word spread rapidly throughout the camp. The men wondered who would be the new chief; the women wondered if they would actually be allowed to contribute.

Dark came early with mountains to the west. Even with the dread and excitement of new leadership, the necessities of camp life continued. Replacement lookouts were posted; three downstream toward the east and one upstream. The horses were tended and firewood was replenished. Babies and young children were tucked in or given strict instructions about their behavior. Almost all the adults in camp planned on being there; a vote for new leadership hadn't transpired since Yellow Bird had been killed many winters ago.

A loose circle of Human Beings gathered around the fire. Pipes were lit and passed. As the last of the tribe joined the group and sat, quiet conversations could be heard. A few youngsters came out and asked for permission to be part of the process. Firewood was added to the fire.

Finally, Stone Foot rose and stood near the fire. The only sounds were of the fire and the stream that flowed nearby. "Soon, we must move to our winter home. The white man is everywhere. The whites take our land and kill our sacred Tatonka. I am old and will soon be with our Thunkashila. You must decide who will lead us through this difficult winter. Then, we must speak about living as captives of the white man. We may be the last tribe living Tawaiciyan like our ancestors. Living free may mean not living at all. We must decide."

There was a moment of silence then quiet but animated conversations broke out around the circle. The old chief waited until he sensed an accord within his people. He held up his hand and the talking stopped. He looked around the circle, made eye contact with all there. "I would follow Broken Knife as my chief and I would trust Leftook with our young warriors. "He looked around and saw more than a few heads nodding.

Broken Knife stood. "I do not want this task. I am just a Human Being, not a great man. All I ever wanted to do was hunt and provide for my family."

Stone Foot stepped close to Broken Knife and pointed around the circle. "This is your family."

Broken Knife looked around the circle. Sitting together were his daughters. His grandchild was cradled in Aponi's arms. Red Feather and Black Elk were there with his family -- were his family. He looked from face to face; he knew them all, the histories, their weaknesses and strengths. He caught Macawi's eye; she looked at him and nodded with respect. Badger and Leftook were also nodding at him, smiling. Kangee patted the earth on his right side as if to say, this is your spot to sit, smiled and nodded his head. Broken Knife faced the old chief for a moment and then dropped his eyes in submission.

"If you will not follow this man, stand and tell us why." Stone Foot looked from face to face. Badger was the first to stand but he did not speak, he placed his hand over his heart. Then in mass, the entire tribe stood and followed suit.

Broken Knife's family came to him and stood close, smiling, hugging him. Many others in the tribe came and shook his hand or just reached out to touch him. There were murmurs of "I will follow." and "Pilamaya."

The new chief faced Stone Foot and said, "You will always be our Thunkashila. I will listen to your advice in all things. Pilamaya!" A loud cheer went up as the old chief sat next to Kangee.

Broken Knife stood in the firelight unsure of what to do next. The faces of his people were expectant, full of admiration. He looked at the old chief who smiled and pointed to Leftook.

"We still have much to decide." the new chief said. He turned to Stone Foot and said, "You advised us to make Leftook our War Chief." Broken Knife turned to the crowd and said, "I trust this man with the security of my family. Stand and speak if you have an opinion about this man as our War Chief."

Conversation broke out again around the circle. Broken Knife could tell that the mutterings were not all positive. Finally, Badger stood and said, "This is a white man. Will our young warriors follow this white man, do as he says?" The talking around the circle got louder, heads nodding.

Black Cloud stood. "This man is a warrior. Is there any here who would fight with this man and win?" "We made him a relative, he is our family. I will follow this man!" He pantomimed a left hook, smiled and sat down.

Stone Foot slowly got to his feet. "This man is a warrior. He knows our ways and he knows the ways of our enemies, the whites. He is a brave man and he has saved us once before. We need this white man to help us understand our enemies." He made eye contact with Leftook, touched his heart then sat down.

Broken Knife walked over to where Leftook and Spoon Woman were sitting. "Will you talk to us about the whites, help us to decide?"

Leftook looked at Spoon Woman as if she could answer for him. She smiled and nodded to him. The big man stood. "I have been a Human Being for three winters. You are my family. I will do whatever my family needs."

Broken Knife smiled at the big man and said, "Your lessons with my daughter have helped you both. You speak our language well."

"I may not have the words to explain the whites. Mouse and Black Elk may need to help me." Leftook hesitated for a moment. "What can I tell you about the whites that I haven't already spoken about?"

Broken Knife thought for a moment. "We must decide to live free as our ancestors or live as the white man wants us to live, under their control. Tell us about the white man so we can decide."

"There is a word in the white's language that I can't translate. *Destiny*." Leftook looked at Mouse and asked, "Do you have this word?"

"We say 'maya owicha paka' which has two meanings in your language." Mouse said. *"It means fate. It also means the person who pushes you off a cliff."*

Leftook laughed sadly. "The white man believes it is his destiny to own this land. It is the fate of the Human Beings to be pushed off this cliff. You are being driven from your land and you have no choice. The whites believe that their God has given them this land. And when a white man owns something, it is like an act of violence. If two men own the same thing, they fight. The white men just fought a terrible war with each other to decide if one man can own another. The winners of this war believe a man cannot own another, and believe that all men are equal. But, the same white men still see the red man, the yellow man and the black man as less than a man. It is in the white man's destiny to have terrible problems in the future because he has not solved the question, *what is a man?*"

Leftook paused for a moment because there were angry conversations beginning around the fire. "The white man is not alone." he said. "The Human Beings are much like the white man in many ways. You believe that Wakan Tanka has made you better. You see the Pawnee and other tribes as less than men. You have warred with them, pushed them off their land. Your beliefs have made these other people your enemies." He looked around at all the shocked faces. "A hundred winters ago, a famous white man said, 'Give me liberty or give me death.' I am a Human Being and I am with you, whatever you decide."

Broken Knife looked around at all the faces, his tribe, and his family. "We must decide. Stand if you wish to move our camp to Ft. Laramie and live with the whites." There was utter silence; not one person moved.

"Stand if you want to move to our winter camp on the plains and continue to live free."

Every person there stood. But there was no joy on those faces, only sadness and fear. They knew their destiny had been stolen and only fate remained.

New Arrivals
1879

"The only good Indian is a dead Indian."

Lieutenant General Philip Henry Sheridan

The vast American prairie was and still is a beautiful and harsh environment, shaped by wind, heat and cold. Two ice ages have passed since the First People arrived on this sea of grass and sage. For more than twenty thousand years, these people were the top predator, balanced and in harmony with their natural world. They lived with minimal agriculture, leaving only blackened fire pits, the only scars on the land to mark their passing.

The year was 1879. Mouse, her new husband and her extended family, their little band of Sioux, had managed to live free. The Indian's victory at Little Big Horn resulted not in more freedom; it only brought white vengeance and more cruelty.

Many others had not been so lucky. The Carlisle Indian School was founded in Pennsylvania in an aggressive U.S. government campaign to "civilize" Indian children. Children from reservations across the West were sent to the school in order to assimilate them into white culture. This assimilation included cutting their hair, burning their clothing and forcing them to wear European American dress. They were strictly forbidden to speak their native language and punishment for infractions was severe. The school was a breeding ground for disease. Many children died there.

* * *

Broken Knife, with advice from Leftook, had found a way to hide from the whites that defied logic. He camped near white towns and settlements. He knew that most whites stayed close to their towns so he always set camp at least an hour's ride away. The tribe always set up their tipis in a depression or ringed by hills so the tipis were not visible from a distance. He also kept scouts out day and night.

During the winter of 1879 and 1880, they camped near a new white town called Garden City, Kansas. The spot Broken Knife chose was east about nine miles near a ridge that overlooked the Arkansas River. From nearby hilltops, his scouts could watch for whites and game yet remain invisible. Game was still somewhat plentiful; elk and deer traveled the river east from the mountains. Near the river was a bluff that was a useful hunting tool. Game animals could be stampeded over the cliff to their deaths.

Ironically, they camped within sight of the Santa Fe Trail, a major east, and west thoroughfare for the whites. It started in Missouri and crossed all of Kansas. At Cimarron, a short cut headed south across the panhandle of Oklahoma. This short cut, the "Dry Route", cut many miles off the trip to Santa Fe but crossed waterless desert. The original trail continued east through Garden City into the Colorado territory to what is now La Junta. There at Ft. Bent, the trail turned south and crossed into New Mexico over the Raton Pass.

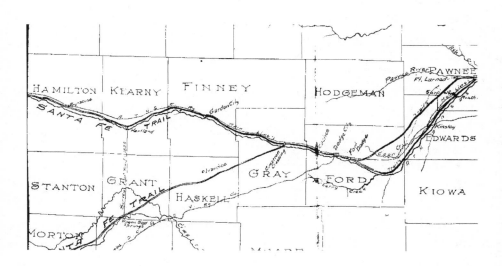

Broken Knife's strategy of hiding in plain sight had worked for several years. It wasn't that they were in plain sight. It was just the opposite, Broken Knife's people hid under the very noses of the whites they were trying to avoid.

* * *

The winter weather in the southwestern part of Kansas tended to be mild and pleasant. Storms, even raging blizzards developed quickly with no mountains or trees to block the wind. Then, just as quickly, the sun would return and mild weather would follow. It was on a day in the last days of 1879 that a large winter storm blew in from the north.

The horses had been edgy all day. The dogs, usually friendly, were surly and nipped at each other. The women complained because the lack of wind kept them from lighting cooking fires. Smoke that was blown away kept the tribe's location secret. Smoke rising from a spot where there should be no smoke meant trouble.

A cloudbank appeared to the north and early in the afternoon, the wind began to blow. It started softly from the south and smelled wet. Within minutes, the wind shifted and began to come from the opposite direction. The change in temperature was abrupt. What had been a pleasant, warm morning became bitterly cold. The wind no longer smelled wet. It smelled of ice.

Broken Knife ordered the women to pound extra stakes around their tipis and tie rope and rawhide to their tipi poles. The buffalo hides that had been raised off the ground to allow air to circulate were dropped and staked. The children were ordered to bring as many arm loads of fuel back to camp as they could. Fires were lit and the smell of burning sage and buffalo chips filled the air.

Those that were alive during the terrible storm fifteen winters ago shuddered as they moved their possessions inside and tethered their horses. Broken Knife sent his fastest scouts on their ponies to the others on lookout. He sent buffalo robes for all and small amounts of dry sage for fires. His orders were to come back to camp before the weather got really bad. He had seen the body of a friend frozen in the snow. His friend had frozen very close to camp because of whiteout conditions.

An early darkness engulfed the camp. The snow began lightly an hour before sunset. By full dark, it was snowing hard. The snow was as deep as a man's ankle and the wind was blowing hard. The two scouts that had been north of camp arrived with their replacements. The horses and the men's buffalo robes were completely caked with snow. They reported very heavy snowfall just behind them. The scouts from the south came back to camp minutes later and reported seeing no whites on the road below their posts until visibility was near zero. The scouts that had been watching west of camp reported in. They had seen no activity at all, only snow.

Broken Knife had sent scouts in all four directions. The only lookouts to not return were those watching east. He ordered two riders to search in a circle using camp as the center when the missing lookouts returned. They brought news.

Word quickly spread through camp that a small covered wagon with five whites was stuck on the road. The wind was growing every hour and the drifts were growing with the wind. The camp was already knee deep in snow but the hilltops were bare. The scouts were late because they had been closely watching the whites. They reported that the driver of the wagon had attempted to take the wagon and its team of two horses through what seemed to be a small drift. The drift had been surprisingly deep and the wagon had become stuck. The driver had tried to pull the horses and wagon through with no luck. The five whites were stuck in the back of a canvas covered wagon with no fire.

A quick council was called. Badger was attending the horses and was the last to arrive. Broken Knife told the men of the situation. His advice was to not intervene. He also insisted that no one from the tribe even approach the wagon let alone salvage supplies from what he was sure to be dead whites. He wanted no hint at all of their presence in the area to be known to the local whites. The other men nodded their heads at this wisdom. There was no vote, only agreement. Then Mouse arrived!

She and Black Elk, her new husband, arrived at Broken Knife's tent wrapped together under a buffalo robe. Even though Mouse's first pregnancy was very evident, she and Black Elk still acted like newlyweds. When they stepped into the tent, Broken Knife smiled at the two young people, so in love and happy together.

His smile was short lived. He knew his daughter better than any person in camp. Mouse and Macawi shared a forceful will; they learned much from each other. Kangee also knew a part of Mouse, the spiritual side; the two of them spent hours together arguing the nature of things. Her new husband knew the lovely and wonderful young woman she had become; he knew the love she was capable of giving. Only Broken Knife knew what was coming. He knew another sort of storm was upon them; he knew his daughter's heart.

Without even a greeting she said, "I must go to help. I speak their language."

Broken Knife stood and faced his daughter. "I speak as your father and also as the protector of our people. These whites will live or die by their own skill. We must not let them know we are here."

Mouse, unable to contain herself blurted out, "In my study of Wakan Tanka, it is said The Other Beings helped us when we were in trouble. Mary, the white woman helped us during the great storm. Here is another storm and whites need our help. They will die. We must help."

Kangee agreed. "We do not know these whites. But some whites are not bad people. Mouse is right about being helped. When our people needed help, help came. We should help these whites."

Badger said, "When I was young and ignorant, Mouse helped me. I will help her."

Broken Knife looked from face to face. Only Leftook had not voted. The huge, white warrior thought a moment then said, "We will bring these whites to our camp. If they are bad people, they will disappear. If they are good, Wakan Tanka will give us favor. We will have friends or two extra horses."

Five riders including Mouse and Black Elk went to rescue the whites. Each was wrapped in a large buffalo skin and each carried an extra. Mouse led a sixth horse that carried food, buffalo skins and water. Her only job was to translate. The snow had stopped and starlight was coldly lighting their way. They were able to avoid the huge drifts. When they rode through snow or smaller drifts, the wind quickly filled in their trail.

Mouse and Black Elk followed the scout that had first seen the whites. Broken Knife and Badger rode together followed by Badger's little brother Dove. The group circled downwind from the wagon and stopped. They hadn't planned how to actually make contact. There was a brief conference then Mouse approached with her husband close behind her.

Mouse rode her horse into the wind shadow of the wagon and said, "*We will help.*"

There was no reaction from inside the wagon. Mouse waited a moment and said louder, "*We will help you!*"

Almost immediately, the canvas at the back of the wagon was thrown back and a face peered out. It was an older man with a gunnysack wrapped around his head. He didn't seem to react. He and Mouse just stared at each other.

Mouse smiled at him and spoke again, "*Can we help you?*"

The man said, "*We?*"

Just then, the rest of Mouse's rescue party rode into view. The man looked at the group and said, "How Coula? *Yes, we could use your help.*"

Another face appeared. This was a younger man, dressed in a fancy, white man's suit. He also had a gunnysack wrapped around his head for warmth. He frowned and spoke to the older man in English, "*Ask them what they want.*"

The older man spoke in broken Sioux, "What do you want from us?"

Mouse replied, *"I speak some of your language. We saw your trouble. We will help."*

"We don't need no help, Redskin!" the younger man snapped.

"Boss", the old man said, *"Rosa's almost dead! The other two are near gone too."*

Mouse looked at the two men then addressed the older one, *"We have warm skins. Our camp is near. We have warm food and fire. We will help you."*

"We ain't goin with no Redskins!" the younger man yelled.

"Well, I'm goin." the older man said. *"We'll die here. We ain't got no choice."* He started to climb down when the younger man pointed a pistol at the man's head. *"Go ahead, shoot me! I'm gonna die here anyway."* He climbed down and walked over to Mouse's horse.

Mouse untied the extra buffalo robe she had and let it drop at the man's feet. The man picked up the large skin and wrapped himself in it.

"Lick-spittle half breed!" the younger man yelled. *"I pays you to drive us and you just leaves us here. Worthless bastard!"*

"You ain't got no choice, boss. If they was gonna kill us, we'd be dead."

Mouse slid off her horse and walked up to the younger man on the wagon. She simply held out her hand to help the man off the wagon. He looked at her for a moment. Instead of shaking her hand, he handed her the pistol. She signaled for Black Elk to ride up. She took the skin from her husband and threw it to the younger man in the wagon. She pointed to the back of the wagon.

The man in the wagon quickly wrapped himself with the robe and motioned with his head for Mouse to come up.

Inside, Mouse found three young women lying on the floor of the wagon. They were dressed in street clothes, no coats, with one blanket between them. The three of them were lying together on a dirty mattress with their arms around each other. The two older women shivered uncontrollably and the youngest seemed to be unconscious. The two looked at Mouse with large eyes. Mouse held her hand to her heart and said, *"I will help you."* She threw back the flap and signaled to Black Elk and her father. The two men handed their extra robes to her. She signaled the women to stand. She wrapped the robes around the two who could stand. The youngest did not respond; she was blue with the cold and barely breathing.

Mouse retrieved the last robe and wrapped it around the unconscious girl.

Badger and the rest of the men including the old man from the wagon pushed and pulled. They finally had to use their horses to pull the wagon and team from the drift.

Mouse told the driver, *"Our camp is not far. Follow."* She then stepped inside the wagon again. The two older women were still shivering uncontrollably. The young woman on the floor had not moved. Mouse went to the two women and put her hand inside their robes and felt their skin. The two were icy cold. Mouse stepped out and signaled Badger and Dove to ride near. She said, "You must ride with a woman. You need to keep them warm inside your robes."

Badger rode up next to the wagon. Mouse pulled the oldest woman out to the back flap. Badger held open his robe. Mouse took the woman's robe and helped lift her in front of Badger. The woman was amazingly cooperative. When Badger wrapped the robe around the two of them, instead of seeming terrified, she snuggled against Badger and laid her cheek on his chest. The warm, intimate connection was almost immediate. Badger wrapped one arm around the woman's waist and felt a wonderful and sensuous connection, contentment he had never before felt but had dreamed of and wanted.

The other woman was not as trusting; she seemed petrified. Mouse had to physically help her climb on Dove's horse. The woman's experiences with men taught her to expect the worst. But when the young Indian man did not grab her breasts or put his hand between her legs, she turned and looked at him. He was young, perhaps younger than she was. And he seemed innocent and shy. But when he wrapped the thick hide around her and pulled her against his chest, she immediately felt something she'd never experienced; she felt protected. Then, as the warmth from his body seeped into hers, she leaned into him and surrendered to feelings she had never experienced, of safety and protection.

Dove's experience was much the same as his brother's. He wrapped the robe around them both and as the warmth of his body seeped into hers, she also allowed herself to be held, softening in his embrace.

The five Sioux and their two passengers rode the ponies. The driver, his "boss" and the youngest woman followed in the wagon.

By the time they arrived at camp, the youngest woman was not breathing. Kangee and Macawi did what they could but the girl was dead. They left her body in the wagon. The two horses were corralled with the tribe's herd and all the humans took shelter in the warmth for the night.

* * *

A Sioux camp is no different than any other small town. Gossip is rampant and each person had his or her own opinion. From the moment the wagon was spotted stuck in the snow until the rescue, there was no other topic of discussion. There were as many opinions as there were people. Broken Knife, like any administrator, wanted control. Leftook, the white warrior, wanted advantage. Kangee simply was curious. Broken Knife and Black Elk simply loved Mouse and yielded to her influence. Some felt fear and most in their hearts felt racial hatred.

What started as a humanitarian, spiritual necessity for Mouse turned awkward, almost dangerous. She saw the rescue as an outreach of Wakan Tanka. As soon as the group returned to camp, the rescued were taken to Broken Knife's tent. His tent was the largest in camp and the usual meeting place for visitors. The four new visitors quickly walked directly to the fire burning in the center of the room. There was an uncomfortable silence. Then, Mouse stepped forward.

Without approval or even consultation, she handed the revolver back to the young male stranger. She said, "*My name is Mouse in your language.*" She held out her hand.

The man holstered his gun but did not respond to Mouse's gesture of welcome. She continued to look into his eyes with her hand out. He quickly broke eye contact and mumbled something no one could understand.

Mouse then turned to the other man. She held out her hand and repeated her greeting.

The man grabbed Mouse's hand and shook her so vigorously that Black Elk and her father almost intervened. The old man grinned hugely and said, "*Howdy! My name's Luther, Luther Bell. You saved our asses! I cain't thank ya enough!*"

Mouse smiled back and said, "*I do not know this word, "Asses". What does it mean in your language?*"

"*What I mean to say little lady is that you saved our lives. I'm much obliged!*"

"*I don't know "Much obliged". What does it mean in your language?*"

Luther replied in broken Sioux, "*I owe you my life. We would have died.*"

Mouse replied in Sioux, "*How Coula? Wakan Tanka wanted you to live.*"

"*I don't go in much for the Wakan Tanka nonsense but I mighty glad you came along. Right girls?*"

The two young women turned from the fire and Mouse could see that they had been crying. They still clutched the buffalo robes to them. Steam was just starting to rise from the melting snow on the pelts. The older of the two smiled weakly at Mouse and asked, "*Is Rosa dead?*"

Mouse looked at Luther and asked, "*The girl in the wagon, is that Rosa?*"

Luther looked at the two women and said, "*Sorry, she didn't make it.*"

The two women looked at each other and began to wail. The sound was at odds with the cheery space, the brightly painted designs and the fire. Language didn't matter. In Sioux or English, all there felt their utter loss, the complete aloneness these women felt.

Mouse stepped between them, took their hands in hers and said, *"You are safe here."*

Moments later, Aponi and Chumani stepped into the big tent carrying hot venison stew and warm corn cakes. Mouse spread her buffalo robe on the floor near the fire. She motioned for the new visitors to do the same. The old driver hustled over and sat near the fire rubbing his hands. The young women sat and looked at Mouse. She said, *"My name is Mouse in your language. What is your name?"*

The older woman was striking. She had long red hair that many of the Sioux kept staring at. She was tall, as tall as most of the men in the room. She wore a long, thin skirt with a checked print. Her top was long sleeved but low cut to show off her ample breasts. She attempted to keep her shawl clutched over her chest and on her broad shoulders. Just seeing her, one got the impression she was fierce and intimidating. Then she spoke. *"Pleased ta meetchu. My name's Julia. This here's Lotti."* Then she did a little curtsy. Her voice and body language did not at all match her look. The impression she gave of herself seemed submissive and childish.

Lotti did not say a word but looked from face to face furtively then looked at her feet. Lotti then curtsied and stood a little closer to Julia.

Mouse said, *"Sit and eat. We will talk later. Please feel welcome."*

Luther, Julia and Lotti sat on their robes near the fire. Aponi and Chumani served the three hot venison stew and corn cakes. Mouse began to cut and cook elk meat on the stone near the fire. The three ate ravenously.

Mouse left the meat cooking and approached the young man sulking near the door. She said, *"Please sit. Eat."* She held out her hand to him again and said, *"My name is Mouse."*

He snapped, *"I ain't eatin none of that Redskin crap!"* and crossed his arms over his chest.

The tension in the room was tangible. The men stood poised with their hands near their knives. The language used meant nothing to them but the man's body language and tone of voices conveyed fear and aggression.

Broken Knife softly said, "We should kill this Wasican now."

Luther and Mouse were the only two in the room that knew the direction their situation was heading. Luther stood and said to Mouse, *"This here's Charles. He's a little ascared of you injuns. He's a city boy and he don't get your ways."* Then Luther looked at Charles and said, *"Boss, you'd better eat a little or these boys will think you don't like um. Take a load off yer feet."*

Charles continued to stand there defiantly. Mouse made eye contact and said softly, *"You are safe here. Get food from the wagon if you won't eat our food."* She turned and sat next to Julie and Lotti.

Julia and Lotti had followed the conversation with their eyes but didn't stop eating. Everyone else relaxed except Charles. They sat down and began to eat roasted elk. The entire group completely and utterly ignored Charles. Slowly, his posture began to change. His shoulders dropped, his hands went to his sides then hesitantly, and he joined the meal.

When the meal was over, Mouse quietly conferred with her men. She then sat and said to their guests, *"It is dark. We will sleep. Tomorrow we talk."* She looked at Charles and Luther and said, *"You will sleep here. This house belongs to this man. His name is Broken Knife in your language. He is my father. He is one of our leaders. The two women, Julia and Lottie, will sleep in my house."*

Charles jumped up, his attitude from before came back. *"These girls are mine! They stays with me!"* He started to grab Julia by the arm when Badger moved between the two. The situation became charged with aggression and fear. The two young men glared at each other.

Mouse stood before Charles, held up her hands palm out and said, *"We do this because of our laws and beliefs. You are safe here. No one will harm you. Tomorrow we will talk. You are welcome to sleep in your wagon. Tonight, Julia and Lottie sleep at my house."* Mouse turned and began to lead the two white women out of her father's tipi.

Lottie stopped, looked at Mouse and said, *"My name is Lottie Johl. Thank you for saving us."* She reached out and gave Mouse a gentle hug.

New Arrivals, New Year's Day
1 8 8 0

During the night, the clouds returned and more snow fell. Mouse did not sleep.

Her night was troubled. She lay awake fretting and thought about the rescue of the whites. In her heart, she knew it was the right thing to do but the reality was different from what she had pictured. In a naïve way, she expected to gain more friends like the white woman Mary. Charles was the opposite, angry, ignorant and dangerous. The two young women, even though they were older than Mouse, seemed more like vulnerable children. The only one of the four who struck her as being at all self-reliant was Luther, and even he seemed like an incomplete person. In comparison, most eight-year old Sioux children seemed more capable than these whites. Mouse was kept awake by the obvious burden she had brought home to her people.

The presence of the two extra bodies asleep in her tipi felt strange and foreign. Black Elk slept through the night but the soft snoring of Lottie made sleep impossible for Mouse. Finally, she got up, fed the fire and examined the shoes the two white women had left by the door. The design, the stitching, and the high heels amazed Mouse. She tried a pair on and walked a short distance across the floor of the tipi. Two steps in the shoes answered the question in her mind. She returned the shoes to the door, and proceeded to find some large scraps of rawhide. By the time the sky began to lighten in the east, Mouse had fashioned two pair of crude leggings for the women. Without them, these white girls wouldn't even be able to step outside the tipi.

The sound of the fire and aromas of roasting corn cakes and elk woke the others. Black Elk rose and dressed quickly. He caressed Mouse, grabbed a cake and stepped outside. Julia and Lottie peered shyly out from under their robe near the fire. Mouse turned two more cakes then handed them to the two white women. She said, "*How Coula. If you need to make water, I'll show you where we go.*"

Lottie sat up and said, "*I really gotta go!*" and began to reach for her shoes.

Mouse opened the tent flap and showed the two the new snowfall. She said, *"Today, you wear these. Tomorrow, we will make warm clothes for you."* She showed the women how to use rawhide and wrap the leggings securely. The three stepped out into the first bright new morning of 1880.

Moments later, Black Elk returned with some disturbing camp news. "There was trouble in the night. The white man pissed in your father's tent. When your father threw him out the door, the white man pointed his gun at him. The old man Luther stepped between them. Your father wants to kill this man who acts like a child."

Mouse sighed. "Bring them to me. We will talk." She returned to cooking.

Minutes later, a small crowd gathered in her once peaceful space. A full range of human emotions was evident in the faces of those who gathered there. Broken Knife was simply furious. Charles acted irate, but he was terrified. Luther seemed baffled and apologetic. Badger seemed amused as he sat down next to Julia. Broken Knife stood near his daughter as though he could protect her from this impending outburst. Only Leftook and Kangee seemed unfazed. Julia and Lottie cringed when Charles entered the tipi.

Mouse stood and spoke to the group. She spoke first in English then in her native tongue. "I brought these whites among us. I will try to teach them our ways." Then in Sioux she said, "Please, all of you leave. There is much anger here."

One by one, the Sioux leadership left the tent, all except Kangee. He said, "I will stay. You will soon talk of our beliefs. I will stay to speak if you need me. I do not understand the white talk but tell me what is said so I may be with you."

Mouse nodded and said, *"This man is Kangee which means Raven in your language. He is our Holy Man, our spiritual teacher. He wishes to stay and learn your ways. He will leave if you wish."*

Charles mumbled, *"I don't give a shit what this injun does."*

Kangee looked directly at Charles as he spoke, "Your voice tells me you are angry. Why?" He then looked at Mouse and asked for her to translate.

After Mouse told Charles, he yelled, *"We don't wanna be here! You killed one of my girls and made us come here! Let us go!"*

Mouse replied, *"We are not enemies. Your enemy would have let you die in the snow."*

"All you Injuns are killers. Let us go!"

"You have no food, no water. You have no way to keep warm. You would be dead", said Mouse. *"If you leave now, you will die."* She looked at the other whites and asked, *"Do you want to leave?"*

The two women shook their heads *"No!"*

Luther said, *"Boss, calm down. We're warm. They fed us. This looks a heap better than that snow out there."*

Kangee looked at each person there then said, "We believe that Wakan Tanka brought you here for a reason. We must talk like men and learn. We must decide if we are enemies or if we are friends. We will be what you decide." He nodded for Mouse to translate.

After Mouse translated what Kangee had said, Charles responded, *"You're nothin but dirty, heathen Injuns! I'm leavin!"* He got up and stepped outside.

"Tell this fool I will help him with the horses." Kangee told Mouse.

Outside, the snow was calf deep. Charles immediately had snow in his shoes and had his arms wrapped around his torso. He'd not brought the buffalo robe and was beginning to shiver in the ten-degree air. He headed for the horse corral.

Kangee went to Badger's tent. "Release the white man's horses." His second stop was at Leftook's tent.

Leftook immediately found the camp's best bowman. "Only if he leaves camp, understand?" The young warrior nodded.

In the meantime, Badger released the two horses.

For the next hour, Charles fumbled with the tack and traces, chased horses and greatly amused the Sioux who watched. He seemed completely oblivious to the frozen woman in the back of the wagon.

While Charles was attempting to hook the horses to the wagon, Mouse was able to talk to Luther and the women. *"Later, we must talk of this woman, Rosa. You must tell us about your beliefs. We will help you send her to Wakan Tanka."* Mouse looked at the women and asked, *"Why are you with this man Charles?"*

Lottie and Julia looked at Mouse then hung their heads. Luther spoke up. *"They work for him. They are his girls."*

Mouse frowned. *"What work? You have no tools. You have nothing but a wagon with a bed."*

"Sportin women. Soiled doves. You know!" said Luther.

Mouse shook her head. *"What does this mean?"*

Luther blushed and said, *"You know, they lay with men for money."*

Mouse shook her head again.

Luther blushed a deep red and said in Sioux, "They kichi yungka, siksil hung."

Mouse was stunned. In Sioux she said, *"White men pay for this? Do all white women do this?"*

Luther shrugged *"I don't know much about women. Better talk to the girls."* His blush grew even deeper.

Mouse turned to the women and asked, *"Why do you get money for a thing that is freely given?"*

Lottie answered. *"We don't get the money. Charles sells us to men. We ain't got no choice."*

"Do you want to do this?" Mouse asked.

Both women shook their heads *"No!"*

"Your people have no slaves. Your leader in the east says so. Why do you go with this man Charles?"

"Well, we owes him money. He says we gots to pay him before we can leave." said Julia.

"Why do you owe this man money?" Mouse asked.

"We was in this orphanage. Nobody wanted us. We was older. Only the babies got adopted," said Lottie.

Mouse looked puzzled. *"What is orphanage?"*

"It's a church place where folks take little kids nobody wants. People comes and pays and gets a baby. Nobody wants no older kids. We was there a long time.", Julia said softly.

"Finally, Charles comes and pays for us to go with him. He says we got to pay him back. We have to pay for our food from him. We have to pay him for everything, even that damn wagon. He was takin us from Dodge City to Colorado to work the gold and silver

camps. He thought he'd get rich on us. We've been with him for almost three years," said Lottie, with a voice that said she had given up long ago

"I don't know much about Rosa and Lottie," Julia shared. *"My dad died and I was the oldest. Mama couldn't keep us so she took us to the orphanage. My little brother and sisters got adopted. I just got in trouble a lot."* Julia said.

"I grew up there." Lottie said. *"Me an' Rosa never knew our families. We were just sorta always there. I took care of Rosa a lot. She was younger and she cried a lot. The Nuns always hit us if we made noise. They made us work all the time."*

"What are Nuns?" asked Mouse.

"Church ladies. Wore black dresses. They made us do all the work." said Julia.

"Why didn't the people in your camp take you, care for you?" asked Mouse.

"Weren't no camp. We lived in a big city. Lotsa kids lived on the street. Didn't have no home, no families. I guess maybe we was lucky but I hated them Nuns," said Lottie.

"Our people believe in many things." Mouse said. *"Our families are very important. We have this word, Wakanisha that says children are sacred. We believe that a strong family means a strong tribe. Do the whites believe this?"*

"Maybe some do." said Lottie. *"We got stuck in that place. We didn't have no family. We hated it! We always hoped a family would take us and we could live happily ever after. All we ever got was dishes to wash and floors to mop, laundry to do. Then, there was church every morning and almost all day Sunday."*

"Did you learn about your Bible and your people?" Mouse asked.

"Didn't learn nothin! Church was in this old language we didn't know. We just sat there and kept our mouths shut." said Julia.

Mouse translated for Kangee. He asked, "Did you have teachers in this place?"

Lottie answered. *"At first we did. The nuns was real mean and hit us if we didn't learn. Then a lot of us, like me and Julia ended up doin' work instead.* That's *what we learned. Just keep our mouths shut and do what we're told."*

Mouse pulled out her cross and said, *"My friend Mary told me about your Bible. She told me that our beliefs and yours are of the same kind. The Bible tells of your God being three things, The Father, The Son and The Holy Spirit. We believe in Wakan Tanka, the name of our God and we also call him The Great Spirit and The Great Mystery. Your Bible tells of a day of judgment for the dead. We also believe this. We believe in a place like your heaven."*

"All I ever learned is that we're sinners." Julia said. Lottie nodded her head in agreement.

"What is sinner?" Mouse asked.

"Everybody's bad! We's born bad and have to go to church before we can go to heaven," said Lottie.

Mouse translated for Kangee. He shook his head and said, "Ask them why new babies are bad."

Lottie snapped back, *"Hell, I don't know. That's just what we was told. We never learned how we was supposed to be good. We just learned how to work and keep quiet."*

Black Elk's voice came from outside, *"May we enter?"* Mouse stood and opened the tent flap.

Outside were Charles, Black Elk and Badger. Charles barged in without an invitation and stood almost on top of the fire; he was shivering violently. Black Elk waited for Mouse to motion them in. He said, "I think the white 'child' has some words for you." He came over to Mouse and put his arm around her.

Luther smiled at Black Elk then said, *"Hey Boss. You look a little cold. Still want to leave?"*

Charles looked from face to face then looked into the fire. *"I've been a damn fool. I'm sorry for bein' rude. I've never really been out of a city before. You're the first Injuns I've ever seen up close. I just thought you was gonna scalp me or somethin'. I'm sorry."*

Mouse picked up the buffalo robe he'd left behind and handed it to him. She said, *"You have much to learn."*

Mouse turned back to Lotti and Julia. *"We must decide about your friend Rosa. How do your people release your dead?"*

Julia said, *"We don't call it release. We calls it a funeral. Our people have a ceremony in church when a person dies. Then we bury 'em."*

Mouse said, *"We also have a ceremony. In our ceremony, we thank the person for being with us and then we release them. We believe their spirit won't leave if it still has something it must do. We tell the person that they are free. We have seen the places you put your dead. We must wait for the earth to not be hard from the cold. When it is warmer, we will hold a ceremony for Rosa."*

Mouse then turned to Charles and made eye contact. *"We also believe each person chooses their own path. These two women have said they no longer want to be with you. We believe they are free to choose their life. As long as they stay with us, they are free to do as they wish."*

Charles coldly glanced at 'his' two girls. *"Well, we'll see about that!"*

Feedback
1 8 8 0

"Nothing is more despicable than respect based on fear."
Albert Camus

"Yea, though I walk through the valley of the shadow of death,
I will fear no evil: for thou art with me;"
Psalm 23: 4

There was no moment of realization, no sudden comprehension of a change. Julia had pitched in on a simple chore some Sioux women were doing and found that she was humming a song she didn't even know she knew. She looked over at Lotti and when she caught her eye, Lotti smiled back. Smiled! Julia realized that she couldn't remember ever having seen Lotti smile.

Later, the two talked. *"You's different."* said Julia. *"Hell, we's worked together forever, never saw you smile."*

Lotti thought for a moment. *"Look at us. We's wearin' skins, workin' our asses off with Injuns. I thought we'd be gettin' raped or killed or scalped or somethin'. But I'm sorta havin' fun, ya know. I like these people."*

"Those two, I think they's brothers. They kinda handsome. They act like little boys around us. They don't treat us like shit." Julia looked up from the skin she was helping scrape. *"The tall one, he always tries to sit by me, seems like he wants to touch me.* Pausing, *" I wish he would."* She laughed.

Lotti stopped and said, *"That's it. They just treats us like people. It's been so strange being here but now that I'm sorta used to it, it's almost like we belong here. Maybe this is what being in a family feels like."* Lotti stole a glance toward the central fire and looked at the men. *"If those two brothers took us on, we'd be sisters!"* she giggled. *"We gotta learn their talk."*

"Are you sayin' you want to stay with these Injuns?" Julia asked. *"What about Charlie?"*

Lotti looked up and, with more confidence than Julia had ever seen, said, "*He's a piece a shit! I'd rather be raped and scalped than go with that sorry excuse of a horse's ass! What about you?*"

Julia paused and thought for a moment. "*Yea, I like it here, to feel just like a regular person. Never felt this way before.*"

"*That little Mouse girl; she's big. Looks like she's gonna pop any day. That fella she's with, damn, he's handsome!*" Lotti said. "*She's so tiny and sorta plain looking; to end up with a guy like that. But he really seems to love her. I sure could use some of that. Wonder when the baby's gonna come?*"

Julia looked up and smiled at another Sioux woman working with her. "*Yea, we gotta learn their talk. It would be nice to talk to these here girls, get the gossip, ya know. I wonder whose idea it was to save us. We could be frozen stiff like Rosa or fuckin' some smelly prospector to make Charlie a dime.*"

"*Yea, they coulda just left us out there to die. That Mouse girl, wonder where she learned to talk English. Ya notice how the men sorta really listen to her, treat her like, well, like a queen or somethin'. Ya know when she talks to us, it's like she's one of us, not all bossy or anythin'. But it's like she's got this power around her. It just makes me want to hug her. I think I love her. Hell, I din't ever think I'd ever say that.*"

* * *

It had been four cold and miserable days since the rescue. Luther pitched in and helped out. He even went out for a hunt and helped skin a nice elk they took down near the river. As soon as he pitched in and offered to help, the others around him began to accept him and his help. The other warriors in the tipi laughed at his stories and were openly curious about life in the white world. Luther just seemed to accept life as it came. He often thanked his rescuers and made it clear he wanted their friendship. If it weren't for Luther and an occasional word from Mouse, Charles would have had no one who would speak to him.

Charles Alan remained sullen and spent most of his time in the new tipi he was assigned along with Luther. He slept with Badger, Dove and several of the other unmarried warriors. He ate when food was offered to him. He kept the fire going in the tipi but did nothing to forage for fuel. His refusal to change from his street clothes and his smell highly offended his tent mates. When he attempted yet another piss in his new tipi, Charles never realized how close he came to death. It was Luther who stepped between Charles and Badger when the dour white man complained about walking in the snow to the common latrine. As Julia, Lottie and Luther became more comfortable in their new surroundings, Charles grew even more morose and defiant.

Gossip is inevitable when people are close-knit and interdependent. When Lotti and Julia joined in the women's work almost from day one, the women of the tribe accepted them and often made positive comments about them. It was obvious to all the women and most of the men that Badger and Dove wanted these white women as wives. Luther, a half-breed, was a rarity to the Sioux. His easy manner and willingness to blend in helped as much as his language. His limited Sioux vocabulary also helped him fit in with his new friends. While he was not terribly smart, he had an uncanny way with horses. The men of the tribe noticed that skill immediately.

Charles was another story entirely. Showing just the opposite of gratitude, his childish, selfish attitude kept the mutual hate between the two races alive. The men of the tribe talked about him constantly; every encounter he had with people of the tribe only fueled that fire. Mouse decided she had better intervene when Black Elk told that there was talk of killing the Wasican.

Late on that fourth day, the sun finally peeked out of the clouds and for a while, the air warmed. Mouse approached the tipi where Charles stayed. His tent mates hated being around him and stayed away during the day. They only returned to their shared tipi to sleep.

Charles was alone. Only a small amount of smoke rose from the top of the tipi and the flap was closed. Mouse and Black Elk stood outside for a moment then she said, *"Charles, may I enter?"* She signaled for black Elk to wait outside.

A long silence ensued. Mouse was almost ready to turn and leave when she heard, *"Whadda ya want?"* The flap opened; Charles sat on the floor looking up at her.

She stood looking at him until he looked away. *"It is polite to invite a guest inside. That is our custom."*

He muttered something under his breath then said in falsetto, *"Won't you please come in?"* The tone of his voice was heavy with sarcasm.

Mouse stepped into the tipi and waited. After a few uncomfortable moments, he said, *"What?"*

"It is also our custom to be offered a seat. An honored guest is offered the seat to the left of the host."

"I don't know your Injun ways. Just sit down," he said.

Mouse painfully sat. Her pregnancy made it hard to do much of anything but sitting was especially difficult. *"The first lesson we teach our children is to learn the ways of any new place they visit. Each tribe has its own family ways. You would have done well to ask and learn our ways."*

"Ya know, I don't really give a crap. As soon as the snow melts, the girls and I are gone. You can have all the Injun ways ya want." He sneered at her and scooted over near the dying fire.

"Lotti and Julia are free to do what they want. If they want to stay, they will stay. That is also our way."

He turned and snarled at her. *"Those fuckin' girls is mine! They owes me money and they be mine till they pays me all they owes me!"*

Mouse calmly stared back at him. *"Your people had a terrible war. It was decided that there would be no slaves. Lotti and Julia are free to do what they want."*

Charles jumped up and whirled to face her. His face was red and his fists were clenched at his sides. *"Ya fuckin little bitch! You cain't tell me what to do with what's mine!"*

Suddenly, with a pained look on her face, Mouse grunted, let out a loud moan and doubled over.

Instantly, Black Elk was through the flap and inside. He saw Charles standing there, face red, fists clenched, with Mouse on the floor doubled over. His reaction was swift and instinctual. In a split second, Charles was on his back, half in the fire with Black Elk at his throat.

Black Elk had one hand around Charles' throat and was pulling his knife when Mouse said, "*Stop! The baby is coming.*"

For Black Elk, his anger was quickly replaced with joy, wonder and a deep concern for Mouse. Charles got up with a look of black, naked hatred on his face, his hand momentarily reaching for the pistol at his side. Then, he relaxed and he began to plan.

* * *

As was their custom, the women took Mouse away from the main encampment. They chose a sheltered spot and erected a small lean-to that broke the bitter winter wind. A small fire was lit in the structure and fuel was stored. The women brought extra hides for bedding, some water and as many fresh sage branches as they could find. The sage was used as a soft cushion for the baby to fall on because Sioux women always stood or squatted during childbirth.

Spoon Woman and Macawi gathered their herbs and powdered bark. As they were about to join the rest of the women, Macawi remained behind for a moment. As Spoon Woman walked away, Macawi stepped into her tipi and closed the flap. Silently, she sank to her knees and wept bitterly in fear and remorse. The guilt she still carried for the death of Ehawee, Itunkala's mother, flowed out of her like a torrent. As her sobs subsided, she lay flat on her stomach and prayed to The Great Spirit for the life of Mouse and the child to be.

The women helped Mouse make the walk to her newly erected shelter just as the sun sank in the west. Macawi, Spoon Woman and Mouse's two sisters were the only women who stayed with Mouse that night. Her contractions quickly escalated until they were almost non-stop. The moon was not even overhead when Mouse's daughter entered the world and by sunrise, the two were snuggled with Black Elk under their warm robes in their tipi by their own fire.

Black Elk marveled at his new daughter as she nursed. She was tiny, an early copy of her mother but her hair, what little she had, was black and shiny as liquid stone. Her eyes, like her mother's, were huge, soulful and intense. Almost without thought, Black Elk said, "She's as tiny as a seed." and the nickname stuck. Sometimes they called her Conala Suthung meaning 'Little Seed' and other times it was Lyusking Suthung, 'Happy Seed'. Mouse smiled to herself and thought, "-to bear fruit, new life, the promise of a future." It was not a name this little girl would carry for long.

***

The sun rose on a bitterly cold day. The fire was almost out and Mouse attempted to jump up to do her usual morning chores, rekindle the fire, heat the stone and begin breakfast. As she sat up, she caught an unfamiliar bundle in her arms and there, looking into her eyes, were the deep, bottomless eyes of her newborn daughter. There was this timeless moment when all of existence narrowed to one thing, the amazing connection that flowed between her and the eyes of this tiny new person. Little Seed smiled and Mouse was overcome with the deepest, most profound emotions she had ever experienced: overpowering love, fierce protectiveness and the belief that her own wants and needs no longer mattered. A sensation that felt like an electrical current passing between her and this new life bonded the two of them completely. They stared into each other's eyes until Mouse pulled her daughter to her breast and profoundly wept.

As Black Elk began to stir, Seed began to nuzzle again at Mouse's breasts. She opened her wrap and began feeding her new daughter. Black Elk awakened and looked over in wonder at his new child then saw his wife's tears. He began to ask what was the matter but Mouse just put her hand to his lips and pulled him close.

Later in the morning, Aponi and Chumani and her two "Aunties" Macawi and Spoon Woman arrived with packets of herbs and a bundle of cloth and skins. The women invited Black Elk to leave, and began the traditional Sioux practice of washing the mother and baby in warm water sweetened with herbs.

Outside, preparations were being made for a feast to celebrate the coming of a new Human Being. Broken Knife sent out several hunters to bring back as much fresh meat as they could find, then went to visit his new grandchild.

As Broken Knife walked through the camp toward Mouse and Black Elk's tipi, Red Feather and Aponi's son, Little Bear, came from another direction. Little Bear screamed "KAKA!" and ran toward his grandfather. Broken Knife squatted down and held out his arms to his grandson. The little boy didn't even make a pretense of slowing down. He crashed into Broken Knife and the two rolled in the snow in a tangle of giggles and tickling. Black Elk was not far behind.

Holding Little Bear, Broken Knife brushed the snow off them both. "Can we enter? I want to see my new granddaughter," he said to the closed tipi flap.

A moment later, they hear Mouse's voice say, "I'm dressing. Just a moment." A short while later, the flap opened and standing there was Mouse holding Little Seed. The warm air from the fire flowed out around those waiting to enter, carrying the smells of the sweet herbs that had washed mother and child.

The three men and one little boy stepped into the warm tipi. They all formed a circle around Mouse and the baby. Mouse stepped up to Broken Knife and handed the child to him as he stepped into the circle. "This is Suthung, your happy little Seed, your granddaughter." Mouse looked into her father's eyes, smiled and said, "Suthung, this is your Thunkashila, your Kaka."

Broken Knife looked into the child's impossibly deep eyes and formed a connection that can only be understood by a grandparent. He looked up at all those gathered around him. He was there in the center of a sacred circle, a circle of love and total acceptance. Slowly, he pulled the child to his chest in an embrace as his tears flowed uncontrollably. Almost simultaneously, his family drew close and closed the circle on this man that had suffered and loved, had lived total Wakanisha.

* * *

Days later, it was still bitterly cold. The ground was frozen but the joyful feast continued. Game was plentiful and the whites had not ventured out on their road near the river. New game was easy to take; the fresh tracks were easy to follow and the young hunters had an easy time taking elk and deer near the partially frozen river.

On the fourth and last day of the celebration of new life, Julia and Lotti approached Leftook. *"Rosa is still frozen stiff in the wagon. It just ain't right to be havin' fun and not bury her,"* Lotti said to him.

"We held a quick council days ago, ladies. You said you wanted her buried like the whites do. We could have put up a platform like these Sioux but we've been waiting for the ground to thaw so we can bury her. We'll have her burial as soon as it warms up." Leftook looked at both of the white women. *"You do want to bury her, don't you?"*

Lotti and Julie looked at each other. *"Yeah, I guess. It just don't seem right to have her layin' out there."* said Julia.

"We'll bury her proper as soon as it warms up. You might want to think about what you want to say over her grave. You knew her better than anybody else."

The following day, the clouds broke and the sun began warming the earth. Leftook and Broken Knife announced that the burial would be early the next day. Julia and Lotti picked a spot a little east of the camp on a hillside that faced the rising sun with a view of the shallow river valley in the distance. Several of the younger men volunteered to dig the grave, and plans were made for the tribe to gather the next morning.

The sun rose. The remaining snow melted quickly as the air warmed and left the sandy soil soft, almost muddy. With the exception of the scouts watching all the approaches to their camp and a couple young warriors watching the horses, the entire tribe gathered near the end of the Luther's wagon. Spoon Woman had made a simple garment of elk and with the help of several other women, dressed the dead white woman for her burial. Lotti and Julia wept softly as several of the men lifted Rosa from the wagon and placed her body on a buffalo hide that was used to carry her to her resting place.

The tribe solemnly walked toward the still-rising sun over the hill to where the grave waited. They were about halfway there when Luther said to Leftook, "*Hey, where's Charlie?*"

Leftook looked over the crowd then said to Luther, "*Go get that worthless bastard. We'll keep on walking; just bring him or he'll answer to me him if he doesn't show.*"

The tribe arrived at the burial site with Julia and Lotti leading the way followed by four young warriors carrying Rosa's body. When they arrived, they all realized that they weren't prepared to just drop Rosa's body like a sack of rocks. Finally, Leftook climbed into the hole and the four warriors handed Rosa to Leftook who held her to his chest almost as if they were lovers. He gently laid her on her back and after one last look at her face, covered her completely with the elk robe.

Lotti and Julia were crying freely now and before the first handful of soil was thrown into the grave, Julia said, "*Lord, I don't know if you're there but it sure feels like it now. So I just wants to say that this ain't a bad girl. Please watch over her and take good care of her. She had a rough life but now, she don't feel no pain.*"

Lotti looked down in the hole then at Julia. "*Amen. Please watch over us all.*"

The silence was shattered by a gunshot.

* * *

Luther walked back to camp and entered the tent he and Charles shared. Inside, Charles was packing his bag he had taken from the wagon. In the bag were his own few belongings in addition to a number of things he thought might be valuable that he'd taken from other tipis -- an old rifle, some decorative arrows, a necklace of claws. Luther said, "*Hey boss, what ya doin, the funeral for Rosa is happenin'. Let's go.*"

Charles grinned coldly. "*This here's our chance. Let's get gone while those red niggers is gone.*"

"*No! It ain't right. They saved us and took us in. I ain't repayin' them by takin' their stuff. I'm goin' to bury Rosa. You'd be obliged to come along.*" Luther motioned toward the door.

"*Fuck that crap! I'm lightin' out while the gettin's good. Let's go! We'll be over the hill and on the road before they come back.*" Charles tried to push past Luther and get out the door.

"*Boss, you're a worthless –*" Luther started to say.

Charles pulled his pistol and shot Luther in the face point blank. Luther went down without a twitch.

Charles ran south toward the road and as he crested the hill, below he saw a team and wagon accompanied by two or three men on horseback headed east.

Charles shouted, "*Wait! Help!*" over and over as he covered the distance between himself and the Santa Fe Trail.

* * *

At the sound of the shot, Leftook, Broken Knife and most of the warriors ran back to camp. They found Luther's body and Charles' tracks in the slush that disappeared over the hill to the south. They gave chase but as they crested the hill, they saw the whites in their wagons and Charles gesturing wildly. Broken Knife briefly considered getting the horses and going after him, but another team and wagon with several riders appeared on the road also headed east toward the new Kansas town, Dodge City.

Charles was almost totally winded as he ran to the wagon. *"Go! Go!"* he gasped as he started to climb aboard. *"Get your guns out and loaded before they attack!"*

"Whoa mister!" said the driver. *"Was those Injuns?"*

"Let's go before they attack! There's a bunch of 'em and they want me dead." Charles was frantic.

The driver looked up at the ridge. *"Hell mister, they's only four or five of 'em and they disappeared. My brother in the next wagon and his boys have lots of guns. Musta scared 'em off. What the hell happened up there?"*

"Let's get rolling if you don't mind. There's a lot of 'em up there and they're mad. I killed a couple of 'em and escaped. They want my scalp! Let's go!" Charles kept looking up at the ridge from where he had just run.

By then, the other wagon and riders had pulled up behind the first. The other driver and all the riders had their guns out and they all gathered around Charles as he sat on the edge of the wagon. The first driver said, *"This guy was them Injun's prisoner and he killed some of 'em and escaped. Hell, he's a hero or somethin."*

Charles looked around him. He was surrounded by a bunch of white men with guns, all of them looking at him with great respect. *"Let's get moving and I'll tell you my story. Where we headin'?"*

"We's 'bout six hours outa Dodge City. Gotta telegraph there. Hell, tell your story there and everybody in town gonna buy you a drink." The driver shook the reins and yelled, *"Geehaw! Gidup!"* *"Now, I wanna hear your story; we got lots of time."*

Charles smiled and began his story. *"About two weeks ago, I was accompanying three ladies to Denver. They hired me as their bodyguard. Damn Injuns attacked us right where you picked me up. Killed my driver and one of the ladies. They kept me tied up in one of their damn tents; took the women someplace else. I heard 'em screamin' off and on. God knows what those red savages was doin' to 'em."*

"Damn!" said the driver. *"How'd you get away? How many of 'em was there?"*

"There was a hundred, maybe more." said Charles.

"*That's a pretty big tribe!*" said the driver.

"*Nope! That was the warriors; musta been at least four hundred in all. They was havin' some heathen ceremony and left me guarded by just three or four warriors. I knocked out one with this here gun and shot 'em all and skeedaddled. The rest of 'em was chasin' me when I got down here. Lucky you came along when you did. Much obliged.*" Charles was really beginning to enjoy the attention.

"*Well!*" said the driver, "*We gotta send out a telegram to the Calvary. Gotta rescue those women!*"

As the wagons rolled east on their bumpy ride toward the land of the whites, Charles continued work on his heroic story.

Wyandotte
Kansas City
The Company will appreciate
concerning

Telegraph Co.
Missouri
suggestions from its patrons
its services.

Day Letter
Night Letter
Urgent **x**

Date
Jan 7, 1880

Time in: 7:40 PM
Time Dlvd: 8:10 PM

To: CMDR FT. LARNED KANSAS

From: J. MASTERSON, MRSL. DODGE CITY

NEED ASSISTANCE — STOP

HOSTILE INDIANS IN VACINITY — STOP

The filing time on the date line on domestic telegrams
is LOCAL TIME at the point of origin.
Time of receipt is LOCAL TIME at point of destination.

Wyandotte
Kansas City
The Company will appreciate
concerning

Telegraph Co.
Missouri
suggestions from its patrons
its services.

Day Letter
Night Letter
Urgent **X**

Date
Jan 7, 1880

Time in: 8:15 PM
Time Dlvd: 8:25 PM

To: MRSL. MASTERSON

From: GEN. W.S. HANCOCK. FT. LARNED

LOCATION? — STOP

SIZE? — STOP

The filing time on the date line on domestic telegrams
is LOCAL TIME at the point of origin.
Time of receipt is LOCAL TIME at point of destination.

Wyandotte
Kansas City
The Company will appreciate
concerning

Telegraph Co.
Missouri
suggestions from its patrons
its services.

Day Letter
Night Letter
Urgent **X**

Date
Jan 7, 1880

Time in: 9:10 PM
Time Dlvd: 9:20 PM

To: Gen. HANCOCK, FT. LARNED, KAN.

From: MASTERSON, DODGE CITY

APPX. 400 — STOP

100 WARRIORS — STOP

The filing time on the date line on domestic telegrams
is LOCAL TIME at the point of origin.
Time of receipt is LOCAL TIME at point of destination.

Wyandotte
Kansas City
The Company will appreciate
concerning

Telegraph Co.
Missouri
suggestions from its patrons
its services.

Day Letter
Night Letter
Urgent **X**

Date
Jan 8, 1880

Time in: 6:50 PM
Time Dlvd: 7:40 PM

To: MRSL. MASTERSON, DODGE CITY

From: CMD. ANDREWS, FT. LARNED

NEED SPECIFIC LOCATION — STOP

WITNESS STATEMENTS — STOP

The filing time on the date line on domestic telegrams
is LOCAL TIME at the point of origin.
Time of receipt is LOCAL TIME at point of destination.

Wyandotte
Kansas City
The Company will appreciate
concerning

Telegraph Co.
Missouri
suggestions from its patrons
its services.

Day Letter
Night Letter
Urgent **X**

Date
Jan 8, 1880

Time in: 8:25 AM
Time Dlvd: 8:40 AM

To: CMDR ANDREWS FT. LARNED, KANS.

From: MASTERSON, DODGE CITY

APPX. TEN MILES E. GARDEN CITY ON RIDGE
ABOVE SANTA FE TRAIL — STOP
WAGON WITH TWO MEN, THREE WOMEN ATTACKED.
TAKEN PRISONER — STOP
ONE MAN, ONE WOMAN KILLED — STOP
MAN ESCAPED, KILLED SEVERAL HOSTILES — STOP
WOMEN MOLESTED — STOP
SEVERAL WITNESSES TO MAN'S ESCAPE — STOP
MAN, WITNESSES CHASED BY INDIANS — STOP
WITNESSES RETURNED FIRE, INDIANS WITHDREW
 — STOP

The filing time on the date line on domestic telegrams
is LOCAL TIME at the point of origin.
Time of receipt is LOCAL TIME at point of destination.

Wyandotte
Kansas City
The Company will appreciate
concerning

Telegraph Co.
Missouri
suggestions from its patrons
its services.

Day Letter
Night Letter
Urgent **X**

Date
Jan 8, 1880

Time in: 9:10 PM
Time Dlvd: 9:20 PM

To: MASTERSON, DODGE CITY

From: CMDR ANDRES, FT. LARNED, KAN

SENDING TWO COMPANIES, EIGHT PLATOON, 200
MEN PLUS 8 PAWNEE SCOUTS — STOP
WILL FOLLOW PAWNEE RIVER & BUCKNER RIVER TO
VACINITY — STOP
DEPART JAN. 9 FIRST LIGHT — STOP
ADVISE IF CHANGES — STOP

*The filing time on the date line on domestic telegrams
is LOCAL TIME at the point of origin.
Time of receipt is LOCAL TIME at point of destination.*

Ft. Larned, Kansas
1 8 8 0

"Wake up peckerwood!" yelled Chester as he kicked the bunk above him. There was no response from his brother Sam so Chester kicked the bunk again. "Hey! Ya turd! Get up!"

The man in the top bunk groaned and rolled over and said, "You cockchafer! Shut your pie hole!" The big man finally put his head over the side of his bed and looked down at his brother. Beside the bed was a reeking puddle of vomit.

Chester tilted his head towards the puddle and said, "Shit man, I didn't know which way to go so I just covered my head. You are such a horse's ass!"

The other men of the platoon had learned long ago to ignore these two brothers. Chester, the older brother, was mean and vindictive. The other brother, Sam, was dim-witted, huge and violent.

Yesterday had been payday and the Ross brothers squandered most of their pay drinking and on the two prostitutes at the Ft. Larned Sutler's store just off post.

Chester Ross and his little brother Sam were a perfect fit for the 19th U.S. Infantry. Little Sam and Chester had been part of the United States military for ten years and both were still privates. The two had been promoted several times but it just didn't last. There was always some charge of drunkenness, petty theft or disobeying orders that resulted in their company commander taking their stripes. But with the Ross brothers, the Army got two boys who had considerable skills; they could shoot, ride, kill and skin any animal (or an Injun) and live on spare rations for weeks at buck private wages.

The 'boys' got three squares a day, a bed, structure and, from time to time, adventure.

Chester and "Little Sam" grew up near what is now called Chanute, Kansas. When they were young boys, there was no city there but only four little communities fighting over which would host the new railroad office. Just before the Civil War began, their mother and father arrived in this area, pregnant and unmarried.

It was 1856 and the westward expansion was in full swing. Chester and Little Sam's mother was just fifteen, their father seventeen when the couple had been kicked out of their respective homes because of the pregnancy. Neither one could read or write, but both had plenty of farming and household skills. And, in the rapidly growing frontier, there was plenty of work to be found.

William Ross, the boys' father, never had a difficult time finding farm work. He knew horses, how to milk cows and do most any chore on any farm in those days. His biggest problem was keeping a job. He always believed he knew more than his employer and, after a few weeks or months; an argument, drunkenness or both would end his current job.

Aida, the boys' mother, usually loved her housemaid work and her employer, the lady of the house. However, after her "husband's" usual Saturday night abuse, she was routinely convinced that there were greener pastures. And there were. As roads and farms pushed rapidly west, William and Aida followed the wave of expansion.

When the war broke out in 1861, Aida's first-born Chester was almost seven years old and Little Sam was five. She and William were working and living on a large farm outside the little settlement of Chicago Junction, Kansas when the call came for Union soldiers to fight in the new Civil War. The town was buzzing with news about the war and saloons were full of boisterous claims of bravery and pride. So, on a Saturday night, after drinking his week's wages, William came home and announced that he was going off to glory and riches. He had signed up to fight without asking for an opinion from the mother of his children. By week's end, he was gone, promising to send half his pay in the letters he would ask someone else to write. They never heard from him again.

"Little Sam" was a bit of a misnomer. Although he was thirteen months younger, Sam was almost seven inches taller and eighty pounds heavier than his older brother Chester. While Chester was the smaller man, there was never any doubt that he was the boss. He had always been a clever boy -- clever like his father. Chester managed to avoid work when he could, and often tricked his younger brother to do it for him. Later, when the petty theft started, usually chickens or garden vegetables, Chester planned the scheme and Little Sam was most often the culprit.

Money was tight in their fatherless household. School was an option but the boys were needed to bring in the extra few cents a week to keep their household afloat. They became educated, instead, by weeding gardens, milking, shoveling walks in the winter and odd jobs on neighboring farms. The boys always managed to 'find' something to bring home after their outings. As they grew older, the boys learned livestock. At a young age, both became experts in castrations, branding, dehorning, anything that seemed to cause immense discomfort to the animals. Not unlike their father, the two boys seemed to enjoy inflicting pain.

* * *

The Sioux, Arapahoe and the Cheyenne couldn't have picked a better time politically to massacre General George A. Custer and his 7th Calvary. The United State's 100th birthday was just weeks away. In May of 1876, President Ulysses S. Grant had opened America's first World's Fair, the U. S. Centennial Exposition in Philadelphia, to great fanfare. News of Custer's defeat shared headlines in the newspapers with the country's centennial celebration.

The general election later that November became the most contentious and controversial presidential election in American history to date. Samuel J. Tilden, Democrat and Rutherford B. Hayes, Republican, disputed 20 electoral votes. There was no clear presidential winner. Congress was divided; the House of Representatives was firmly in the hands of the Democrats and the Senate voted Republican. The presidential election wasn't cleared up until 1877 with "The Great Betrayal." The Compromise of 1877 gave the White House to Hayes in an unwritten "deal." In exchange for the presidency Hayes agreed to remove federal troops from the South, ending Reconstruction. As troops and funding were removed from South Carolina, Florida and Louisiana, many white Republicans left as well, leaving those states firmly controlled by the Democrats.

All this political turmoil gave The First People a bit of breathing room and freedom before the will of the United States government focused again on the free roaming Indians.

* * *

Winters in the barracks at Ft. Larned, Kansas were a dismal affair. Many of the enlisted men, including Little Sam Ross and his brother Chester, rarely bathed. The men played cards and checkers and when they could get out of the barracks; there was billiards, bowling, gambling and a prostitute or two at the Sutler's store. There was also plenty of cheap whisky.

Chester and Sam were generally outcasts. Chester cheated at cards, stole from his platoon mates, and regularly lied to their platoon sergeant when confronted. The other platoon members finally gave up trying for any justice because Little Sam, at his brother's instructions, enforced his brother's will.

When they could, the Ross brothers took their horses and hunted in the countryside. They often brought back fresh meat; buffalo when they could find it. Hunting was a diversion to the boring life in the barracks but what the two lived for were raids on Indian camps. The only unpaid sexual experiences the brothers had ever had were the rape and murder of Indian girls. The brothers considered the bloodlust of destroying an Indian village the best experience they'd ever had. The army officers rarely took part in anything but gunfire, but encouraged and watched as the enlisted men took their satisfaction.

When word began to circulate around the barracks that a raid was being organized, the Ross brothers and many other troops were overjoyed. There had been very little to do around the fort except for shit details, like painting rocks, shoveling the company commander's walk and general upkeep.

It was late winter and the weather had been unmercifully cold. The barracks windows had been kept closed and the smell of unwashed men was overpowering. The men were suffering from an acute case of 'cabin fever' and wanted out for some action. The hunting had been terrible. They managed to take a deer once in a while but the buffalo were almost completely extinct by then. The outright slaughter of buffalo was meant to crush the plains Indians into accepting life on a reservation under the government's thumb. Many of the soldiers realized that the upcoming raid might just be their last moment of glory.

The irony was completely lost on the Ross boys; they put on their very best behavior in order to be chosen to participate in an action that broke three of the Ten Commandments. What little conscience they had was clear. As Chester always said, "Them damn Injuns are like the niggers, they ain't human."

A Cruel God?
1 8 8 0

"Belief in a cruel God makes a cruel man."
  Thomas Paine

"While I know myself as a creation of God, I am also obligated
to realize and remember that everyone else and everything else
are also God's creation."
  Maya Angelou

When Charlie ran away from the tribe, it was hard to believe that he was also a child of God. Along with his selfish, hate-centered personality, went Charlie's knowledge of the tribe's location and number. Every member of the tribe realized at some level that his actions would dictate their very existence.

Leftook quickly called the leadership together and said, "We must leave! Now! That wasican knows too much about us! He knows where we are, how small and weak we are. A fair sized posse of local ranchers could come in and destroy us."

Mouse walked up holding Happy Seed and joined her husband in this distressed group of men. "I think Lotti and Julia want to walk the Red Road with us but Charles is full of hate. I brought this on us. What can I do?"

Kangee put his arm around her shoulder and hugged her. "Your spirit is pure Little One. You helped these whites like the Human Beings were helped many winters ago. We gave him many chances to release his bad feelings. We live free so we must move. It is not you but the whites who force us to live as we do."

Mouse looked from man to man. Some met her eyes; some did not. "I brought these whites among us. What would you have me do?" A loose circle of people had gathered around this cruel drama being played out. She looked around at her people, her family. Some faces showed anger, some fear. Mouse looked for answers in these faces; should she ride out and kill this white man who would bring disaster? What simple act would undo the damage this one, angry white man could do to her people? Finally, she looked up at her father. "Ate', what can I do?"

Broken Knife reached out and put the palm of his hand on her cheek. "Be my daughter. Be a mother to this child. Be a wife to this man. You are a Human Being. You chose life and to honor our ways. You have not done wrong." He pulled his daughter into a rough embrace as he looked from face to face, challenging anyone there to speak differently.

* * *

"Tench HUT!" yelled Captain Jacob Andrews. He looked out over the assembled troops standing in the snow. "Parade REST!" he bellowed.

Virtually all the soldiers of the 19th U. S. Infantry stationed at Ft. Larned stood attentively on the parade grounds. There were four companies of four platoons of twenty men. Nearly 350 men stood at parade rest and waited for what "The Old Man" had to say. Rumors of an Indian raid swirled around the barracks ever since the first telegram arrived. Almost every soldier hoped to be assigned to the force sent out to enforce President Grant's executive order that all Indians report to their assigned reservation. That order was over four years old and the 19th had not been on an Indian raid for over a year. The boys were itching for some action.

"Listen up! General Hancock will brief you on our mission. General, Sir." said Captain Andrews as the general took the stand.

The general struck a dramatic pose and looked out over the assembled troops for at least thirty seconds before he began to speak. "At ease men. We've received word that a large group of hostile Indians are in our territory. They attacked civilians and took hostages. Some of those hostages were killed but there may be two white women being held in their camp. Your primary mission is to rescue these two women. Your secondary mission is to force any remaining hostiles onto their proper reservation." He paused for effect then continued. "Captain Andrews here will give the specifics of your mission."

The captain faced forward and yelled, "Tench HUT!" The assembled crowd snapped to attention and saluted as the general made his way back to his warm quarters and his political aspirations.

"As the general said, our main mission is the rescue of these white women. We will rely on our Pawnee scouts to locate the enemy camp. We will approach by stealth. One platoon from Company A will act as a decoy to draw the warriors away from the camp. The rest of Company A will secure the camp and rescue these women. Company B will flank the warriors and engage them if they resist. Any survivors" he winked at the men "will be escorted to Ft. Laramie." Pvt. Chester Ross nudged his brother Little Sam and smiled an evil smile.

* * *

Anger and fear are more closely related than brothers; one is usually the result of the other. There were plenty of both as the Sioux broke camp. Leftook, with the backing of their chief Broken Knife, ordered the men to assist the women in readying the camp for a forced march. Husband and wife barked at each other, children were scolded. Mouse reluctantly gave little Suthung to Kangee to hold while she and Black Elk disassembled their tipi for travel. She was still sore and uncomfortable from recently giving birth but she did not complain.

Lotti and Julia were amazing during the breakdown of camp. They seemed to be everywhere, helping everybody. Both the men and the women smiled at them and thanked them for their help. The children had lost most of their shyness around these white women and gave them tentative affectionate touches. The irony of the situation was not lost on Mouse; she got angry glances and one syllable grunts from her own people.

But she understood. It was her naïve practices of traditional Sioux beliefs that brought this threat to her people. In her heart, she knew she'd been right but at what cost?

The tribe was on the move well before mid-day. Broken Knife and several of the other men decided their best destination would be their traditional wintering ground, Dry Lake. The trip was a hard day's journey almost due north. Most of the men were on horseback and scouting in a complete circle around their direction of travel. Leftook was frustrated and frightened because the ground was so wet and muddy; their tracks could not be erased.

To a bird looking down on this group of humanity on the move, it would resemble an amoeba. The nucleus was the women and children. They lead or rode the horses, towing their belongings on travois. For security, the men ranged for miles in all directions and surrounded the women and children. At the very center was Mouse, encircled but not near any of the other women. Their anger and resentment was still evident.

Her isolation would have been complete if it were not for her sleeping daughter. Little Seed snuggled in a pack Mouse carried over her shoulder. Mouse led her horse that pulled the possessions of her life. Behind her were the skins and poles that were her home; the home of her new husband and child. Wrapped tightly was her cooking stone that once had belonged to the mother she never knew. Around her waist was the knife she had carried almost all her life. Around her neck, she wore the chain and cross; a reminder that the whites also believed in a God, perhaps the same God that permeated her life. It was her profound belief in that God that had brought her here, isolated, in danger and shunned by her own people. Mouse wondered if her people would turn her over to the whites if it meant no risk to them. For the first time in her life, she wished she could dig a hole in the prairie, pull the sod over her head and hide from the world.

The spring sun beat down on her head as she trudged along. She slipped into a hypnotic place; the prairie rolled by as her thoughts randomly flowed from memory to memory. It was in this transcendental place where the miles slipped by, that boredom was replaced by fantasies of better outcomes, of happy times to come, of places where all people shared and lived in peace.

Her reverie was abruptly interrupted when Lotti said, "*It's a right purty day.*" Mouse looked up and realized that Lotti and Julia were walking beside her. They may have been there for miles. Mouse smiled at the two and said, "*Sorry, I was dream walking.*"

Lotti looked uncomfortably at Julia, cleared her throat and began. "*We's been talkin.*" She stuttered a couple of times then said, "*We's only been with you folks a week or so but we feel different; good. Don't know how to splain it xactly, just, well, we feels good with you people. Before, our life was crap but now, we feels like we belongs here, like you just sees us as people, like we belong. We's never felt that before.*"

Mouse smiled at them both. "*It was always your choice. Charles chose his path. You chose another path; you chose to respect us. I am glad you stayed.*"

"*They's more!*" Julia said. "*Now that we's here, free an' all, we feels somethin's with us, somethin big, joy like. I cain't splain it either but, well, its like we's connected to somethin, something good, holy I guess. Do you feel it too?*"

Mouse reached out with her free hand and took Julia's hand in hers. "*I feel it all the time. It's Wakan Tanka, God. He is with us always.*"

"*Couldja tell us about it. We wants to know.*" Julia looked back and forth between Mouse and her friend Lotti.

Little Seed moved a little so Mouse touched her affectionately and adjusted her sling. As the baby snuggled against her back, Mouse began to speak:

"*Two things are of the greatest value to us. The first is our tawaiciyan. Your word is freedom. The other is wakanisha. That means children are holy, a blessing. Our children are our greatest treasure. We protect them and never harm them. When you came and decided to live with us, our people treated you like our children, like you were perfect, that you had no sin. It was your choice to be like us and that is when you began to feel what we call The Great Spirit.*

We believe in Wakan Tanka, God. And like the whites, we believe in three different ways he blesses us. We call him Wakan Tanka but we also call him The Great Spirit and The Great Mystery. It is the Spirit that you feel, that you see working in everything. We believe that The Great Spirit is in everything, the rocks and the trees, in us. We call him The Great Mystery because we cannot understand how Wakan Tanka created everything and is in everything. He is everything.

We believe that when we die, the part of The Great Spirit that lives within us returns to Wakan Tanka. That is why you hear us thank the spirit of an animal we kill for food. We believe the animal's spirit returns to Wakan Tanka. We thank the spirit of Wakan Tanka for giving us our lives because we know our spirit will return home someday.

About two thousand winters ago, The Human Beings were in a very bad place and there was a famine. We had lost our beliefs. White Buffalo Woman came from the stars to remind us that we had forgotten our beliefs. She stayed with our people for four days and taught us again what we had forgotten.

We believe the whole world is our church. We try to be with Wakan Tanka always."

* * *

Company A. and Company B. of the 19th U.S. Infantry stopped about mid-day where Buckner Creek flowed into the Pawnee River. They had been traveling hard almost due west. They had a quick meal, watered their horses and began traveling southwest following the creek. The maps carried by the two company commanders showed that the headwaters of Buckner Creek originated within only a few miles of their destination. It had been a cold, wet winter but the early spring sun had melted the snow and the traveling was easy. Game was plentiful and several deer and an elk carcass rode on the following wagon promising fresh meat rather than hardtack and salt pork for their dinner.

Just before sunset, the 19th crested a small hill and in the distance, there was a tiny oxbow on the creek. There was a shallow pool with shade from huge cottonwood trees. The two lieutenants nodded to each other and called for the non-commissioned officers to order a camp set up. Lookouts were posted, the Pawnee scouts were sent out to patrol their perimeter and several cooking fires were lit. The supply wagon was brought up near the water and the cooks finally began to clean the deer and elk. The legs, heads and entrails of their game were thrown into the creek. The cooks made their tired jokes about always drinking upstream from the cook's wagon

The officers claimed one elk backstrap and set up their tents away from the rest of the men. The non-commissioned officers claimed the meat they wanted and then the feeding frenzy began. Little Sam waded through most of the other men and cut a large strip off the elk rump and returned to eat with his brother.

As Little Sam roasted the elk meat over the fire, Pvt. Chester Ross began laying out his plan. "If we get the chance, we gotta get us some souvenirs, ya know. This may be our last chance."

Little Sam looked over the fire at his brother. "Whadda ya mean bud? Ya mean get more of that squaw meat." He chuckled to himself.

"I mean", said Chester, "we get us a couple tobacco pouches, ya know, like the other guys."

Several bottles appeared and by the time the men turned in, there had been several fights, but only one minor injury. The left over bones, broken bottles and other trash were thrown into the creek.

The following morning, several of the men had to be nearly dragged out of their tents; there were headaches, sore heads, bruised ribs and a lot of complaining. As usual, the non-coms had to use harsh, vile language to intimidate the rest of the men into some semblance of a formation. Finally, after the men had secured most of their gear and seen to their horses, the ranking lieutenant spoke to the men. *"By lunch time today, we could be within hearing of the Indians we're seeking. All your gear must be silenced; there will be absolutely no gunfire unless we're attacked. If I hear so much as a canteen clank or spoons rattling, I will personally dump your gear on the ground and we will leave you there. Any questions? We ride in half an hour. Saddle up and silence your gear."* Several men took the opportunity to use the creek as a latrine. An hour later, they were headed southwest.

* * *

Broken Knife and Leftook pushed the tribe hard. Scouts roamed for miles in all directions watching for threats. Scouts returned regularly to report updates. Red Feather and two other young warriors on their fastest horses rode ahead to scout out the vicinity of Dry Lake.

About mid-day, Red Feather thundered back to the tribe with disturbing news. There was a herd of cattle surrounding Dry Lake. No whites had been spotted but where there were cattle, the white cowboys would not be far away. Broken Knife conferred with Leftook and Kangee. "I know of a spot where there are some small springs that flow in wet years. There are many small hills there. It will be a good place to hide."

By late afternoon, the tribe arrived at a spot that was an hour's ride south of Dry Lake. The spot they chose resembled a shallow bowl surrounded by rolling hills. This land, later to become the Breyfogle Ranch, was rich in buffalo grass, yucca and sage. The springs were indeed flowing and the surrounding countryside held no tracks of the white man's cattle. The tribe stopped and immediately began to erect their homes. Familiar age-old chores were carried out; children gathered fuel, the women erected the tipis, the men began scouting for game. Lookouts were posted on all the surrounding hills as a normal pattern of life returned.

* * *

The sun was not quite directly overhead when the 19th cavalry crossed a rough, little used wagon trail that ran north and south. The two lieutenants called a halt for lunch as they conferred. The two officers pulled out their maps and compasses and correctly guessed that they were directly north of the new settlement on the Santé Fe trail called Cimarron.

They rode north toward the creek and stopped at the tiny settlement of Buckner. The town consisted of several houses, a blacksmith shop and livery and a general store. The men were ordered to stay in a smart formation and to not dismount. One officer rode into the village and asked if there had been any Indian activity in the vicinity. The baffled town folk said there had been no sighting and begged the officer for any news. He assured them there was no danger and rode away. Rumors spread like wildfire through the little town and the countryside. These humble white farmers lived in terror of Indian attack for weeks.

The cavalry continued on their southwest ride until late in the day. The officers knew they were close to the place where the Indians were reported. Scouts were about to be sent out when they crossed an obvious Indian trail. Tracks of many unshod horses with the telltale markings of travois being dragged north across the prairie were obvious. The officers gave the order to halt and conferred again. They briefly considered splitting the two companies with one going north to follow the trail and the other to report to the actual place where the Indians had been sighted. The two officers only conferred for a minute; they decided not to split up because they predicted the Indians had left the area. Their thinking was that the Indians must realize the man that escaped would report their location.

Sentries were posted and tents were pitched. The men were ordered to be as quiet as possible; there would be no gunfire, no drinking and no cooking fires of any kind. The cook in the supply wagon passed out hardtack and salt pork and the men ate their rations. After dinner, the officers and non-coms talked strategy while the rest of the men played cards, wandered around or just relaxed in their tents. One of the men rolled a smoke and was about to light it when a non-com slapped the cigarette out of the man's mouth and bellowed, "*Ya dunce! Those redskins could smell that ten miles away. Ya want 'em slippin' here in the night and cuttin' yer stupid throat?*"

Chester and Little Sam snuck their last bottle into their two-man tent and settled in for the night. "*This is how I sees it.*" said Chester. "*We finds a tipi with the flap closed. I go to the door. You wait behind the tipi on the other side. When I give the signal, I'll pull the flap open and step back. You slice open the hide with your bayonet, lean in and shoot the squaw like we tried last time. I'll step in and cut us off a couple pouches and we'll have our souvenirs. Just don't shoot me. Shoot toward the door; I'll be off to the side. That last squaw damn near stuck me. She was crazy!*"

* * *

Mouse stepped outside carrying Happy Seed. They watched as the sun slid below the hills and the vast sky became coppery shot with violet. She felt truly lonely for the first time in her short life. Almost all of the men were either hunting or on the lookout for any telltale signs of approaching threats. Black Elk, her father, Red Feather, Kangee, any person who would talk to her, acknowledge her were off dealing with the situation she knew she brought upon her people. The other women still refused to even look at her. She dreaded the knowledge that if even one person in her tribe was hurt or killed because of her actions, the weight of guilt might crush her.

Julia and Lotti now seemed to have gained favored status with the other women. The two were truly kind hearted and seemed to know intuitively what needed to be done and never hesitated to help out. They were also picking up some words and phrases in Sioux much to the amusement of all who were with them. One of their endearing mistakes was the result of Lotti overhearing the men talking about the horses. Both Lotti and Julia began using the word "chesli" they thought meant horse but really meant horse manure.

The sky was turning from a deep blue to indigo when several riders came trotting in from the north. Black Elk was one of the riders much to Mouse's relief. With him were Red Feather, Badger and Lark.

Red Feather smiled at Mouse and said, "It's all clear out there. I may go out later but I want to see your sister."

Black Elk accepted Little Seed from Mouse and he gave them both a hug. The three sat quietly outside their tipi and watched the stars appear one by one in their cold brilliance. Finally, he asked, "Has the anger left the women?"

Mouse shook her head "No" without looking at him. He put his arm around her shoulders and they just sat quietly. Little Seed began to fuss so Black Elk passed the little girl back to Mouse. The baby nuzzled Mouse so she undid her wrap and began to nurse her daughter. Shortly, the tiny girl fell asleep.

The two of them sat there, leaning against their tipi, lost in their own thoughts. It was almost full dark when Julia and Lotti appeared in front of them followed by the two brothers, Badger and Lark. The two young men looked sheepish and ill at ease, something only seen when they were around these two white women. Julia's long red hair, normally kept tied, was loose and freshly combed out. Both Julia and Lotti were nicely cleaned up but looked somewhat perplexed.

Julia looked at Lotti, cleared her throat and began to speak. She stopped, looked at Lotti again and blushed a deep red. Then, she just blurted out, *"We's wonderin. If a man and woman wants to be, ya know, together, is there some law or somethin against it?"*

Mouse smiled. *"If you like this man, be with him. If you could understand what the others are saying, you would know that our people approve of you being with him. We have been wondering how long this would take. Love is a blessing."*

Julia stared at Mouse and slowly smiled. She turned around and took Badger by the hand. Lotti followed suit and the two couples disappeared into the night.

Black Elk stood and held out his hand to Mouse. That didn't need a translation." He smiled as he pulled her to her feet. "Let's go in, we need to talk."

Mouse stepped through into their tipi and gently put Happy Seed to bed. Black Elk followed her into their space and she closed the flap. They sat on their bedding and faced each other. She reached out and took his hands in hers. "Do you think we should have let the whites freeze?" Her face was more sorrowful than he had ever seen it. "Do you think I was wrong?"

He shook his head and looked into her eyes for a moment. "You follow your spirit but the whites will come. Today, tomorrow, next week, next year, they will come. We must talk about our family, about Little Seed."

"Husband, what is there to talk about? We try to live as the Great Spirit has taught us. If we live free or on the terms of the white man: will that change our bond with The Great Mystery?"

Angrily, he replied, "Yes, our lives will change! I lived under the white man's rule for two years. They took everything from us. They sent the children away to learn the white man's ways. Your sister led us back to you because she was afraid for her child. I want our Little Seed to be a Human Being."

"Husband", she said softly, "I too want our child to be a child of Wakan Tanka. But we do not know his will. It is enough to know that we have his wóyawašte and we know our spirit will return to him when he calls."

"I am so afraid." he said as he began to cry. "I am afraid the time will come that I cannot protect you and our child."

"They cannot steal our love or the spirit of Wakan Tanka living inside us." She pulled him under the warm hide they had been sitting on. She held him and the warmth of their bodies connected them, bonded them yet again. As their waking nightmares receded, she said, "This, they cannot steal from us."

* * *

The tents of the 19th cavalry and the tipis of the Sioux were warmed by the rising sun in equal measure. The sun and God gave no sign of preference in the beliefs the humans harbored below. Their bodily needs were identical; they slept, ate and guarded their lives with a fierce instinct. Their slight difference is skin color was no indicator of the vast gulf of difference that separated these two people. What divided these two races was not biology or their belief in God. They both believed in their sovereign right to live on this land. The difference, the gulf that separated them was how they lived their beliefs.

* * *

Mouse woke early from a disturbing dream. What she could remember of the dream was familiar but the full memory just wouldn't come. In her dream, there had been two men, sometimes protecting, sometimes threatening. She found herself under her warm buffalo robes between her husband and child. Her child was already awake, looking at her with those deep, soulful eyes. Her memory of that disquieting dream was replaced instantly with that ancient connection between mother and child. Mouse pulled her infant to her and the two nourished each other.

Outside, she could hear Leftook already up, giving orders. Sentries were being assigned areas to monitor; the warriors were being kept close to camp. She smiled to herself as she heard Leftook roust Badger and Lark. She heard them complaining and some of the other men teasing them good-naturedly. Mouse lay warm and comfortable, nursing Happy Little Seed; the sounds of camp sounded familiar and comforting. The only hint of trouble was the urgency in Leftook's voice.

Seed finally stopped nursing and just seemed happy to be held. Mouse sat up with her and patted the baby's back. Seed attempted to hold up her head as she produced a surprisingly man-like belch. Black Elk stirred and smiled up at them. "Go back to sleep husband. Leftook will be here soon to take you away. I'll make us some breakfast." Mouse laid the baby down near her husband and began to fan the flame of their banked cooking fire. She got the fire going and heated her mother's cooking stone. She mixed some dried, chopped buffalo meat in with some of the very last corn meal she had and began frying up cakes.

"May I come in?" Mouse recognized her father's voice and invited him in. Black Elk sat up as Broken Knife came in and accepted the first warm cake from his daughter. "We will need you soon." Broken Knife said to Black Elk. "We just don't have enough men. We need sentries in all directions, we need to hunt and we need to keep warriors in camp. We may need to think about eating a horse unless our luck changes."

Black Elk stood, dressed and accepted a cake and a kiss from his wife. "Tell me where you need me and it will be done."

"Stay in camp with Leftook. You and Itunkala may be needed to tell the warriors that stay here in camp what Leftook tells them to do. I'm taking Red Feather to the lake. We may bring back one of the white's cattle." Broken Knife smiled grimly. "We might get lucky and be back with an elk." He picked up Little Seed, gave her a small squeeze and said, "Take care of your mother for me." He smiled at Mouse, stepped outside, called for Red Feather and was gone. She listened as the hoof beats of her father and best friend receded into the distance.

Broken Knife and Red Feather rode north out of camp, glad to be away from the intensity and fear. It was a fine spring morning; the wind was beginning to blow briskly from the west; the two of them briefly discussed approaching the lake from the east to take advantage of the wind. They changed direction and swung their horses in a southeasterly direction hoping to come in behind any game. They rode directly into a full platoon of white soldiers.

* * *

Lieutenant Bart Ashby woke with a start. He could tell from the light coming through the canvas tent that the sun was far from up. There was almost no sound. He heard the occasional chuffing of a horse but nothing else. Some sixth sense alerted him to a strangeness of the morning. He reached out and pulled his tent flap aside.

The morning had a definite surreal quality. There was no wind at all. A fine mist hung in the air and gave the scene a washed out, faded photographic quality. Every man in his company was up and nearly ready to ride. Lt. Ashby's tent was the only one still standing. Like a photograph, the men did not move but stood there staring at him, expecting him to emerge and start the day. Squatted within feet of his tent opening were three of the eight Pawnee scouts. They too were staring at him.

Lt. Ashby was taken aback but not surprised. He had seen this same behavior many times before. The men, usually contentious and hard to manage, always seemed to sense a coming action when they would be allowed to kill with impunity. On these days when the men knew that their animalistic instincts could run wild, they became the most focused.

Lt. Ashby and the other Lieutenant conferred with the Pawnee scouts as the two officers ate their breakfast. The scouts reported a small band of Sioux less than four miles away to the northwest. The camp was estimated at perhaps fifty Indians but a count was difficult because during the night, several Sioux lookouts had exchanged places. They estimated that there might be as few as twenty warriors to worry about.

Lt. Ashby called the entire two companies into a formation. *"We are approximately four miles away from a small Sioux encampment. Company A will approach the camp from downwind.*

Company B will split in two, two platoons flanking the camp from the south and the other two platoons flanking the camp from the north. Our faithful Pawnee scouts will circle the camp and take out their sentries by stealth. Then, the Pawnees will approach by horseback from upwind, steal a few of the Sioux horses and lead their warriors into our vise. Company A will secure the camp. For our strategy to work, you must be absolutely silent. At the first sound of gunfire, advance and take any non-hostile prisoners. Any question?"

* * *

A few women were up, sharing the communal cooking fire as the early morning sun warmed the air. The women did not speak to Mouse but they also did not leave the fire as Mouse and Little Seed joined them. It was a small improvement over the shunning of yesterday.

Julia and Lotti joined Mouse and the other women at the central fire. As Mouse smiled at her two new white friends, she noticed a subtle but obvious change. Outwardly, Julia and Lotti still appeared the same but the aura they projected, their foreignness; their whiteness was almost gone. They felt like a Human Being, as one of the people.

"Híŋhaŋni wašté." said Lotti. She smiled at Mouse and touched Seed affectionately.

"Good morning to you!" replied Mouse. She smiled as the two women sat down by the fire.

"We was talkin' again, Julia and me. Last night between, well, when the boys was sleepin. We's been with lotsa men, ya know. But until last night, it seems like every man we's been with were mad, little boys; mean ya know, sorta stupid. But the boys last night were like, babies and real men at the same time, can't splain it xactly. It's just, well, they's touched us on the inside, not just our bodies. It just wasn't fuckin; we was connected, like friends sort a, like we feels close to you. I guess it's like ya said, love is a blessing. Didn't know it was possible but we's happy; didn't know that was even possible. Pilamaya!"

One by one, some of the other women appeared but seemed reluctant to sit with Mouse and the white women. Julia finally asked, *"What's with them? They still mad atcha?"*

Mouse looked at them both. *"It was my idea to not let you die in the snow. Many in the tribe think the problems caused by Charles are my fault."*

"That's bullshit!" Julia got up and walked over to several of the women she had help out days before. She grabbed one by the hand and motioned to the others to join them at the fire. Reluctantly, the women came over and sat down.

Within minutes, all the women were laughing and having a wonderful time gossiping. Mouse was there but excluded in an odd way; she translated but didn't really join in. Untreated hides came out; clothes that needed mending were fetched. Mouse continued to translate as the women did their daily chores.

The morning passed pleasantly. As the sun rose and the air warmed, a breeze began to blow in from the west, making the morning even more pleasant. Julia and Lotti were now, more than ever, part of this amazing, extended family. There was much laughter around the fire as the two white women attempted to learn more Sioux vocabulary. They all laughed hysterically when Mouse finally corrected their use of the word chesli. Julia and Lotti had heard chesli used in relations to horses and thought that's what it meant. Its real meaning was horse manure. All the women were laughing so hard, some of the men came over to check on them. This only made the women laugh even harder.

Late morning, the sound of gunfire echoed across the hills from the north. In both languages, Mouse said, "I hope my father and Red Feather bring back an elk. They went to the lake to hunt." There was no way of knowing that her father and Red Feather had become the hunted.

Minutes later, there was a major disturbance from the west side of the camp. The women heard the men shouting, "Pawnee! They're stealing horses!"

All of the warriors defending camp rushed to their horses to give chase. Leftook yelled, "Stay! Do not leave!" without avail. Black Elk and Kangee were the only men in camp that heeded Leftook's orders. The rest rode madly west out of camp to chase their mortal enemies, the Pawnee.

Leftook grabbed Black Elk by the arm and pleaded, "Ride out; bring them back! We cannot leave the camp unguarded."

Black Elk nodded, ran to his horse and rode off after the men of the village. When he crested the hill, he saw the warriors in front of him riding into a funnel of cavalry. They were hopelessly outnumbered and as the first warrior fired his rifle, as many as eighty rifles cut the warriors down in seconds. Black Elk simply dismounted, sat on the prairie and began to pray. He was the only Sioux male to survive.

Seconds later, as many as eighty mounted cavalry soldiers appeared over the hill from the east, shouting and firing their weapons into the village. All the women scattered back to their tipis, to children, older parents.

Mouse hugged Little Seed to her as she ran to her tipi. Quickly, she ducked inside and closed the flap. Mouse looked down at her daughter in her arms. The two made eye contact. Mouse hoped her daughter, instead of seeing the fear in her eyes, saw the prayer in her heart. "Please be quiet, little one." Mouse said as she tucked the baby under the thick hide they all slept under. Mouse drew her knife and stood guard facing the door.

Kangee solemnly walked toward the charging soldiers, hand up in greeting. The advancing soldiers simply rode over him. Macawi saw Kangee being trampled and ran to give him aid. She was cut down by gunfire.

Leftook saw the charge, grabbed Spoon Woman and ran for their tipi. The moment they arrived, he began changing back to Lt. John Dunn. As he was transforming himself back to a white man, a U. S. Army officer, he heard gunfire and screams from all parts of his village. The process was frustratingly slow; all the brass buttons, the boots, the holster and hat. He knew he had to be convincing but the chaos outside terrified him.

Finally, Leftook whispered to Spoon Woman to stay down, hide under their bedding and he stepped outside. He saw several women face down, not moving. He also saw many of the soldiers running into tipis, laughing, some even waiting their turn. Macawi was still alive but bleeding profusely. He knew she was mortally wounded; he began to run across to her when he saw was a huge cavalry man using his bayonet to slice open Mouse's tipi. The man leaned in and shot once, then stuck his head inside to look around. Leftook saw another private step into Mouse's tipi.

Mouse felt a terrible pain and a severe blow to her left side. The impact threw her face down, almost on top of her child. The intense pain she felt in her back and left breast quickly disappeared, replaced by a quiet calm, a sense of release and rest. A brilliant, white light, a beckoning, immediately replaced the blackness that overtook her. She felt herself receding and at the same time, being more than herself, somehow held and comforted. She looked down calmly and saw her child, beneath the buffalo robe where she and her husband had loved each other and conceived this child.

Leftook ran up behind this soldier and yelled, *"PRIVATE! STAND DOWN!"*

As Private Ross spun around to look at Leftook, he said, *"Yes sir! – Who the fuck is you?"* He lifted his rifle and lunged at Leftook. Leftook deflected the bayonet blade and hit the man with his right fist so hard the private's boots came off the ground several feet. The big private went down and did not move.

Mouse heard Leftook's voice from a great distance. She felt more than heard her name being called from all around her. Leftook's voice was receding and seemed so unimportant but the voice calling to her was compelling, commanding, and compassionate. The screaming and gunshots lost their meaning as Mouse listened to the call of another, a woman whose voice comforted her, called her to a place of peace.

Leftook quickly moved to the opening of Mouse's tipi when a smaller man, also a private stepped out.

The second private stepped out and said, *"Hey you dumb shit, you gotta aim better. I only got one."* Then he saw the man in front of him was not who he thought. *"Where'd you come from?"*

"Itunkala" the voice said to Mouse, "I have been waiting."

When Leftook saw what the man had in his bloody hand, he simply pulled his revolver and shot the man through the forehead.   He swallowed hard and stepped into the tipi. Mouse lay on her back; her chest was a complete ruin but her face looked serene, the hint of a smile touched her lips. Her eyes were open; Leftook knew immediately that she was gone. That brilliance, that doorway to the Great Spirit was gone. He gently closed her eyes and pulled her buckskin blouse up so she looked asleep.

It was when Leftook wrapped Itunkala in her buffalo skin blanket that he found the baby. She lay quietly and stared up at him. For an instant, the insanity, the horrible sounds coming from all directions ceased to exist as Leftook looked into Little Seed's eyes. The sensation was familiar; he felt as if he were falling into a better place, a place where God actually existed, a place he had felt every time he had looked into the eyes of his mentor, his friend, a tiny woman with a huge spirit.

Leftook wasn't sure how long the moment lasted; the sounds, his reality rushed back and overwhelmed him. Then, Little Seed reached out to him.

Mouse turned toward the voice. She had been looking down and felt so sad for the people she seemed to remember from a dream. They were so angry, so unhappy. As she turned to the voice calling her, she seemed relieved to leave the strife she was watching from such a distance and to embrace the peace and wholeness she felt calling her.

The gunfire in the camp had completely ceased. The only sounds that registered on Leftook's consciousness were the laughter and grunting of the white men and the screams and groans of the women coming from inside their tipis.

The violence and bloodshed below seemed even more of a dream as Mouse lifted her eyes up from her family below. Beside her was an ancient woman dressed in the most beautiful white robe Mouse had ever seen. The old woman radiated peace and acceptance and as she held out her hand to Mouse she smiled and said, "Itunkala, I am Maya Owichapaha. We have been waiting for you."

Several enlisted men discovered Lotti and Julia cowering in the tipi where they had spent the night in with the two brothers. Lotti and Julia were brought to the center of camp. *"We got em sir."*, the men yelled. *"We saved the white women!"*

Lt. Ashby said to the troops gathering in the center of the village, *"Good work men! Is this camp secure?"*

"We?" asked Mouse. The world below her seemed to be disappearing, dreamlike, as if she were awaking. "Who is waiting for me? " The old woman smiled and touched Mouse on the heart. Mouse looked down and saw not her ruined body but a perfect white robe covered in the finest beadwork she had ever seen. For a moment, her question seemed so unimportant; her wonder and growing joy almost made her curiosity seem like it didn't matter.

"Your Thunkashila is waiting, your mother is here and her mother. All the People who ever were are here and all those to come. We have work to do."

Lotti and Julia were weeping and terrified. Then, they saw Leftook emerge from Mouse's tipi. He was carrying Little Seed. His face was nearly white and he was openly weeping. The two women shook off the hands of their "saviors" and ran to Leftook and clung to him.

Mouse felt a stab of sadness, regret; she had a distant residual memory of her life from before that wouldn't be realized. She pictured Black Elk's face on the first day they met. She remembered the intense joy she felt the first moment Little Seed nuzzled her. "Work?" she said to the old woman. "I am a child here."

At that moment, Little Sam stumbled from behind Mouse's tipi, looked at the dead man on the ground and shouted, *"This fucker killed my brother!"* He raised his rifle and aimed at Leftook's chest. Julia stepped in front of Leftook and screamed at them all, "You butchers! You all can go to hell!" Several other soldiers restrained "Little Sam" as Lt. Ashby turned to question "Lt. Dunn."

Leftook ignored Lt. Ashby and the soldiers around him. He turned his back on the lieutenant who was questioning him and stood in front of Julia and Lotti. He gently handed Little Seed to Lotti and said as he looked around, "Take the spirit of these people with you." He then gave them a small silver cross on a chain and a large, slightly rusty knife.

Mouse looked down on this exchange then looked at Maya Owichapaha. The old woman smiled at Mouse and began to speak. As the old woman spoke, the same words were in Itunkala's heart and she spoke them also.

Below, Mouse heard Leftook, Lotti and Julia say the same words. "Wakanisha. Wakanisha in all things."

Epilogue

Before any final solution to American history can occur, reconciliation must be effected between the spiritual owner of the land – American Indians – and the political owner of the land – American Whites. Guilt and accusations cannot continue to revolve in a vacuum without some effort at reaching a solution.

Vine Deloria, Jr.

Consider the vast amount of time the Native American cultures existed on the American continents. White European culture arrived approximately six hundred years ago. The Native Americans have been on this same land as much as fifty times as long, thirty thousand years.

During the six hundred years the white culture spread across the Americas, many of the approximately five hundred tribal groups were lost to posterity. These people and their language, religion, culture and unique knowledge simply vanished. The expertise these Human Beings had that allowed them to thrive in their distinctive ecological niches no longer exists. That knowledge, that could have enriched us all, is gone forever.

For other tribal groups like the Sioux, the six hundred years has been but an interruption, a disruption that continues. Life for many Native Americans is grim. With the near destruction of their culture replaced by an artificial and forced dependency, many First People live in poverty and addiction. In many cases, their children, the absolute future of any people, were ripped away from their culture and education and were forced to live, poorly, in the culture of their conquerors.

There are still many more Wasicans than Warriors but things are slowly changing. The Indian Wars never stopped. Many tribes are actively relearning their culture, language and ways of life. Warriors are now using the courts, technology and education to preserve and reclaim their heritage. One such warrior, Yellow Bird Woman (Elouise P. Cobell), sued the United States Government in a class action lawsuit for mismanagement of reservation resources. She and her team won a $3.4 billion settlement for her people as well as $60 million for a scholarship fund, the largest ever class action lawsuit against the U. S. Government.

Now, more and more people of all colors are becoming warriors. Many people simply own less and share more. Others speak out against the rapid loss of habitat or the poisonous air and water. More and more people question the economic model for the necessity of continued growth on an earth with finite resources. Others simply see and practice the connection between the food that they eat and the spirituality of the land that sustains us all. It is by that spirit that we all live.

> *Who will find peace with the lands? The future of humankind lies waiting for those who will come to understand their lives and take up their responsibilities to all living things. Who will listen to the trees, the animals and birds, the voices of the places of the land? As the long forgotten peoples of the respective continents rise and begin to reclaim their ancient heritage, they will discover the meaning of the lands of their ancestors. That is when the invaders of the North American continent will finally discover that for this land, God is red.*
>
> *Vine Deloria, Jr.*

Acknowledgements and Thanks

Thanks to David Foster, my brother. He owns the land where this story begins and ends. His single-minded devotion to the land, its history and integrity has kept the Breyfogle Ranch unbroken. It is a few square miles of native American prairie in a sea of industrial farmland. It is as it was when the original Americans arrived millennia ago. This land is a treasure in the Kansas heartland both for the fauna and flora that live there as well as for generations of humans to come.

Thanks to Caroline Bloomfield, my editor and friend. In her heart, she walks the Red Road.

Thanks to Dr. Bill Sarnoff, my mentor. Your gentle and compassionate suggestions made this book more gentle and compassionate.

Many thanks to my son and author Aaron Foster. His novel and mine were published almost simultaneously. Without his technical skills and reality checks, Wakanisha would still be a pile of unformatted and separate files. He repeatedly transitioned my analog mindset into digital magic with grace and patience. He is father to my grandchildren, our Wakanisha.

Most of all thanks to Mary. For her, Wakanisha is both a noun and a verb. Without her this story and my story would not have been.

Aho Mitakuye Oyasin

All my relations. I honor you in this circle of life with me today. I am grateful for this opportunity to acknowledge you in this prayer....

To the Creator, for the ultimate gift of life, I thank you.

To the mineral nation that has built and maintained my bones and all foundations of life experience, I thank you.

To the plant nation that sustains my organs and body and gives me healing herbs for sickness, I thank you.

To the animal nation that feeds me from your own flesh and offers your loyal companionship in this walk of life, I thank you.

To the human nation that shares my path as a soul upon the sacred wheel of Earthly life, I thank you.

To the Spirit nation that guides me invisibly through the ups and downs of life and for carrying the torch of light through the Ages, I thank you.

To the Four Winds of Change and Growth, I thank you.

You are all my relations, my relatives, without whom I would not live. We are in the circle of life together, co-existing, co-dependent, co-creating our destiny. One, not more important than the other. One nation evolving from the other and yet each dependent upon the one above and the one below. All of us a part of the Great Mystery.

Thank you for this Life.

Made in the USA
Charleston, SC
28 August 2016